Stimulus of Sin
Selected Writings of John Broderick

Stimulus of Sin

Selected Writings of John Broderick

edited by Madeline Kingston

with a foreword by Colm Tóibín

THE LILLIPUT PRESS
DUBLIN

First published 2007 by
THE LILLIPUT PRESS
62–63 Sitric Road, Arbour Hill,
Dublin 7, Ireland
www.lilliputpress.ie

A CIP record for this title is available from
The British Library.

1 3 5 7 9 10 8 6 4 2

ISBN   978 1 84351 096 3

Set in 10 on 13.5 pt Hoefler by Marsha Swan
Printed in the UK by Athenaeum Press Ltd, Tyne and Wear

Contents

Acknowledgments

I am personally indebted to two people for their help in the preparation of this book. My thanks to Desmond Green of Athlone and Europe for his generous practical help and encouragment, which made this project possible, and to Gearoid O'Brien of Athlone Public Library for his unfailing interest and his endless readiness to answer questions, return phonecalls, transmit photocopies and typescripts in all directions, and engage in the most arcane discussions, possible only with those who have spent lengthy periods absorbed in the life and work of John Broderick.

Madeline Kingston, Editor, 2007

Foreword

In his book on the painter Tony O'Malley, Brian Fallon has written:

> In a country town, everybody knows you and your family, or at
> least knows about you; every birth or death is a kind of com-
> munal event, and there is a certain sense of an enveloping
> cocoon of fatalism, of a pre-ordained round ending in the local
> churchyard. It is a difficult thing to put into words, but it is felt
> by everyone and permeates the small, tight world; and though
> the town itself may be left behind, you are marked in certain
> ways for life.

In this world, certain small things – how light falls on stone,
for example, or the way family likeness makes its way from one
generation to the next, or systems of speech and dialect, or a tiny
detail in streetscape or landscape – can become nourishing energy,
constant inspiration. In the work of Tony O'Malley, this sense of
small things – a scene on the outside of a town or the very interior shape of the landscape – can slowly become a distilled form
of personal iconography, close to mythology. It can be nourished
further, oddly enough, as it hits against the outside world, in
O'Malley's case as he came across the work of certain English contemporaries who worked with landscape, and as he experienced
the light of the Caribbean in later years.

For many Irish writers, the contours of an exact landscape
and the system of speech and local cadence have not only marked
them but made their way into the very core of the writers' poetic
diction and style and vision. In prose, Eugene McCabe's Monaghan, John McGahern's Leitrim and John Broderick's Athlone, to

take just three examples, have been conjured up as enveloping cocoon. The landscape, the systems of speech, the legacy of memory are allowed places in the fictional world as though they were characters. Indeed, character itself is often seen as a precise function of place, and community as a kind of poisonous stream in which the solitary conscience has to wade uneasily.

The possibility of escape from the cocoon of fatalism thus becomes an important engine in the drama, making the city of Dublin for both McGahern and for Broderick as important a stage as the one where their characters were born or come from. McGahern's northside in some of his best short stories and in his novels *The Leavetaking* and *The Pornographer* is a place of solitary freedom, just as the Fitzwilliam Square of John Broderick's best novel *The Trial of Father Dillingham* allows him to make his drama free of family and small-town destiny.

Both writers, then, used the local when it served their purposes, just as Tony O'Malley could, when the mood took him, paint in an Irish idiom with Irish light. Both writers wrote about family and locality and isolation because they were fascinated by the literary possibilities of Catholic ritual and rural romance. Both of them also knew that power of sexual imagery and sexual frankness in a world where such things were not often mentioned. 'McGahern is an uncompromising puritan,' Broderick wrote. Both he and McGahern managed to contain and discard a native Puritanism all the more powerfully to work it and its precise opposite into the very body of their fiction.

As two of John Broderick's unpublished stories, published here for the first time, make clear, he was interested in the literary possibilities also of sexual disappointment, of love long ago lost and now recollected. His world in 'Two Pieces of Sevres' and 'The Young Poet' was close to that of Kate O'Brien. Both writers came from an upper middle-class Catholic world and they felt more at ease describing prize possessions rather than the shadows of dispossession which darken most Irish fiction.

It is interesting, too, to watch Broderick work in an idiom at odds with his own natural tone. In the story 'The Marked Man', he moved into the world of Synge and folk tale to dramatize the fatalism that usually made its way into his work in a more comfortable setting. In 'Untitled Story', which is an exploration of his own sense of disappointment and isolation as a novelist and an artist, Broderick described his own world. He changed the bakery in Athlone which he inherited, making it a woolen mills; he allowed his mother to die at his birth rather than re-marry as she did in 1936 when he was twelve, his father having died when he was three. In merging his own work with that of Kate O'Brien in the story, he managed to do justice to the shape of his background and to what his main themes and topics were.

In 'Untitled Story':

> Dowling had published seven novels and two volumes of short stories, all obviously inspired by the life of the richer middle-class merchants in the large midland town in Ireland where he was born. He had been an only child, his mother died at his birth, and he had been brought up by his spinster aunt. His father died when he was sixteen and left him his large interest in the local woollen mills, shares which he was still in possession of at the time of his death ... He was the first author to tap a hitherto neglected mine of material. Irish life up to this time had been treated as if it consisted of a passionately poetic peasantry, and a romantically rakish Anglo-Irish gentry. The solid, Jansenistic, purse-proud, insular, ruthless, hypocritical, conservative junta which has emerged as the ruling class since the Rebellion, has remained unchronicled for the simple reason that it had not produced a renegade of genius from within its own ranks. Roger Dowling was the first child among them to take notes. He wrote about them with a clinical detachment, a profound acquaintance with their household gods, which could only have been done by a man who was one of themselves.

Broderick did not become a writer merely because he possessed such detachment and such close knowledge. He also loved books and had a great literary curiosity. He was a most exacting and careful reader. For many of us who read his reviews as they appeared in *Hibernia* and *The Irish Times*, he could seem at times deeply cantankerous. A review opening 'If an author will not take the trouble to write a book properly ...' or 'I am sick and tired of novelists who write novels about novelists writing novels about novelists' could only have been Broderick. He could dismiss whole movements in a flick of his wrist: 'Of all the various fads which have rippled across the literary scene over the past two hundred years symbolism was undoubtedly the silliest, and the most sterile.' And the axe of Athlone could be wielded on the neck of even the most famous writers: 'W.B. Yeats was much impressed by this twaddle, and I am not in the least surprised. The old poseur spent his life fooling the mob with mystical roses, most of them artificial.' Or: 'Joyce will revert, if he has not already done so, to the universities.'

But it is important to remember that Broderick also reviewed books and authors that he loved and wrote with enthusiasm and warmth when he thought it was appropriate.

Thus his piece on Liam O'Flaherty in *Hibernia* in 1969 was pure praise. 'That he is a great short-story writer is universally acknowledged; but he is also a great novelist – a very rare combination. *The Informer* will always be read for its mastery story-telling, its sinister undertones of brutish violence, and its lurid camera-like glimpses of the Dublin slums.'

I vividly remember two of these reviews appearing for the first time in *Hibernia* in the early 1970s. I had not read Broderick himself at the time, and did not know anything about him. His review of Francis Stuart's *Black List, Section H* in 1972 and John Banville's *Birchwood* in 1973 created a first audience for these two books. Broderick did not praise easily or often, and he could when it pleased him play the common man, the mouth of the midlands that choked on pretentious literature. But he had in his possession a certain magisterial tone which he could also use and which he dusted down on these two important literary occasions. I know I am not alone in having read these two books quite soon after they appeared because of what Broderick wrote. He declared Francis Stuart to have 'produced some of the most profound and mysterious novels in modern literature' of which *Black List, Section H* 'is, in my opinion, the most important of them all.'

And he declared John Banville to be 'the finest Irish stylist of his generation'.

Two years before he died, Broderick, who like Kate O'Brien, produced a body of journalism and travel writing, as well as literary reviewing, read Lorna Reynolds's informative and affectionate portrait of her friend Kate O'Brien, where Reynolds makes a case for *Without My Cloak* to be included among O'Brien's better novels. Broderick, who like O'Brien, spent his last years sadly and unhappily in the English provinces, wrote:

> Reading her chapter on this much loved book is a very moving experience; a sort of recreation of one's youth; and in her magnificent last paragraphs Lorna Reynolds brought back for me the very voice – a rarely beautiful one – and personality of a great and noble woman, who wrote so movingly and with such grave dignity of the 'holiness of the heart's affections'.

So, too, reading these pages of Broderick's journalism and his unpublished stories is a very moving experience. He was a complicated figure, exacting and difficult, whose own uneven body of work reflects the dilemma of a man of his class and his time and his temperament. His constant efforts to praise what he loved and his work to maintain standards, including his own, have much to teach us. He remains not only the chief chronicler of the Irish midlands, but also someone who found in books a way of both enriching and deepening his own experience of the world.

Colm Tóibín

Stimulus of Sin
Selected Writings of John Broderick

I.

Reviews

John Broderick's first review was published in *The Irish Times* in 1956, and his last in the *Irish Independent* in 1988. Between those dates he produced over 300 review columns, many of them dealing with more than one title and ranging in length between 500 and 2500 words. He reviewed fiction, travel books, biography, history, collections of essays and anthologies. The columns reprinted here have been selected (with considerable difficulty) to suggest the range of interests, knowledge, passion and judgment he brought to the reading of books new and old.

The Consul and the Headhunters

Borneo People by Malcolm MacDonald. Jonathan Cape, 32s 6d

It is said of Queen Elizabeth I that she played the virginal well – for a queen. The role of the proconsul in the arts has been somewhat more professional: a formidable number of diplomatists have engaged in literature more or less successfully since Confucius was Minister for Justice in Chung-tu.

Mr Malcolm MacDonald was Governor General of Malaya and British Borneo from 1946 to 1948; and this book clearly proves that he cannot be accused, as a distinguished literary colleague of his once was, of observing life through an embassy window. *Borneo People* is mainly a record of his administrative journeys up and down the state of Sarawak by jeep, sampan, launch, bicycle and on foot. Mr MacDonald has had unique opportunities, and his book can be read as a straightforward travel book, or as an indirect account of British colonial administration in the twentieth century. Either way it is vastly interesting: the author has a keen ear and a sympathetic eye; he is not only interested in people, he likes them, and his observations add up to a most companionable and comprehensive record of a strange and little-known way of life.

The country itself is fascinating, possessing in abundance those three natural Rs, rapids, ritual and romance, without which no remote place can qualify for a travel book. It is, of course, widely known for its white Rajahs, the Brookes, who not unnaturally caught the imagination of the world, and who ceded their fabulous principality to Britain in 1945. It is also inhabited by many colourful tribes of different racial stock; it has huge tracts of unexplored jungle; wildlife abounds; native chieftains have sufficient leisure and authority to develop colourful eccentricities, and their daughters are uncommonly graceful.

Whether he is describing a bath taken in a temple hung about with heads, the trial marriages of the Ibans, the monkey dances of the Kayans, or life in a communal longhouse, Mr MacDonald remains a most agreeable travelling companion, with a pleasantly dry sense of humour. *Borneo People* is a leisurely book and some of Mr MacDonald's descriptions have the colourful amplitude and the careful detail of an Academy picture by Sir Gerald Kelly. The whole thing has a rich and curiously old-fashioned air: one had forgotten that there were natives so grateful and so good, or that law and order could still sail down an equatorial river with such bland assurance.

But there can be no question of the sincerity of Mr MacDonald's intentions: he has an almost mystic sense of duty, and like all imperialists, he is a great romantic. (Someday someone will write a learned tome on imperialism and the romantic ideal.) He is much concerned with leading the Borneans along the well-ordered paths of Western education, medicine and religion, and his observations on this process have a more than passing interest. (Whether or not the jungle tribes would be happier gaily cutting off one another's heads is, of course, an open question.) Mr MacDonald is fully aware that he is the agent of something inexorable, and his portrait of the young native girl Segura, who left her family and took to lipstick and perms, is strangely touching. It is this self-knowledge that gives the book its peculiar charm, and lifts it out of the ordinary run of travel literature.

The Irish Times, 15 December 1956

Pilgrim's Progress

The Road to Santiago by Walter Starkie. John Murray, 25*s*

Every book – I am speaking of literature – has a centre of gravity, a paragraph, or a sentence, which gives us the key to the whole thing. 'As we grow older,' says Dr Starkie, 'we become more and more obsessed by the longing to undertake a hidden journey which will remind us gently of the ultimate one, and evoke for us countless shadowy spirits who, though they have long since been ferried across to the further bank of the last river, yet continue to haunt us when we plod along the road.' In *The Road to Santiago*, a history of the famous shrine, and a record of a pilgrimage made to it in 1954, this sentiment is magnificently realized.

The Spaniards were an imperial nation, and their saints are apt to be warlike. The Apostle James, patron of Spain, whose shrine at Compostella is one of the greatest in Europe, distinguished himself particularly in this respect – especially after his death. He disliked being described as a fisherman, and, appearing in a vision to the Greek bishop Estiano, indicated that he preferred to be known as a knight; he was called the Moor-slayer, and he helped Cortés to slaughter innumerable Indians. Little is known of his real character, and his adoption by the Spaniards as their patron, with all the legends that this inspired, is an interesting study in national hagiology. Yet in this ferocious Spanish single-mindedness there is a certain magnificent unity. As Unamuno puts it: 'It is a monotheistic landscape, this infinite plain where a man is made small without losing his self, and where amid the parched fields he is made to feel the parched places in his soul.'

Although the bookshelves groan under the weight of books about Spain, there is need for such a one as this. Dr Starkie is not here concerned with the harsh enchantment of flamenco, or the cut-glass radiance of Moorish fountains under the moon, but with an older, harder Spain, forever troubled by that vision of mortality which made St Teresa of Avila cry out in her autobiography: 'There is no happiness that is secure and nothing that does not change.' This never deterred that remarkable woman from glorying in life, and the humanist will find *The Road to Santiago* a gloriously lively progress.

Dr Starkie began his pilgrimage at Arles in Provence, travelling along one of the old pilgrim roads through Toulouse, and across the Pyrenees into Spain. It is a journey through history: every town and village along the way yields its story, its legend or its miracle. It is a living history: in Santo Domingo de la Calzada, in Castile, Dr Starkie gets himself into trouble because he questions the authenticity of the local legend of St James, which dates from the fifteenth century.

The author's great erudition – he is steeped in the lore of a thousand years of Santiago – his rich personality, and his ability to make stones live combine to give an effect of timelessness, which is truly remarkable. He is as much at home with the pilgrims he meets along the way, and the bus conductors, strolling players, cowboys and bagpipers, as he is with the princes, popes, knights and gypsies who have gone down the road before him. Only the very superficial imagine that life is composed of today: it is made up also of all our yesterdays. We are, as T.S. Eliot puts it, born with the dead. It is this extraordinary sense of the past, and the ability to place it side by side with the passing moment, that makes *The Road to Santiago* such enthralling reading.

The Irish Times, 4 May 1957

Stimulus of Sin

Mémoires Intérieures by François Mauriac. Eyre and Spottiswoode, 21s

The creative artist is a bridge between the present and the past, between himself and the outer world, even, if he is a great artist, between appearance and reality. When this always-fragile bridge collapses he ceases to be a creative artist, and becomes either a sterile egoist or a hopeful cipher. This is precisely what has happened to M. François Mauriac, who has for some years now been burning all his bridges. He has immured himself in the past and is interested only in the future: the heavenly future.

Few writers care to admit this. That is why his memoirs make such a fascinating and, I think, important, document. It is a subtle, wise, sensitive, powerful, intelligent, inconsistent and deeply depressing book. M. Mauriac refuses to 'tell all'; for which we may be grateful in these days when so many writers confuse the naked flesh with the naked soul. His reflections follow two paths: the memory of his youth, which his old home near Bordeaux inspires in him, and the books which he read long ago, and continues to read as if contemporary literature never existed. He has given up reading novels and poetry, and is interested only in memoirs and philosophy. He has in a sense retired from life and waits to be released from mortal coils.

But even now this great writer has not quite succeeded in stifling his genius. The atmosphere of the landscape round Malagar is evoked with all the dangerous and compelling power of his great creative period in the twenties. There are passages in the *Mémoires*, which might have come out of *Thérèse* and *Le Baiser au Lépreux*; even once or twice from the torrid *Le Fleuve de Feu*.

The literary reflections, always neat, thoughtful and enthusiastic, are less remarkable. Benjamin Constant, Baudelaire and Emily Brontë among others have been more potently evoked elsewhere. And one wonders at the end of a long passage if he has succeeded in solving the enigma of Gide – who fascinates him, as he fascinated all the Catholic intellectuals of his day – any more successfully than Gide himself. Not surprisingly he admires Pascal and Racine, but one was not prepared for such a wholehearted admiration of Proust and Tolstoy. M. Mauriac's literary musings are essentially personal and sentimental.

Why has this great novelist turned his back on his art? Because, he implies, he is interested in saving his soul, and writing novels is no way to do it. Perhaps. Nevertheless one suspects that there is some confusion here. If he is so sensitive to Catholic criticism, why is he not inspired by transcendental Catholic themes? There is a sublime need here. One has only to mention the greatest name in European literature – Dante.

The truth is that M. Mauriac's imagination is stimulated only by sin. Virtue, goodness, mysticism bore him as a creative artist: he is obsessed by death, disease, decay and putrefaction. He would, one feels, like to have written *Les Fleurs du Mal*. He has come to terms with this and ceased to write novels. It is a noble gesture, and this book of memoirs is his testament. 'For a poet, to save his life is to lose it,' he remarks. Surely this is not true; but clearly M. Mauriac thinks it is for him and one must respect his decision.

The novels, however, remain – novels, which at their best place him in the forefront of that modern literature that he despises. M. Mauriac has, in fact, done something which few people have achieved since the world began; he has had it both ways.

The Irish Times, 10 December 1960

The West Awake

The Middle Passage by V.S. Naipaul. Andre Deutsch, 25s

It is unfortunate that most travel books are written by people whose only talent is for travel. The creative travel writer, the man who has imagination and the gift of words, is one of the rarest things in literature. And when we do come across one he is apt to be a novelist taking time off from the strenuous business of revealing the truth through instinct. Mr V.S. Naipaul is a distinguished novelist who has accepted a commission from the government of his native Trinidad to write a book about the Caribbean.

Whatever one may think about the dilemma of the creative artist when presented with a commission, there can be no two opinions about Mr Naipaul's talent. He is a born writer; with the novelist's gift – so embarrassing to the world at large – of seeing below the surface of things. Instead of a dreary journal soaked in synthetic sunshine and bound with platitudes, he presents us with a book packed not with place names, but with the essence of his experience. He can create a character, paint a scene and reveal a situation with that kind of talent, which, as Henry James put it, converts the very pulses of the air into revelations. Some of his conclusions must, to put it mildly, be a slight embarrassment to the government that commissioned him. But then no real writer can ever be bought. And, after all, politicians come and go: good books live on.

Mr Naipaul is at his best in Trinidad and British Guiana. He is brilliant on Surinam, but with the oblique brilliance of an outsider.

He is unfair to Martinique; but good again on Jamaica, to which he devotes far too little space.

Trinidad is unique in the West Indies in that its society has not hardened around the institution of slavery as it has done elsewhere. But for all its colour and noise it is a dull little island with no real culture of its own: a typical product of the materialistic colonial society that founded it. There is much ostentation and great poverty, and very real tension between the Indians and the Negroes. Mr Naipaul's analysis of this tension – he is an Indian himself – is subtle, profound, and in the circumstances, extremely objective. Here, as throughout the book, he is able to enliven his sociological findings with character studies and some admirable pieces of descriptive writing.

In British Guiana we come bang up against the slave complex, the curse of the West Indies. Slavery, as Mr Naipaul remarks, has always produced a society, which is at once revolutionary and intensely reactionary. For the Negro, with the guilt and shame of slavery in his blood, the white man is at once the object of hatred and emulation. This results in all kinds of social and psychological complications. The Indians have a certain rigid culture of their own; the Negroes have nothing, except the superimposed shibboleths of their former owners. The result is the emergence of a kind of subculture of protest, and protest is always ultimately negative. In Africa the Negro has the opportunity of developing his own culture, since he is quite simply an African. In the West Indies the problem that confronts this gifted and horribly ill-treated race is appalling. The situation there is explosive. It is difficult to know how it will develop without further bloodshed and violence. Here, as elsewhere, the white race is reaping the terrible harvest of an unjust sowing.

The Irish Times, 18 August 1962

All At Sea

The Mountbattens by Alden Hatch. W.H. Allen, 50*s*

The British have always distrusted brilliance in their leaders, and they usually get the sort of politicians and princes they deserve. Winston Churchill was kept out of Downing Street until the moment was desperate, and thrown out when he had served his purpose. Stanley Baldwin was perhaps the prototype of the sort of statesman they feel comfortable with, a calm, dull exterior concealing depths of cleverness and ruthlessness. Dash, flair, glamour are deeply suspect qualities, which they prefer to see exercised outside the political arena, but not in the vicinity of the royal palaces whose occupants are expected to possess every virtue except spontaneity, without which good works are apt to be academic. It is all rather complicated, but then the British are not a logical people. If they were they would not be human.

It is good even now to be royal in England, but what if those royals possess ambition and genuine ability? Such a family are the Mountbattens. In his book Mr Hatch tells us that they are one of the most unpopular families in the kingdom, in spite of having served their adopted country brilliantly and well for the better part of a century. There seems to me to be some exaggeration here, but one can see what he means.

This is a three-decker book and in Victorian times would probably have been published in separate volumes, weighty, exquisitely printed and deadly dull. Mr Hatch is far from dull and has a pleasantly astringent sense of humour. He has obviously studied his naval form; and the book should delight all those who love the sea. But it is chiefly remarkable as a study of three remarkable men: Prince Louis of Battenberg who became 1st Marquis of Milford Haven; Lord Louis Mountbatten, who became Earl Mountbatten of Burma; and Prince Philip of Greece who became the Duke of Edinburgh. The metamorphoses of these men are celebrated in truly mythical style by their changes of titles; and their legends are among the most colourful of recent times.

Prince Louis of Battenberg was the son of Prince Alexander of Hesse and Countess Julie Hauke. He was born in 1854 and died in 1921. Instead of entering the service of Austria, Russia or Prussia whose monarchs were all relations of his, he elected to join the British navy and became a British subject. He had a most distinguished career and in spite of his royal connections, ended up as a First Sea Lord in 1912. He was one of the most popular officers in the service, and no one has ever doubted his ability, which indeed was extraordinary. He was, like his son afterwards, in favour of every modern innovation; and was the first of his family to get on the wrong side of the dinosaurs. Because of his German birth and connections he was forced to resign in 1914. (Logically, King George V might well have been asked to do the same.) A veil of mystery still surrounds this hysterical affair. Winston Churchill, who was at the Admiralty at the time, glosses over it in *The World Crisis* and clearly suffered from a sense of guilt about it for the rest of his life. Mr Hatch makes it clear that Prince Louis was, in fact, thrown out.

No one ever succeeded in doing the same by his son, although he became one of the most controversial figures of his time. A member of the royal family who voted Labour and whose wife was, according to Lord Attlee, 'very, very left': a head of Combined Operations who was responsible for the disastrous Dieppe raid in 1942; the last viceroy who presided over the liquidation of the Indian Empire; and as if all that were not enough, the chief of the defence staff who pushed through the very necessary unification of land, sea and air forces into a single ministry, thereby enraging the brass hats of every service. And all this Lord Mount-batten has done with superb aplomb, glitter and energy. No wonder he has his enemies. But he has more than proved the democratic right of the aristocrat to pursue the prize with the same zest and ruthlessness as anybody else. With disabilities such as an aunt who was the last Empress of Russia, would Mr Wilson ever have made Downing Street?

Of the Duke of Edinburgh, who made the most brilliant connection of all the Mountbattens by marrying the future Queen of England, Mr Hatch has little to say. Indeed what is there to say? Prince Philip is obviously a man of ability, and in business would probably have ended up as a self-made millionaire. But his scope is limited by his position; his promising career in the navy was cut short; and in some ways he is rather a tragic figure. On the other hand he is not dead yet; he is a hard worker and one of the best public speakers in England. But at the moment he looks like a man whose future is all too certain: lots of glory and no power at all: a sailor who goes down to the sea in a yacht.

The Irish Times, 12 March 1966

Consumer Goods

The English Ruling Class edited by W.L. Guttsman. Weidenfield & Nicolson, 50s
The Victorian Mind edited and selected by Gerald B. Kauvar and Gerald C. Sorenson. Cassell, 45s

If an author will not take the trouble to write a book properly, I see no reason why a reviewer should strain his eyesight to read it. This, I know, is an unfashionable view; since more than half the space in book pages and magazines today is filled with totally irrelevant critiques of completely unnecessary non-books put out by publishers to push up their turnover for American interests. It is time someone took a firm stand on this matter, and informed the public of sharp practice in an area of consumer goods, which they might, in their innocence, confuse with the ancient and honourable trade of writing.

The two objects under review give me an admirable opportunity to do this; for they bear no more relation to a real book than a wax figure does to a man. The features are similar as in the wax image, in the sense that they are printed on paper and suitably bound; but of that spark of life, which all genuine books possess in common with living persons, they are absolutely devoid.

Many years ago, in a broadcast, I remarked that the day would come when books would be sold by weight like soap, and bear the same relation to literature as a packet of detergent. That time has now arrived; and it is proper that the public should be told about it. The modern mania for 'information' has reached such a pitch that people will buy anything that claims to put them in possession of the facts. To this end the written word, with all the prestige bestowed upon it by generations of great creative writers, is being gradually prostituted.

To the public at large a book is still a book; something valuable and even slightly awesome in its own right; but dazed as they are by publicity stunts of all kinds, their discrimination, such as it is, is being gradually eroded. Any pretentious hack can get together a collection of facts and figures by burying his nose in the reference books of a public library, string them together and present them to the public as a 'book', and think of himself, quite erroneously, as an 'author'. The end product is then placed on the shelves of a bookshop in the company of Gibbon, Macaulay and Hazlitt; or if the arrangements be haphazard, worse still, in the company of Shakespeare, Goethe and Dante. Thus are the goats confused with the great; and the average reader conned into thinking that he is buying something of literary value.

I have indicated that I have not read these objects, which I am now reviewing. 'You say I am repeating something I have said before, I shall say it again.' How comforting are those charmingly arrogant lines of Eliot to the indignant reviewer. How then can I condemn them? It is quite simple. When I began to review books a hundred years ago, I had to read at least fifty pages before I knew whether they were going to be any good. After about half a century, I knew after the first chapter. Now I can tell by the first paragraph. (This does not say that I stop there: I read on most carefully when the book is informed by any sort of creative spirit.) But I merely dipped through this pair; and that is as far as I am prepared to go with either of them. After all, I assume that I am writing for an intelligent public, who will realize that non-books deserve a non-review – the first, I should like to think, of its kind.

The English Ruling Class is a collection of essays, extracts, and bits and pieces by various authors, mostly nineteenth-century, on the title subject. The writers themselves are distinguished and include Burke, Coleridge, Disraeli, Bagehot and Newman: a digest in short of various opinions on a subject that is as futile as it is boring. Of all the delusions that have exercised the minds of uncertified lunatics since the world began, that of power is the most ridiculous. Those who have what is termed 'power' very soon discover how very limited it is; those who have not got it, or think they have not, project their idle fancies onto various public dummies who in time actually begin to believe in their own myths.

I very much doubt if there is, or ever has been, such a thing as a ruling class in any country. There is privilege certainly, arising from money, birth or personal achievement; but that is very different from 'ruling'. On the whole, countries, even when they are run by dictators, muddle along in a welter of conflicting interests, with no one section really holding any sure monopoly of power – whatever that may mean – for any great length of time. So that the title of this non-book, attractive though it may be to the gullible, is misleading from the outset.

And to stick together a collection of pieces by various authors – bleeding hunks, you might say – on a largely meaningless subject, which sounds important, is simply to foist upon the public a pretentious successor to those annuals, birthday books and photographic albums of famous beauties, which predated the coffee-table volumes of today. The editor of this scrapbook is, needless to say, a university librarian. No wonder the students are rebelling.

The Victorian Mind might just as aptly be entitled *The Modern Mind*. The plan is the same as that followed in the object mentioned above: a collection of bits and pieces on education, social welfare, religion, science and art, by Victorian writers. Apart from the fact that the Victorian mind did not differ greatly from ours, I see no reason at all why this volume should be published. The Victorians dressed differently, they had their own hypocrisies; otherwise they were not, individually, either better or worse than we are.

Handling these objects, I was reminded of the words of a real writer – the speech Congreve put in Mirabell's mouth long ago: 'You had the leisure to entertain a herd of fools; things who visit you from their excessive idleness; bestowing on your easiness that time which is the encumbrance of their lives. How can you find delight in such society?'

One last word. Not having a scales handy, I did not weigh these goods; but I did smell them. I beg to advise the prospective consumer that they smell exactly the same as the real thing. So does tinned soup.

The Irish Times, 1 December 1969

Liam O'Flaherty: A Partial View

It is not often that a critic is able to make a virtue of his limitations. Too frequently the mantle of omniscience is forced upon him by an intensive knowledge of his subject; or, if he is a fraud, by his pretensions. Ideally he should of course know as much as possible of his subject, have studied it thoroughly and possess the faculty, so sadly lacking in modern academic critics, of projecting his imagination into the world of the author he is writing about. If he is capable of the latter it is not always necessary for him to have read every word of every book produced by the subject of his study. Instinct, a certain creative sympathy, and a civilized appreciation of the importance of literature as distinct from information, will often be of greater benefit to him than the pedantic nose and the gimlet eye. And after all it is not necessary to eat an entire Christmas pudding to discover its quality – or lack of it.

Thus do I make my excuses for not having read the complete works of Liam O'Flaherty. In such a predicament one tries to present oneself in as favourable a light as possible; and certainly I should be aware of a certain element of boasting when I say that I am no academic critic. One does not want to give the impression of too much superiority. On the credit side however there remains the fact that I have not read even half of O'Flaherty's novels; and none at all of his general works such as *Shame the Devil, Life of Tim Healey* and *A Tourist's Guide to Ireland*. I have a shrewd suspicion that these books have not added greatly to O'Flaherty's enormous reputation; nevertheless one would like to have them. But the novels are a more serious matter; and I stress the fact that I have not read so many of them in order to highlight a deplorable state of affairs concerning Ireland's greatest living writer. I would read every book he has written if I could get them. But I can't. They are not available.

In France, collected editions of Mauriac, Colette, Gide, Camus and other lesser figures have long since been published. In England, Graham Greene, Evelyn Waugh, Joyce Cary and our own Elizabeth Bowen have all had their collected editions. Yet O'Flaherty, who is at least as great as any of those writers, and better than one or two, is almost totally absent from the bookshops. So far as I can ascertain, only two of his books are at present available in the shops – *The Informer*, which is always with us, and the 'collected' stories, which are in fact a selection from three separate volumes.

Some people might argue that the stories contain the best of O'Flaherty; and so they do, but not all of it. That he is a great short-story writer is universally acknowledged; but he is also a great novelist – a very rare combination. *The Informer* will always be read for its masterly story-telling, its sinister undertones of brutish violence, and its lurid camera-like glimpses of the Dublin slums. Its portrayal of the physical reactions of the characters is also extraordinarily acute and has not yet been equalled by any other Irish writer. And of course the theme of the informer is buried deep in the Irish subconscious: he is a nightmare archetype. But it is not a great book for the simple reason that it is impossible to write a great book about an ape, which is what Gypo Nolan is.

The Black Soul, one of the few other O'Flaherty novels I possess, is breathtaking in its force. Its characters are primitive but human; and its evocation of the island of Inverara in all seasons is both realistic and mythical, like the moors in *Wuthering Heights*. A prose poem if you like, but with no purple passages, no self-conscious 'atmospherics', it exists in its own right as a force of nature, elemental, lyrical and rock-like.

There is a hardness about O'Flaherty, a true ring of steel, which one is conscious of in the work of all great writers. Unlike

Hemingway, with whom he has sometimes been compared, there is no soft centre in his best work. Of all the Irish writers who have written in English, he is the most Gaelic in style and temperament. Indeed his stories sometimes read like translations from the Irish; and for all I know they may well be. Now, the Irish are not a sentimental people, like the Americans and the English. They are clear-eyed, realistic and hard as nails, in spite of a certain superficial sweetness and an elaborate code of manners. But they have never lacked courage; above all the ability to survive. Those people, and they are not all visitors, newly established planters or tourists, who think of the Irish as a race of easy-going charmers, given to the philosophy of *dolce far niente*, have clearly not read their O'Flaherty. Consider his treatment of animals. His animal stories, which are justly famous, are light years apart from the cosy English attitude of attributing human characteristics to all manner of beasts. They identify themselves with them in a way that would be less alarming if it were also less suburban.

O'Flaherty never makes this mistake. His approach to animals is completely unsentimental, which greatly heightens his natural sympathy and understanding; and the result is marvellously vivid, clear-cut and vital. Hardly any other writer has equalled him in this particular field.

But to appreciate him at his best one must read *Famine*. I do not think anyone can have a proper understanding of the Irish character without a knowledge of this tremendous book. It is in my view by far the greatest Irish novel in the mainstream tradition written in this century. Joyce and Beckett are outside this tradition; and if the reader does not understand why, it would need another article to enlighten him. The power of this novel is real, heartfelt and strong as bone, its narrative flow as overwhelming as a tidal wave; its drawing and development of character on the grand scale; its message of courage, endurance and pain, universal. By literary standards it is a masterpiece; and has long since been accepted as such.

But it is something more. I suspect that many fine writers never realize their full potential because they never hit upon a theme that stirs the deepest instincts of their beings. Sometimes this is due to timidity, sometimes to ill luck; yet again, more often than is supposed, to an excess of intellectual enquiry. Genius is blazingly bright; but it has its blind side, and occasionally, groping in the dark, it stumbles on the vein of gold that provides the material for a work of art that is made to last. I do not know how O'Flaherty discovered this mine; but it seems to me that he is one of those writers who were sent into the world to write a particular book, just as Emily Brontë was born to write *Wuthering Heights* and Samuel Beckett *Waiting for Godot*. *Famine* has the true ring of inevitability.

It is accepted almost without question that the Rebellion of 1916 was the great watershed of modern Irish history. It wasn't. Yeats's 'terrible beauty' turned out to be stillborn, which is not surprising, since that popular poet was always wrong. I very much doubt if the Ireland of 1925 was in essence very different from the Ireland of 1910. But the Famine was another matter. Before it, there was a different sort of Ireland; and after it something had happened to the national spirit, a tremendous wound, which has not healed to this day. It was a cataclysm in which the entire nation was involved, body and soul, as it most certainly was not in the War of Independence. It is this tremendous theme that O'Flaherty has tackled in *Famine* with such complete success that if he had never written another book he would still be accorded a place among the greatest writers of his time.

This one novel is a national glory. That so little of his other work is available is a national disgrace. A very Irish dilemma.

Hibernia, 19 December 1969

Marianne and the Bookject

The Myth of France by Raymond Rudorff. Hamish Hamilton, 42*s*

There has been a great deal of discussion about the superfluous man. Russian literature in particular is full of it; and the choicest examples are to be found in the novels and tales of Turgenev, who may be said to have invented the type with Tchulkaturin in *The Diary of a Superfluous Man*. [...]

Far less has been said about the superfluous book. For one genuine masterpiece of creative fiction, there are at least a thousand of them; for every honest novel at least a hundred. They are usually concerned with facts, theses and the lives of famous persons supposed to have influenced the fate of nations. The formula is simple. Take a subject, preferably political or historical, add references from newspapers, files, letters and other earlier books of the same sort, garnish with prejudice; and ten to one you will find some critic to take you seriously, swallow your concoction, and swear that it makes him feel a fuller man.

Books about countries, as distinct from travel books, which often have real literary merit, are particularly popular and particularly superfluous. Of necessity they must deal with matters political, touch upon the influence of famous men whose names always impress the ignorant, and give unlimited scope for sweeping generalizations to which everybody, including myself, is prone. The fact that most of the things that can be said about one country can also be said about another, is neither here nor there. Most people are convinced that Spaniards are different from Italians, Greeks from Turks, and Irish from English, as if they did not all share a common humanity, and given the circumstances and the chance would not all act in exactly the same manner. [...]

What purpose does this particular bookject serve? None. It is entirely superfluous. The matter? France and all it stands for is a fake from beginning to end, and especially since the French Revolution, which Mr Rudorff seems to deplore. Indeed his opinions here are exactly the same as the most hidebound conservative, although he presents himself as a progressive. This is just one instance of where a completely prejudiced view will land one. You deplore police brutality in one breath and lament the Bourbons in the next. French colonial history is deplorable; and the country is little better than a police state, and a particularly brutal one at that. The much-vaunted French culture is a sham and a fraud, and nothing of value in the arts is now being produced in France.

The French all hate one another like poison; they gang up only when their pockets are threatened. They are the meanest people in the world, and also of course the rudest. The men are obsessed by sex, and are convinced that they are the greatest lovers in the world, and all others pigs by comparison. And so on and so on. You name a prejudice against France and the French, and Mr Rudorff comes up with it with all the subtlety of a politician abusing an opposition candidate at an election.

Some of his charges are of course true. France has a bad colonial record. But since only one side of the question is given in all other matters, one quickly loses confidence in the author's judgment. His arguments are so ham-handed that they are not worth disputing, though if the book had any merit one would try. [...]

I therefore dub this production a bookject. It is an easy word to remember, and I hope it catches on, for it describes exactly the type of article now being produced in great numbers. I bear no malice towards Mr Rudorff, and for his sake hope that he will be remembered as the author of the first named bookject. It is the only immortality he is likely to achieve.

The Irish Times, 2 May 1970

Untitled

Their Good Names by H. Montgomery Hyde. Hamish
Hamilton, 63*s*

Mr Montgomery Hyde started life as a barrister-at-law, served a
term as an Ulster MP, and has ended up as a bookmaker. His latest volume is a transcript of various trials, all sensational and
mostly scandalous. Since the processes of law are as obscure to me
as military tactics, I never read court cases unless I have to. But I
must confess that many of the trials here recorded are outra-
geously funny. Never were so many lies told with such pompous
and ponderous dignity. My own favourite is the Liberace case. The
spectacle of the flashy entertainer appearing in the dock and con-
founding his prosecutor in the manner of a pious, prosperous and
highly respectable Catholic stockbroker falsely accused of stealing
the altar wine, is one of the funniest things I have ever read. That
surely was the greatest performance of his life; and British justice,
with that impartiality for which it is famous, took him at his word
and awarded him enormous damages on the strength of his blue
business suit.

This is, of course, a bookject and has no literary merit whatsoever. There seems to be an enormous public for this sort of
thing; and I have no doubt at all that this particular specimen will
be a bestseller. But I hope most sincerely, for Mr Hyde's sake, that
he wrote it for the money, and the money alone.

The Irish Times, 25 July 1970

Papal Bulls

The Bad Popes by E.R. Chamberlin. Hamish Hamilton, 60s
A Thousand Afternoons edited by Peter Haining. Peter Owen, 45s

It might not appear on the face of it that the popes of Rome had anything in common with the bullfighters of Spain; but on reflection one begins to see that they share more characteristics than is generally supposed.

It is doubtful, of course, if the papacy can be officially classified as a sport; but then, bullfighting is not recognized by many people as a reputable game either. What cannot be denied is that they are both great institutions, which give rise to violent passions, for and against. At the moment both are going through a crisis. The authority of the papacy is being questioned by turbulent elements panting for what Mrs Patrick Campbell called the deep, deep peace of the marriage bed after the hurly-burly of the chaise longue; and bullfighters are being driven off the pitch by soccer fans.

The analogy can be taken a few steps further. The Pope and the bullfighter, strikingly and sometimes gorgeously attired, and surrounded by attendants only a little less so, are both ultimately at the moment of truth utterly and completely alone. Their respective roles are both heavily weighed with symbolism, not altogether dissimilar. Both are preoccupied with death and how it can be surmounted by skill, cunning or bravery: the one fighting for the life of the soul, a process which sometimes involves some highly complicated theological sidestepping; the other courting death for the purpose of showing his complete disregard for it; since neither Pope nor bullfighter can admit for a moment that death holds any fear for him if he abides by the rules of the game. In each case it is interesting to note that the adversary is horned; but not so dangerously, either in Spain or in Rome, as he once was. The devil in recent times has become as mangy and tame as one of El Cordobes's bulls.

Again, this all takes place in public. The Pope, representing a far greater and older institution, commands a much bigger audience, many of whom, like the aficionados, are consumed with religious fervour, and many more merely curious, hoping in a half-hearted sort of way that something spectacular will happen. This is more likely in Spain than in Rome.

And finally, behind the scenes in both arenas, there are similar intrigues, plots, plans, jealousies and violent partisanships, whether the horned monster be wrested or not. He never is. There is an unending supply of bright young bulls ready to charge the scarlet cloak. When the day dawns that the breed dies out, when the gorgeous regalia and the implements of battle, crozier and estoque are laid aside, both Pope and matador will have had their chips.

It is, therefore, not altogether inappropriate that these two books should be lumped together in one review, with the warning that there is one important difference. It is possible that bullfighting may be destroyed, bulls or no bulls, by the ineptitude of the men who practise it; but an institution that has survived the seven incumbents portrayed in Mr Chamberlin's book – and there were many others quite as unworthy – is clearly designed by providence to survive anything, as Cardinal Baronius, the first great papal historian, pointed out in the sixteenth century.

Mr Chamberlin's selection is not as arbitrary as it might first appear. Each of the popes he writes about precipitated a crisis in the affairs of the Church through the interaction of a defective personality and theoretically unlimited power. He does not deal with the fine theological point that the waters of grace can pour through the foulest conduit, provided it is consecrated. This is a highly significant doctrine, which to me at least seems self-evident. After all, 'bad' men differ from 'good' ones only in the magnitude of their crimes: all are tainted. The man who does not understand this is not likely to have any profound religious sense, and in particular no understanding at all of the Roman Catholic Church.

Certainly the seven pontiffs selected by Mr Chamberlin stank to high heaven as conduits of anything. Only two, Urban VI (1378–89), and the bastard Medici, Clement VII (1523–34) were chaste according to our priggish modern notions; the first became unhinged after his election, fought with everyone and widened the greatest schism the Church had hitherto suffered; so that after his death there were three popes instead of one. While Clement was so false, double-dealing and vacillating that he brought about the sack of Rome by the armies of Charles V, greatest of the Hapsburgs and as faithful a Catholic as ever lived; and as if that were not enough ensured the triumph of Lutheranism by failing to call a council, and evading the whole issue. So much for celibacy.

The others were profligates. John XII, elected in 955 at the age of sixteen, was no advertisement for teenagers. He was obsessed by the temporal power of the papacy; and failed both as Pope and king. He founded the Holy Roman Empire with the first Otto, and turned the Lateran into a brothel, where he was murdered by an outraged husband who found him in bed with his wife. No one was much shocked by this: it was his weakness as a king that destroyed him.

Benedict IX (1032–46) subjected the papacy to its greatest indignity: he sold it to the highest bidder for 1500 pounds of gold, having been elected at the age of fourteen, the first pop-pope. On the other hand, Boniface VIII was over sixty when he was given the redeemed keys in 1294. He was magnificent in his way; but he took his title as 'ruler of the world' literally, carried the temporal claims to heights never dreamed of before or since, and was crushed in the process.

Alexander VI, whose career is well known, prepared the way for the Reformation in style; and the legitimate Medici, Leo X, made it inevitable with his wild extravagance, which necessitated the sale of indulgences and inflamed Martin Luther, who in other ways was no model of rectitude himself.

All this makes a sorry tale, and Mr Chamberlin tells it with complete fairness and objectivity. Yet it is far from unedifying, and read in the right spirit is likely to do more good than a handful of Catholic Truth Society pamphlets, especially for those who imagine that the present crisis in the Church is unique. It is mild compared to many that have gone before – Rome will survive. It always does.

A Thousand Afternoons is an anthology of bullfighting. All the old familiar names are included, from the hairy high camp of Hemingway to the boozy bathos of Norman Mailer. Whatever one may think of bullfighting, no one can deny that more nonsense has been written about it than any other object under the sun, with the possible exception of the British royal family. The connoisseur of offbeat humour will find plenty to chuckle about here. That article, for instance, on El Cordobes by the crusty old Tory, Mr Kenneth Tynan. If ever two clowns were made for each other it is this grisly pair.

The book has two remarkable features: an article by John Steinbeck, and a short story by D.H. Lawrence. Both take us behind the scenes to reveal the sort of men who run this racket, without benefit of grace, as they really are. The Lawrence story, 'None of That', which I had not read before, is magnificent. No one who reads these two pieces should ever be able to look at a bullfighter again without shuddering. Which alone makes the book worth acquiring.

The Irish Times, 8 August 1970

The Rose and the Ring

Axel by Villiers de L'Isle-Adam. The Dolmen Press, 40s
Sugar Ray by Sugar Ray Robinson, with Dave Anderson.
Putnam, 36s

In the sixth book of *The Wings of the Dove*, one comes across one of those sentences that flash out so often like lighted matches among the dusty cobwebs of Henry James's later style: 'Anything was boomable enough when nothing else was more so; the author of the "rotten" book, the beauty who has no beauty, the heiress, who was only that – the creature in fine as to whom spangles or spots of any sufficiently marked and applied sort could be loudly enough predicated.'

Well, here are two 'rotten' books, so completely different in kind that they might be taken as illustrations of the extreme limits of literature at either end of the pole of sanity. One is so self-conscious that it is absolutely divorced from life; the other so pre-occupied with giving an instant impression of life in the raw that no hint of a mind shaping, moulding, creating in its own individual way can be sensed behind it. They are both symptoms of a malaise. *Axel* might be likened to consumption, once so prevalent, now almost conquered; while *Sugar Ray* is bang up-to-date and highly fashionable, like cancer and slipped discs. From the literary point of view, both are poisonous.

Villiers de L'Isle-Adam's play is one of the great monuments of the symbolist movement: an ivory tower which on closer inspection is discovered to be fashioned out of chalk. It is a prime example of what that great journalist, James Agate, used to call the higher tosh. A four-act drama that takes five hours to perform, it is unactable, unreadable, urnal and generally a cod. It survives because it captures in a unique way the mood of a period long since dead, as a diseased organ might be preserved in a jar in a scientist's laboratory in the interests of medical history.

Of all the various fads that have rippled across the literary scene over the past two hundred years, symbolism was undoubtedly the silliest, and the most sterile. It was a total rejection of flesh and blood in favour of the torturous fantasies of the mind, and it reached its culminating point in *Finnegans Wake* in which the hero sleeps his way through 628 pages, accompanied after about ten paragraphs by the reader.

It is really too easy to make fun of this sort of thing, and one feels almost ashamed to do so. Nevertheless, *Axel* does have a plot, and honesty demands that a short sketch of it be given. Count Axel is a virile lily who lives in a Gothic castle in the Black Forest, where he has retired from the world to give himself up to what I have always suspected were those practices realized so vividly by John McGahern in *The Dark*, but which are described by the author as a study of the hermetic philosophy of the alchemists and the mystery of the rose, otherwise Rosicrucianism. A rose is a pose is a pose.

Buried in a castle is an enormous treasure of gold hidden by Axel's father for the people of Frankfurt before the advent of Napoleon. A rude cousin, Commander Kasper, arrives and declares 'I am real life', which means that he has his eye on the main chance. Axel's sensitive soul is shattered, and after many, many long speeches that would exhaust a relay of Gielguds, the Count runs him through with a sword in a duel. Kasper 'utters a short raucous cry which leadenly smothers itself, etc., etc'. Ethel M. Dell could not have done better at her hottest.

In the meantime, dirty doings are going on in a convent in old French Flanders. One of the novices, Sara, has discovered the secret of the whereabouts of the treasure in a book of hours belonging to Axel's mother. Trust the nuns to sniff out a piece of information like that. After this, wild horses would not drag her back to the cloister, for which in any case she has no vocation. She makes her way to Axel's castle, where he surprises her in the vaults up to her knees in the treasure; she attempts to shoot him with two pistols that she has handy, but succeeds only in slightly wounding him. This is a subtle piece of plotting, for otherwise the epic could not proceed. Nobody seems to think of de L'Isle-Adam as the father of the television serial. He missed his vocation.

After this hectic episode the couple take, as the saying goes, one look at each other, and fall madly in love. Clearly a shotgun affair. Sara turns out to be a Rosicrucian, too; her escape from the convent has been signalized by the blooming of the mystic rose. She tries to persuade Axel to take a world cruise with the money in language that would do credit to a tourist brochure at its fruitiest. But our hero is having none of this. Here he makes his celebrated remark, afterwards cogged, like so many other cracks from French literature, by Wilde; 'Live? Our servants will do that for us.' Sara suggests a night in bed. Nothing doing. Presumably the servants can do that for them also. At last, beaten to the ropes, the idiotic girl is persuaded that the only way to live is to die. They drink a goblet of poison together and perish in a rapture.

The whole thing reads like a Wagner libretto. *In der Goldes Scheine wie leuchtest du schon!* A sort of mixture of *Rheingold* and *Tristan* complete with *Liebestod*. Wagner, as everybody knows, was an execrable poet, but a composer of genius. Set to music by Debussy, *Axel* might be acceptable, since no one expects an operatic libretto to make any kind of sense. On its own it reads like nothing on earth, and not even the valiant efforts of Marilyn Gaddis Rose, the new translator, can bring it to life.

W.B. Yeats was much impressed by this twaddle, and I am not in the least surprised. The old poseur spent his life fooling the mob with mystical roses, most of them artificial. His preface to an earlier translation is reprinted in this new one. It is the mixture as before. Nevertheless, The Dolmen Press has performed a really useful function in bringing out this beautifully printed reissue. It should be given to every embryo poet and dramatist by their best friends – if they have any – as a warning. For this reason alone I sincerely hope that it has a wide sale. The plain reader like myself can always read it for laughs.

And now from the rose to the ring. Since I have never attended a prizefight, and have never to my knowledge met a professional boxer in my life, I can only judge Sugar Ray Robinson's autobiography on its literary merits, which are non-existent. It is obviously ghostwritten, taped, and the result is a bookject. But at least it gives some useful information about the tragic career of one of the greatest fighters of his time.

Those who are interested in boxing will of course read it; they will need no recommendation from me; and they will get none. After which the bell rings for the end of this particular round.

The Irish Times, 12 September 1970

Untitled

Black List, Section H by Francis Stuart. Southern Illinois
University Press, $10.00

It is not often that a reviewer's plea for mercy is answered. In the
last issue I was complaining about novels that were chic, modish
and artificial, composed of characters that bore little resemblance
to human beings. I was prepared to settle for something minor
and unpretentious, provided it made some attempt, however feeble, to grapple with the problems of living, which in spite of passing fashions, do not really change. Instead of such a book I find
myself presented with a great one: the sort of novel that is likely
to provoke discussion, argument and controversy for many years
to come.

For a long time now anyone at all in this country who has the
slightest interest in literature most have been aware of the presence in their midst of a great solitary artist. They must have wondered at his long silence. They must have asked themselves why he
never took part in any public activity; or engaged in any of those
pursuits, such as reviewing, broadcasting or lecturing, which writers are apt to take up when they are between books, and sometimes in the case of a particular temperament even when they are
in the middle of a novel, a play or a poem.

In short, people must have been wondering what had become
of Francis Stuart. He is a founder member of the Irish Academy of

Letters. He is the author of nineteen novels, many of which have been acclaimed both at home and abroad in a manner accorded to few Irish writers during their lifetime. At the age of fifty he had already made a contribution to literature that would have ensured him a place in any short list of great Irish novelists. Now, after all these years he has produced a book that may well prove to be his masterpiece. The publication of *Black List, Section H* is an important literary event; and it is as such that it should be treated.

It is entirely autobiographical, beginning with the author's first attempt at writing poetry and ending with his imprisonment in Germany after the last war. It is an extraordinary story, and it is told in an extraordinary fashion. Many people will miss the point of it because of the manner of its telling. It is here, I think, that a reviewer may be of some use in attempting to illuminate the method used by this great writer in this summing-up of a lifetime's experience.

First of all it is extremely easy to read, which may lead some people to suppose that it is in some way trivial. They would be very much mistaken. Certainly the writing is on the whole smooth and lucid; but it is lit up on almost every page by some vivid poetic image that brands itself in the imagination and leaves no doubt in the mind that the novelist is also a poet. I would liken it to a pond at the edge of a wood upon which an autumnal sun is gleaming. At first sight everything appears to be smooth, quiet, unruffled. Then suddenly a ray of sunlight dances across the glassy water and one looks closer. The gleam disappears, and looking down into the pond one becomes aware of strange moving objects swimming to and fro under the surface; and at the bottom that fathomless mystery, which is the spring of all our lives. It is a book to be interpreted on many levels, but certainly not on the surface.

The narrator calls himself H for the most part. He begins with his very early and highly romantic marriage to Iseult Gonne, the daughter of the mythical Madame MacBride. As Stuart tells it, it is one of the most profound recreations of an unhappy alliance since George Eliot's analysis of the Casaubon ménage in *Middlemarch*. Iseult emerges as a strange, pathetic creature, maddening but sympathetic. The reader will, I think, find himself haunted by her curiously potent image. H himself is anything but pathetic; and the only thing one can say about this marriage, which is evoked with such powerful realism that one feels almost an intruder in even commenting upon it, is that it is fatal for a boy of seventeen to marry anyone.

Few authors have revealed themselves in such uncompromising terms as Stuart has in this novel. Some readers may find the portrait repulsive; but this would be to take a superficial view. What really makes a book is the personality of the author. All through this exciting story, one is aware of a strange, mysterious personage lurking between the lines: egotistical often, sometimes ruthless, yet always vulnerable. His various experiments with life, love, religion, politics, horses, chicken farming and mysticism are all attempts to expand his experience of the human condition in general, and of his own in particular. This is true of every writer. Some of them acquire a high social gloss and are very good company; but always behind the mask there is a detached intelligence at work: noting, observing, making use of everything and everybody. Anyone who really gets to know a genuine creative writer always in the end retires with a sense of icy shock. No one in recent times has made this more clear than Francis Stuart. And it is this honesty that makes the novel so important.

He wants, above all, to isolate himself from all conventional attitudes. Any writer worth his salt succeeds in doing this; but few of them set it down with such cool precision. No apology is made for his staying in Berlin during the Nazi regime; and none in my opinion is called for. All this has nothing to do with literature; but it has a great deal to do with the personality of the writer. No more unfashionable attitude could have been adopted by any novelist working in this century than that taken by Stuart. He has left himself wide open to public disapproval of every sort; and he has survived, because in the end he has in a large measure found himself the 'lonely old artist man' as Henry James put it. There are many roads to this. Stuart has chosen, not altogether willingly, the most unpopular one. And one notices at the end that the callow youth of the beginning has become a mature man, purged through suffering, and capable of the most courageous kind of loyalty and affection. His affaire and the slow growth of his love for the girl he meets in Germany during the war is most moving and rings absolutely true. Yet even here the ending is left open. One feels that with this writer the quest for the absolute will end only with death. So it is with all of us; but how many have the courage to state it?

This novel may be read as an adventure story of a most unusual man of our time; but in a much more important sense it is a journey into the interior of the spirit: a harrowing revelation of the fires through which a creative writer must pass if he is to fulfil his destiny. In the case of Francis Stuart it is a very strange one indeed; but it has produced some of the most profound and mysterious novels in modern literature. *Black List, Section H* is, in my opinion, the most important of them all: a true poetic pilgrimage of a soul that could quite easily be damned. That it is not is perhaps his greatest achievement. That and the telling of this remarkable story. The surface, as I said, is smooth; but what hidden depths it contains.

The book is published by the Southern Illinois University Press. I do not know if any arrangements have been made to bring it out in England or in this country. I hope so. If not, the general reading public on this side of the Atlantic will have been robbed of one of the most important experiences of recent times. It is a book for everyone; and whether they approve of it or not, it will last. It is outside politics, outside convention, outside every set of values except purely literary ones. And in the end that is what really matters.

Hibernia, 31 March 1972

A Backward Glance

Thy Tears Might Cease by Michael Farrell. Hutchinson, £3.00

This is a retrospective exhibition in more ways than one. It is now nine years since Michael Farrell's posthumous novel was first published. It was received with enormous enthusiasm by critics and public alike, went into four impressions, and subsequently had an even larger success in paperback. It is now reprinted again in hardback, a most unusual occurrence, which would seem to suggest that the publishers believe that it has that kind of universal and timeless appeal that is usually associated with the classics. Or is it that it is topical again, now that 'the Troubles' in Ireland have flared up once more? A little of both, I suppose.

I read it when it first appeared, and thought it immensely readable, although at the time it struck me as sentimental, and almost completely lacking in those qualities of power and passion that are such a striking feature of all great epic novels. I can see now that I was mistaken. Much stress was laid on the heroic side of Farrell's book when it first appeared by all sorts and conditions of reviewers. One was given to understand that it expressed the soul of a nation in turmoil: Ireland in the ten years following 1910. I think I must have been expecting something like *War and Peace*. Naturally I was disappointed, for manifestly *Thy Tears Might Cease* is not in this class. As a result it was all too easy to dismiss it as just another attempt to write the Great Irish Novel; although I was aware in the years that followed of certain scenes lingering in my mind with a sort of haunting intensity.

Rereading it now, I realize that I had first approached it from an entirely wrong angle; and I expect many other people did the same. It is not an epic, in spite of being set against the turbulent background of rebellion and swift social change; it is essentially a domestic novel, preoccupied with the household gods of a boy growing to manhood during a significant period of our history. And on this level, it is, I think now, quite superb.

The hero, Martin Matthew Reilly, is ten years of age when the story begins, twenty-two at the end. While one would not describe him as ordinary, he is far from being extraordinary. Sensitive, intelligent, affectionate, egotistical and slightly limp, he is a very typical product of his time and class – the pre-1914 Irish Catholic bourgeoisie. He certainly has a more poetic sensibility than most of the specimens thrown up by that particular order; but his vision of life is conditioned by it, and he never really escapes from it. He is forever looking back, remembering old places, old acquaintances, old loyalties. The book is steeped in nostalgia, a minor emotion that always inhibits greatness, but one which most of us share, particularly if we are Irish. In no country in the world is it so much indulged; we are forever harking back, retracing our steps in some banquet hall deserted, listening for the echo of some half-forgotten song we seem to have sung or heard in our youth. Farrell has captured this side of the national character with a glowing, elegiac grace. It is a book which, I imagine, has been much loved; and now I can see why.

It is not surprising that Martin Reilly is the only character who develops and grows in the whole course of 590 pages. The others, despite the many misfortunes that befall them, remain the same; older, of course, in changed circumstances, but essentially the same as when we first met them. Farrell does not want his people to change; one gets the impression at times that he is turning over the leaves of a family photograph album. 'This is Aunt Mary, and this is Aunt Eileen, and this is Grandmother Reilly. Do you remember?' Yes, we remember. This is the great charm of this book; it is also the reason why it is not a great one.

But it is wonderfully companionable. Which of us has not had a relation, teacher or friend that we loved long ago – and lost – and cannot imagine them being any other way except as they were? During the First World War a French soldier, standing up in the midst of his dead comrades, uttered a strange and magnificent cry, which is part of the French consciousness, and is itself a line of pure poetry: 'Debout les morts!' It might have served as an epigraph for this book.

Young Reilly sees some action in the War of Independence. He joins the movement, goes on the run, takes part in an attack on a police barracks, and ironically, after leaving the 'rebels' in disgust at their bigoted patriotism, is captured and tortured by the Auxiliaries. All these incidents are vividly described, and do not by any means stick out like a sore thumb. But young Martin's instincts are really domestic and personal; and the sections of the book that one remembers best are those in which he is emotionally involved with others, and with the landscape that he loves.

The famous description of the Easter Rising of 1916 is unforgettable: one of the finest things in modern Irish literature. This, one feels, is exactly how it must have appeared to those who were not personally involved. The other scenes I had remembered since my first reading were the little boy watching for the 'waits' at Christmas; and the marvellous description of Martin Reilly rowing his dying friend, Norman Dempsey, down the river after an ambush. But in fact the book is full of haunting moments, less memorable perhaps than those mentioned, but almost equally evocative and vivid.

Martin's rejection of his faith seemed to me when I first read the book to be unconvincing; now I am inclined to think it is one of the best things in it. Nothing dramatic; just a quiet, inevitable sloughing-off of old beliefs, still respected for the good they contained, but impossible to accept because of the way they were applied. It is a very subtle portrait of interior adolescent revolt.

The writing is sometimes powerful; but Farrell is at his best in a quieter vein. His lyrical passages are delicate, poetic and unobtrusive. On a second reading, one realizes how very good they are.

I am very glad to have had the opportunity of reconsidering this remarkable novel. Many others will no doubt want to do the same; and I hope that the generation that has grown up since 1963 will now read it for the first time. Many of them will find themselves mirrored in it, for it has a timeless quality.

The Irish Times, 9 December 1972

Untitled

Birchwood by John Banville. Secker and Warburg, £2.00

It might be said of the Irish that while they have lost many a battle, they have not yet been defeated in a war. On the other hand, this small country has some victories it can boast about; and one of the most glorious of them all has been, on the whole, a bloodless one. It is the conquest of the English language. Few Englishmen since Shakespeare have used their own tongue with such peculiar mastery as those Irishmen who have taken to writing in what is to them essentially a foreign method of communication. This applies not only to the native Irish, but even more to those whose ancestors settled here three or four hundred years ago, and who never spoke Gaelic.

But there is such a thing as a spirit, a rhythm of the air; and in this country it has proved contagious. The Anglo-Irish literary tradition is one of the greatest in Europe; and it persists to this day. In modern times English writers have become more and more limp; less and less preoccupied with the beauty and subtlcty of their own heritage. It is true that there are several novelists now active who are real stylists – Anthony Powell, for instance – and many good young poets, but one has only to take up any of the great British newspapers to realize how far standards have fallen. Journalism, that much maligned profession, is the best indicator I know of the state of the language in any country. And there are no

43

great journalists in England today; which means that the mass of people are quite incapable of telling the difference between good and bad. Yet, decade after decade Ireland throws up a young writer who uses English as if he were discovering it for the first time; playing with words as if they were newly minted coins made for the express purpose of throwing into the air; and if a few get lost in the process, so what? English in these hands is not the language of misers.

The latest in this long and distinguished list, and the most exciting new talent in this island for many a long year, is Mr John Banville, who at the early age of twenty-seven has just published his third novel, *Birchwood*. I am ashamed to say that before this book passed into my hands I had never heard of him. Unless I am much mistaken, every literary person will soon be equally ashamed; for of course there is no justice in this world, and hardly any critical standards left. It may be that Mr Banville will remain a writer for connoisseurs. I hope not; but the fact remains that the Anglo-Irish tradition has done it again, and produced a magician. Only envy or ignorance could deny Mr Banville the right to be acclaimed as the finest Irish stylist of his generation.

How to describe this extraordinary book? Marvellous, yes. One could trot out all the adjectives, all the superlatives, and all of them would be justified. But critical usage has become dulled with overwork; and when a reviewer is dealing with a work of the calibre of *Birchwood* he is well advised to remember those lines of Eliot:

> The word neither diffident nor ostentatious,
> An easy commerce of the old and the new,
> The common word exact without vulgarity,
> The formal word precise but not pedantic.

When I say, therefore, that this young writer displays a touch of genius, neither more nor less than that, I am weighing my words very carefully; for I do not want to be accused of an easy over-enthusiasm.

The first thing that strikes one about *Birchwood* is the use of words. They flash and shimmer, forming the most complicated and exquisite mosaic. If I were to begin to quote from the book, I should never finish this notice, for there is a striking image on every page. It is not easy reading; but it is a most exciting and rewarding experience, as all great craftsmanship must be. And although Mr Banville may be intoxicated with words, he is not drunk with them, for nothing in this curious story ever goes on too long.

It is the story of one Gabriel Godkin, and it is at once clear that this is not another Irish autobiographical novelist. Certain incidents may very well correspond with experiences of the author; but on the whole he would appear to be one of those rare novelists who is genuinely creative. When work of this kind falls into the hands of a certain type of sterile hack, posing as a critic, it usually causes them to foam at both ends with frustrated rage. I was not, therefore, surprised to find *Birchwood* dismissed in a famous English Sunday newspaper as a 'rapt but rather leaden exercise in Irish Gothick'. We are further informed that Mr Banville writes a 'poet's prose, but only in the sense that he is given to such expressions as: "Violets and cowshit, my life has been ever thus". ' Thus far have the once proud English fallen, that they must pick a phrase out of context, which shows this author at less than his best, so terrified are they of the singing mastery he brings to their own language. Of course when a novelist is writing at such a pitch there are bound to be lapses; but the compensations are so rich that they do not matter at all.

Gabriel is in search of his past, well aware of the fact that it is another country. Thus time and place become entangled; and a vision of life takes over. It is a poet's vision, full of echoes, sun, shadows and sudden unexplained beginnings and endings: in short, a celebration. The Godkins are a curious family, wild, passionate and untamed. The description of the boy's upbringing among such horror and beauty haunts the mind. Birchwood is decaying, and so are its inhabitants. Family secrets are hinted at and half-explained to the boy, as such things always are; and in the end he runs away with a travelling circus, the description of which is as gaudy, tragic, comic and ribald as life itself. This is a marvellous section, worthy of Joyce. In the end, Gabriel comes back, discovers most of the secrets, and sets himself the task of reconstructing the past. One extract only:

> We imagine that we remember things as they were, while in fact all we carry into the future are fragments which reconstruct a wholly illusory past. That first death we witness will always be a murmur of voices down a corridor and a clock falling silent in the darkened room, the end of love is forever two spent cigarettes in a saucer and a white door closing.

There is a story, of course, and a particularly savage one. The book can be read for that alone. The characters do not develop, with the exception of the narrator: in this book it is life itself that is seen to unfold before us, like a series of plants and flowers photographed by a slow-moving lens. Yet most of the characters are extremely vivid. Gabriel's father, forever a dark, brooding, dangerous figure; his wild and tragic aunt, Martha; his gorgeous gorgon of a grandmother; his sly, stunted little grandfather. And all the circus folk spring to life without exception with a pounce. They are true creatures of memory: vivid, larger than life, shouting to get out.

Finally, Mr Banville has a glorious sense of comedy. Anyone who can play with words as he can usually has; but no one who reads this book will ever forget the awful black humour of Granny Godkin's death, or the sheer hilarity of Gabriel's first love, Rosie, whose heart he won with mathematics! Yes, algebra to be exact. The funniest piece of wooing I have come across in many a long year.

I have devoted a great deal of space to this novel, and I hope given some indication of its quality. But it really must be read; and I think it is time also that Mr Banville was acclaimed. He is young, possessed of enormous talent, and has already achieved much. A great Irish banking group are, I believe, looking for a book by a young Irish writer on which to bestow a prize. If they pass up this one, they will not only fail in their duty: it will be a triumph of old apathy again. And I hope they will not judge the book by the cover, which is awful.

Hibernia, 16 February 1973

The Labelling of Lee Dunne

The number of authors banned by the Irish Censorship Board over the past forty years is so incredible that it is necessary to set them down again from time to time. They include Joyce Cary, Theodore Dreiser, William Faulkner, Scott Fitzgerald, Anatole France, André Gide, Graham Greene, Knut Hamsun, Ernest Hemingway, Aldous Huxley, Thomas Mann, Marcel Proust, Ignazio Silone, John Steinbeck, H.G. Wells and the Church of England. This list includes at least seven Nobel Prize winners, and must strike some younger readers as a clear case of lunacy, either on my part or on that of the censors. For, of course, the works of all those writers were later 'unbanned', and are largely available, according to the printing situation, for those lucky young men and women of twenty who can afford to buy them in paperback. However, I can assure them that all of those writers, together with a publication issued by the Church of England, were at one time labelled 'indecent and/or obscene' by the Censorship Board in this country. All of which would seem to suggest that this mysterious committee was frequently wrong in its moral judgment.

Of recent years this iniquitous law has not been much employed; but it still remains on the statute books; and over the past forty years it has been used to brand the work of practically every well-known Irish writer of merit. We remain the only country in the Western world of which this can be said. I repeat this, because I do not think it is sufficiently appreciated and known. Either our writers are particularly immoral persons, or there is something gravely wrong with the Censorship Board. The fact that a great many Irish artists, branded by mysterious officials in their own country as purveyors of goods that are 'obscene', are acclaimed elsewhere as honourable members of their craft, would seem to suggest that our laws governing the publication of books are iniquitous and unjust. And to prove the point that the censors are ignorant and undemocratic, it has been deemed necessary to revoke their decisions in very many cases over the years, thus holding the law, such as it is, up to ridicule and contempt.

And these mysterious officials are still at it. When, as the popular song has it, will they ever learn? Last November Mr Lee Dunne's latest novel *Paddy Maguire is Dead* was banned, and quite recently this 'judgment' was upheld by the Appeal Board. Mr Dunne is a professional writer, whose books in paperback have a large circulation in Ireland, thus making it possible for him to live here, in a very modest manner, as everybody connected with writing knows. And now the censors, with a stroke of the pen, have taken his means of livelihood away from him. So much for justice.

This novel was published in paperback first, thus making it possible for a larger number of people to buy it. Insofar as one can read the minds of men who ban books in this country, it would appear that this cheap edition had something to do with the banning. What is 'safe' for a man with money is dangerous for those who have to count their pennies. Here again we come upon a situation unique in Western Europe. But the banning of this book poses an even more serious question. Do the censors know what they are doing? And in particular do they know what this novel is all about? If they do, then they are a truly sinister body; and if they do not, they are an ignorant and arrogant bunch who have once again made the Republic of Ireland ridiculous: the home of obscurantism and imbecility.

It will be argued that *Paddy Maguire is Dead* has many passages which deal with the sexual act between men and women in a manner which might be described as 'raw'. It has. So have many other paperbacks on sale freely in this country. They are, however, by foreign authors; and their sex passages are just that and no more. Whereas the sexual descriptions in Mr Dunne's novel are of a special nature. They reveal, together with everything else in the book, the character and temperament of an alcoholic. This story is the most detailed and horrifying exposé of alcoholism ever written in this country. Every incident, every character, every act of the anti-hero, Maguire, is motivated and overshadowed by the effects of this frightful disease. In any other country, it would be regarded as didactic. Here it is branded as 'indecent and/or obscene' because it reveals exactly and honestly what it is really like to be an alcoholic. I mentioned above that if the censors know this, then they are truly sinister, because it would appear that they do not want people to know the real truth of this condition. I would, however, prefer to think that they are ignorant. But ignorance of this problem on the part of persons invested with such power is almost criminal. They are confusing sex with disease.

From the beginning of this novel, it is made clear that Maguire is a potential alcoholic. He suffers from blackouts whenever he drinks. His sexual exploits are of a 'special nature' because they are not the actions of a responsible man. The desperation, the loneliness, the craving for affection and the wild pursuit of it, are characteristics of this disease, and are instantly recognizable to anyone who has any experience of it; as is the sense of guilt with which Maguire is riddled. Nothing is glossed over; nothing is glorified: his sexual exploits are revealed for what they are, figments of a phantasmagoric world. Some of the scenes are Hogarthian; and all of them take place in a working-class setting.

I doubt if this novel could have been written against any other background. Dickens would have made a great masterpiece of it. Lee Dunne writes in the language of the Dublin slums. Evidently the censors, no doubt well-educated nonentities, disapprove of this. Have they ever really listened to it? Do they know anything of alcoholism? If they do, and then quite deliberately suppress this book, then God forgive them. If they don't, it is about time they learned. Because at the end Lee Dunne indicates how this disease can be arrested; although it cannot be cured. The real worth of the book can, I suppose, only be appreciated by those who have themselves been through this hell; but it would be a very good thing if the many others who have not, but may well be heading for it, could be allowed to read about what may be in store for them.

Nowadays we have many public meetings, many seminars dedicated to the discussion of alcoholism. Bishops have the gall to get up and tell us how terrible it is, one unctuous platitude following another. Yet, when someone writes a book revealing the real truth of alcoholism, it is banned, and labelled 'obscene'. The real obscenity is to be found among those who say all the right things, and do nothing about it, except to ban a book that might enlighten many who are in need of it. And does so in their own language.

After the rejection by the Appeal Board, I do not know exactly what the legal position is. But there are in the present government many enlightened and civilized men. Surely it is possible to have this scandalous banning quietly rescinded, and this highly moral novel restored to general circulation. Since the members of the Censorship Board and the Appeal Board are all faceless men, they have no face to lose. And if they are really ignorant of the effects of alcoholism as a disease, I know of many people who would be only too happy to explain it to them. After that, unless they are completely ossified, they will see this extraordinary book in a completely new light, the lurid glow of a terrible and widespread disease.

Hibernia, 11 May 1973

Untitled

The Wonder-Worker by Dan Jacobson. Weidenfeld and
Nicolson, £2.25
Hide and Seek by Dennis Potter. Deutsch, £2.25

I am sick and tired of novelists who write novels about novelists
writing novels about novelists. It is all so bogus. An anecdote that
might amuse or interest the reader in a short story of 5000 words
is stretched out by a technical trick so that he may be overpow-
ered by the weight of 50 or 60,000. And puzzled; so that in the
process he may come to the conclusion that what he is reading
with so much effort is a very profound piece of work, instead of a
blueprint for a literary construction with an elaborate front wall
and nothing behind it. The novel within a novel was an interesting experiment first brought to perfection by André Gide in *Les
Faux-Monnayeurs* in 1925, and not really capable of development, as
has been amply proved by its imitators ever since. Gide was perhaps the most distinguished man of letters of his time, but he was
not by nature a novelist. Neither are the two writers whose books
nearly drove me mad in an effort to read them for the purpose of
this review.

    Mr Dan Jacobson comes to us with the worst possible refer-
ences. Long experience has taught me to distrust any writer of fiction praised by Messrs Cyril Connolly and Philip Toynbee. The
former hates novels, and the latter likes them only when they are

obscure and preferably kinky. On the dust cover of *The Wonder-Worker* this jaded pair pay lavish tribute to Mr Jacobson's last novel; and if that were not enough he comes to us also with a strong recommendation from that well-known public relations officer, Lady Antonia Fraser. With this unholy trinity plugging for him I expected the worst, and got it.

The Wonder-Worker is all about a character called Timothy and his creator, the so-called Narrator. Timothy is born in London in circumstances so portentous that they recall to mind the Gospel story of the birth of Jesus Christ. Mr Jacobson's hero, however, unlike Christ, is an intolerably fey character who is supposed to possess extraordinary powers which even the Son of Man would have hesitated to claim for Himself. One of them, so far as I could make out, is the ability to turn himself into precious stones. He is, however, endowed by Mr Jacobson with one unforgettable characteristic, which nobody can deny, and which I can assure all who are interested that he absolutely possesses, and that is the power of boring the bejasus out of the reader, to an extent unread of even in recent fiction.

Interspersed with Timothy's wonderful works we are introduced to the Narrator, who is supposed to be writing the novel, creating the characters from a luxury hotel in Switzerland. In the end we discover that the hotel is a lunatic asylum, and the Narrator apparently quite dotty, as would anybody be who invested £2.25 in this pretentious chi-chi. So please, Mr Jacobson, on my knees, Mr Jacobson, don't put your theories on the page.

The same plea might be made to Mr Dennis Potter. He takes the technique a step further. He has a character called Daniel Miller who is convinced that he is a character called Daniel Miller in a novel. This seems to me to be pretty obvious, but to Mr Potter it is clearly of enormous significance. We then are introduced to the writer who is writing about Daniel Miller, and after a while it seems to be apparent that he is in fact writing about himself. But he isn't. That is to say, not entirely so. He is writing about himself, yes, but he is also writing about a writer who is not only writing about Daniel Miller and himself, but in addition about the

poet Coleridge and a friend of his, that is to say a friend of the
composite person who is Miller and the writer, called Richard. I
trust I make myself plain. It took me two nights of closely applied
reading to arrive at this lucid solution.

In spite of the irritation he has caused me I cannot feel quite
as furious with Mr Potter as any reviewer who imagines that he is
still more or less in possession of his faculties might be. Am I
writing this notice, or am I writing about the person who is writing a review of a review of a review? I begin to wonder. If I began
to express myself in that way people would very soon cease to read
this column. So why should they take upon themselves the
penance of ploughing through a novel within a novelist within a
novel called *Hide and Seek*? I doubt very much if many will; and it
is entirely Mr Potter's own fault.

He is, in fact, a writer of great power. Like so many people
who use this technique, he is essentially an essayist. Yet there is
one scene in this book that reveals him as a writer with a true creative streak. It takes place between pages 96 and 106 and con-
cerns the encounter between the writer who is not quite Miller
and not quite Richard, and not quite himself, and the prostitute
he imagines is an aloof and beautiful girl. This is superb writing by
any standard; but it is immediately followed by a piece of D.H.
Lawrence greenery-fernery in which God turns out to be an Italian sodomite. No doubt He is, among many other things. But one
thing I am prepared to bet He is not: and that is a Creator who
cannot make up His mind what He is. If that were the case He
would long ago have appeared to St Jean-Paul Sartre and assured
him that he, St Jean-Paul, was an absurdity. Mr Potter has had no
such revelation. He clearly believes he is a novelist, which really is
absurd. But what a pity Messrs Connolly and Toynbee did not get
their hands on this one. It would serve them right.

Hibernia, 16 November 1973

Fallon's Poetic Genius

Collected Poems by Padraic Fallon. The Dolmen Press, £3.00

Whenever I was asked, anytime since the death of Kavanagh, who, in my opinion, was now the greatest living poet in Ireland, I always replied without any hesitation at all – Padraic Fallon. People were apt to be puzzled by this and enquired where they could get his poems. To this I had to reply that as yet they had not been published; and as a result received many a curious look; for people have no opinion of a poet who has never appeared between the covers of a book; and unless those people had a more than passing interest in poetry, they were not likely to have kept the various magazines and newspapers in which the work of this great poet appeared for a period of thirty years or more. Many had, of course, heard his magnificent verse plays performed on Radio Éireann; but had they been published? They had not. So all in all, I was not able to give real satisfaction in this matter.

Padraic Fallon has had a curious career, as a poet. He always steadfastly refused to have his poems brought out in book form, which makes him unique in poetry circles here or elsewhere. When at last a few years ago he was persuaded to prepare a collected edition, he did so, I am told, with the greatest reluctance; and it is only now at the age of sixty-nine that he has made a selection of his poems, and literature is the richer for this remarkable volume. It is the most important book since the *Collected Poems* of Patrick Kavanagh.

On reading the first line we know we are in the presence of a master.

> A man must go naked to an island,
> Let the weather lend
> A skin till he grows one, the rock fit
> The beat of the surftop to
> His feet.

Fallon is particularly sensitive to the sea, and to the men who draw a precarious livelihood from it, especially when they are old, no longer fit for work and merely sit on a wall looking out at the implacable ocean. The poems in this first section are magnificent, although they are all by no means about fishermen. 'Johnstown Castle' is, by any standard, and by that I mean an international one, a great poem. In it the poet comes face to face with his identity, and the difficulty facing all poets. He is characteristically humble, although I suspect he knows his real worth.

> The monologue intrudes, my words let me
> Into a poem, not into the poetry.

I wish very much that other poets would learn those lines; and indeed learn the whole of this magnificent poem by heart. It is the voice of a master: quiet, uneasy, yet in perfect command of his medium. No one knows better than Fallon how hard a trade he is following, and his humility is only possible because he does know.

It would appear that Fallon passed through a Yeats period. It is no coincidence that the poems written under this influence are the weakest in the collection. I simply refuse to believe in 'Yeats at Athenry Perhaps'. The 'Perhaps' is too telling, a complete give-away in fact. But this temporary lapse is more than made up for by the marvellous Raftery dialogues, than which there is nothing more impressive in modern Irish literature. One can only marvel at such ease, identification and sheer poetic power. The book was worth publishing for these alone; and many a lesser poet would have long ago made his reputation out of them.

> A lovely instrument. One finds all
> Silence in a note.

Fallon almost remained silent; but now it is revealed that his genius was a lovely instrument. Yet not lovely only. Consider a poem like 'The Head', which might easily become an anthology piece, but which I hope will not. It is strong, brutal and frightening. Fallon's poems are always strong and sometimes they are overwhelming. One could go on quoting forever; but I have always refused to do so, since I think it is a form of cheating on the part of a reviewer: it fills up space. Let the reader take my word for it – he doesn't have to – that this is the work of a very great poet; and if he wants to prove it, let him buy it, it is a precious volume. We have had to wait a long time for it; but it is worth it.

Since this notice was written I have heard that Padraic Fallon has died. The loss is a great one to literature; yet I think he has fulfilled himself. But what a very curious swansong. To live the life of a poet, intensely and quietly, for the best part of forty years; to publish that quantity of verse that he wants preserved; and then to die. A strange event indeed. Now his words are curiously prophetic:

> Around me now from this great height
> Is a vision I did not seek.

He was the first of our poets, and is at rest. Who will take his place? Kinsella, I suppose, while among the under-forties I would be prepared to lay a bet on Desmond Egan. I know I am laying myself open to assault, but since I do not frequent Dublin literary pubs, I can afford to be objective. Who cares what people say? Not me. Although I say so myself, I was one of those who fought a lone battle for Fallon for years. Perhaps we were right after all. May his gentle and poetic soul rest in peace.

Hibernia, 25 October 1974

Memory and Desire

The Leavetaking by John McGahern. Faber, £2.50

After the death of Joyce in 1941 it seemed to many that novel
writing had come to an end in Ireland; or perhaps it would be
more correct to say that novelists of Irish birth using the English
language had ceased to function, since Joyce spent most of his life
abroad. This idea of a wasteland was largely created by university
professors and similar parasites to whom the author of *Ulysses* and
Finnegans Wake came as a godsend. Since few people could understand the last work of the master, the commentators took it upon
themselves to interpret him to the multitude, much in the same
way as the exegetists are forever explaining the more obscure
parts of Holy Writ. Thus was the Joyce industry born; and in spite
of the fact that most of its products were studied by other university professors and students, and hardly at all by the general
public, it did untold harm to writing in Ireland.

For, of course, Irish writers continued to produce novels in
the forties and fifties; and very distinguished work it was. One
thinks in particular of Elizabeth Bowen, Kate O'Brien, Mary
Lavin – whose novels are scandalously neglected – Francis Mac-
Manus, Benedict Kiely and Brian Moore. The two latter are still
with us, now in their prime, and still producing novels that are
marvels of creative energy and style, while Mary Lavin has confined herself entirely to the short story, in which form she is probably the greatest living master. Now that the Joyce industry is

beginning to wane, these writers are in their turn becoming the subject of learned studies and ponderous critical tomes. Since Bowen, MacManus and O'Brien are dead, and their work is completed, the vultures cannot harm them; but I fear for the others. It is, I suppose, gratifying to be hailed as a classic in one's lifetime; but it can be an embarrassment, for such is the critic's passion for classification that writers like Kiely, Moore and Mervyn Wall will inevitably be branded as products of the forties and fifties because they began to be published in those decades. They will be hailed as the courageous few, who, at a time when the Censorship Board was particularly vicious, kept the flag of literature flying, produced brilliant work and prepared the way for the novelists of the sixties.

And no doubt in time there will be critical studies of the writers of this decade also, either individually or as a group. For there is very much a school of the sixties, and in one particular it is unique. Starting in 1960 there followed in quick succession Edna O'Brien, William Trevor, Aidan Higgins, John McGahern, Maurice Leitch, Patrick Boyle, James Plunkett, Kevin Casey and Anthony Cronin. The brilliant John Banville was first published in January 1970; and two years later came Jennifer Johnston. Michael Farrell's *Thy Tears Might Cease* was published in 1963, and became an international bestseller, as did Plunkett's *Strumpet City*. Farrell was, of course, dead when his novel was published, so he cannot be considered entirely typical of this school. Another feature of the sixties was the emergence of the popular 'middlebrow' novel as exemplified in the work of Terence de Vere White, Christy Brown and Brian Cleeve. So that never before have so many novelists, as distinct from poets and playwrights, been at work in Ireland, or at any rate dealing with Irish life and themes. And many of them dealt with subjects never before discussed in Irish fiction; in itself a sufficient reason to make them important.

If I were asked which of all those novelists showed the greatest sign of all-round excellence I should answer without any hesitation at all – John McGahern. His first novel, *The Barracks*, was published in 1963 and created a sensation. *The Dark*, which came out two years later, created a sensation of a somewhat different kind. It was banned; the author lost his job as a result and had to emigrate. Since then he has brought out a volume of short stories. And now after far too long of an interval we have his third novel, *The Leavetaking.*

Let me say at once that it was well worth waiting for. The first hundred pages of this novel are so sensitive, so deeply moving, and so brilliantly written that they constitute a triumph that might well serve as a model for all younger writers, and, of course, a joy for all connoisseurs of fiction. About the last eighty pages I am not so sure; except to say that they would make the reputation of a lesser writer.

The story is told in the first person, by a narrator called Moran. It is largely autobiographical, as McGahern's novels tend to be. It deals with the growing-up of a young boy in what might be called the McGahern country; and it is the most sensitive as well as the most powerful portrayal of adolescence in modern Irish literature. One has to go back to Joyce to find anything to equal it; but *The Leavetaking* displays a quality that the author of *Ulysses* on the whole lacks: tenderness. This is particularly true of the young boy's relationship with his mother. This is a theme which can so easily turn into mawkishness; but McGahern handles it with such restraint that the effect is shattering. Only a writer of the first rank and the greatest integrity could achieve this.

And as for his power, there are at least two scenes that I doubt if even Joyce could have brought off with such poetic truth and strength. One is the death scene, where the furniture of the house is dismantled while Moran's mother is dying; the other the episode where the boy hides in the laurels with an alarm clock as the time approaches when his mother is due to be buried, since he is not allowed to attend the funeral. Only talent of the rarest kind could write of these things with such perfection.

About the second half of the book I am not so sure. Moran becomes a teacher, and the scenes in the Dublin school are vintage McGahern; but when he goes off to London and has an affair with a divorced American girl, the author's touch is not so sure.

For one thing the girl does not come to life, although her father, a truly horrible person, does. It is a corrupt milieu; very much Henry James country; and since McGahern is an uncompromising puritan, he is not at all easy in it. Not that his narrator is supposed to be: this is made quite plain.

'I can't be rid of the whole mess quick enough.' This is the way Moran feels about those awful Americans; and I can't say I blame him. But this section is not entirely successful; although the love affair with the girl, Isobel, is beautifully treated.

As in all this writer's work, there are passages of marvellous lyrical beauty; throughout the book they light up like sunlight on snow. It is the work of a supremely gifted novelist; and I hope very much that we do not have to wait another ten years for his next book. One feels, particularly in the London scenes, that McGahern is at a crossroads. With a writer of such importance it must be a matter of the greatest interest to watch what way he will go. For novelists like this are rare indeed.

Hibernia, 10 January 1975

The Apotheosis of Wilde

Oscar Wilde by H. Montgomery Hyde. Eyre Methuen, £6.95

There is nothing new to say about Oscar Wilde; yet people will go on saying it. For some years now he has been deified in the literary sense; and since one hardly ever encounters criticism of his work, as distinct from his personality and trials, it might be salutary to point out that his writing, apart from one play, is second-rate, and often worse.

On the whole he was a very bad writer indeed; and to read his books today is an embarrassing experience.

Such a view of Wilde may strike many people as new; but in fact it is not: it is merely unfashionable. One of the clearest and most objective views of Wilde can be found in an essay on the playwright written thirty years ago by James Agate, one of the greatest journalists of this century.

He makes no effort to deny that *The Importance of Being Ernest* is one of the best light comedies in the English language. He then proceeds to dissect the other four plays, exposing them for the worthless, stilted pieces they are. They will survive, Agate writes, as long as actors and actresses like dressing up, and stage producers like functioning as dressers.

In the beginning of his essay the great critic quotes a passage from *De Profundis*, which is more than usually awful, even for Wilde:

> The gods had given me almost everything. I had genius, a distinguished name, high social position, brilliancy, intellectual

daring; I made art a philosophy and philosophy an art; I altered the minds of men, and the colours of things ... Whatever I touched I made beautiful in a new mode of beauty ... I awoke the imagination of my century so that it created myth and legend around me. I summed up all systems in a phrase and all existence in an epigram.

There are worse passages than that in *De Profundis*, a work full of a sort of quivering self-pity, fruity, purple passages, and a great many second-hand ideas. Wilde had not genius; he was deluding himself if he imagined he had a high social position; and he had no intellectual daring whatsoever. Such ideas as are to be found in his essays and other prose writings are nearly always borrowings, usually from French writers and philosophers. And far from being a creature of myth and legend, he was entirely a product of publicity. If a public relations officer can be said to have genius, then Wilde had it.

He was the prototype of those Irishmen and women who go to England, determined to make their name at any cost. He had one great advantage: he was a superb talker and a brilliant wit, even if most of his jokes are basically epicene. Sydney Smith was an equally fine conversationalist, and a far more profound wit; but how many people have heard of him? About as many, I should say, as know Tibullus and Montaigne. Wilde's dressing-up as an aesthete in that ridiculous outfit was on the same level as Brendan Behan's efforts to draw attention to himself, sixty years later.

It killed both of them. But Behan was a more sensitive and altogether more vulnerable person, with a tiny but genuine lyrical talent. Wilde was tougher, more ambitious, and was a great deal less scrupulous. I think it is too much to say that he deliberately chose jail and exile at the height of his career; but there is small doubt that, subconsciously at any rate, he brought ruin on himself. And posthumous glory, which had nothing to do with literature.

Wilde had a coarse, vulgar streak. Instead of putting his undoubted talents to their best use, working hard at his trade, and achieving a decent reputation, he settled for the tinsel of publicity, was flattered by it and eventually obsessed by it.

All his biographers claim that he was an immensely good-natured and kind-hearted man; and indeed he seems to have been. But I have always suspected that it was a very theatrical sort of amiability: a desire to please, which is forgotten as soon as the subject of it has departed. There were at least three people whom Wilde did not consider when he embarked upon his reckless course to ruin, which was to make him far more famous than his writing could ever have done; and these people were his wife and two sons. I know it is terribly old-fashioned to say so, but good nature begins at home.

Mr Montgomery Hyde's new biography is perhaps the best of the lot and certainly the most accurate. He does not give much space to consideration of Wilde's books, poems and plays, which is wise of him. But everything else gets full and detailed treatment, including aspects of Wilde's sexual life, which, not to put too fine a point on it, are disgusting. Does it really add to one's knowledge of anybody to examine bedlinen?

However, there are some interesting new facts about Wilde's ancestry. It was always understood that his paternal great-grandfather was a builder who came from the northeast of England to follow his trade in Dublin. Now it appears that the Wildes were descended from a Colonel de Wilde, a Dutch officer, who accompanied William of Orange to Ireland, and for his services was granted land in Connaught.

Although I have always thought Oscar Wilde to be a repulsive person, it must be said that this is a first-rate biography of a spectacular career. Mr Montgomery Hyde's book is likely to remain the standard one for many years. Unless, of course, someone sets out to treat this subject in the spirit of an Agate. That would be really worth waiting for.

Irish Independent, 24 May 1976

Bards and Bullets

The Heart Grown Brutal by Peter Costello. Gill & Macmillan, Rowman & Littlefield, £12.00

Mr Costello deals with the Irish revolution in literature, from Parnell to the death of Yeats. I had not read more than half a dozen pages of this wise and often brilliant history when I was forced to leave it down and think.

He is concerned with 'the extent to which writers influenced political leaders and revolutionaries, as well as vice versa'. That a period of violence should make its mark upon literary men seems self-evident; but how many political upheavals have been assisted, consciously or otherwise, by genuine creative artists, as distinct from propagandists? Take three great names at random. Shakespeare had no political influence at all; and his immediate concern would seem to have been the turning of a fast buck at the box office. Goethe had great social prestige, and found a ready response in the German heart for the wise saws he incorporated into his work. (*Tages Arbeit*, *Abendes Gastei*, and so on.) But he had no sympathy with the idea of German reunification. And Milton, although he was anti-prelatical, and served in Cromwell's government, cannot be said to have influenced the course of events in his time in any way.

Yet Mr Costello quotes W.B. Yeats, in a letter to a friend, wondering after the 1916 Rising if some of the responsibility was not his. This is a fascinating theory, and one which gives rise to several questions. Would the Rebellion have taken place without the literary renaissance? No doubt it would. But I think on the whole that Mr Costello is right in claiming that it would have been different. Ireland towards the end of the last century was unique in the sense that it was a country rediscovering its ancient past, which had moreover taken place in an almost dead language. It must have been a heady experience for the young poets of those days to make the acquaintance of Cú Chulainn and company. It did not seem to have occurred to any of them that that particular man of war, stripped of all the poetics, was just another Ulster thug. But the myths are potent; and we have not escaped from them even today.

At the turn of the century there was a great deal of idealism about the making of a nation. This was particularly evident among the poets. Herein lay the seeds of disaster.

None of the leaders of the 1916 Rebellion were really practical men. Revolutions may be made by poets; but it is a depressing fact that they are sustained by pedants. Even Connolly, who was so realistic in so many ways, had a dotty side. He imagined that a socialist state would be compatible with a revival of ancient Celtic Ireland. All one can say is that with the leaders' heads stuffed with Yeats's ersatz gods and goddesses, their own notions of blood sacrifice and Connolly's flawed syndicalism, it is a great wonder that the Rebellion was not even a greater fiasco than it actually turned out to be.

The prose writers, who might be described as the manure of literature, as distinct from the poets' flowering shrubs, perceived that the great mass of the people did not give a tinker's curse for mythical heroes. They had their own shibboleths. Ireland free meant Ireland pure, Catholic and racist. The credit for publishing this at that time must go to George Moore, a novelist whose writing had much greater influence on James Joyce than that unfrocked Jesuit ever admitted. Mr Costello gives Moore his rightful place in Irish literature, for the first time, I think.

It was the prose writers also who expressed the inevitable disillusionment that followed upon the establishment of the Free State. This was no land for heroes to live in. Mr Costello makes the very important distinction between a revolution and a rebellion. Most of the patriot-politicians were content with the latter: more than willing to take over existing institutions, rather than change them. As a result, all that happened was that the country ended up with new backsides in the old saddles; and most of them could not even ride.

Mr Costello finds Michael Farrell's novel *Thy Tears Might Cease* a perfect illustration of his thesis: romance, confusion, disillusionment. This may get him into trouble with the higher critics. Farrell's novel is not a great one, but it is by far the best and most sensitive record of those crucial years of pre-war peace, armed chaos and resulting bitterness. Its immense success with the public has led to its being underestimated.

Mr Costello deals with all the famous figures with sympathy, insight and wit. But it seems to me that one of the most important aspects of the book lies in his treatment of the more unexpected figures of the revival: Gerald O'Donovan for instance. The novels of this ex-priest are now all to seek; but he gave a clear enough, if rather over-kind picture of the real Ireland that was likely to emerge after the Civil War. And some readers may be surprised to discover that Edith Somerville also saw the way things were going. This remarkable woman went even further. She was clear-sighted enough to see both sides of the red line. 'When the British lost the support of Irish people like Edith Somerville,' writes Mr Costello, 'there was nothing left to fight for.' That too was a tragedy.

It is impossible to give more than an indication of the scope of this enthralling book. I would like to devote space to the treatment of Jack B. Yeats in one of the later chapters. This extraordinary man was in many ways a far greater figure than his brother, and in the context of Irish history he has his own special place, as Mr Costello demonstrates. *The Heart Grown Brutal* is full of such special and unexpected insights. It is one of those books which opens up endless areas for discussion, and which makes one feel, after reading it, a little more effective than before.

The Irish Times, 10 December 1977

Proper Studies

The Human Situation by Aldous Huxley. Chatto and
Windus, £4.95

In the storm of argument, approval and controversy provoked by
the activities of the Catholic Church since the Second Vatican
Council, it seems to me that the real issue and its effects have
been forgotten. Minor irrelevancies have clouded the minds of
the laity, and, one suspects, the clerical consciousness also. Nuns
tripping about in hideous 'modern' garb, and priests flinging shirt
buttons and discretion to the winds, have, together with M.
Lefebvre, obscured the central issue.

The Roman Church has always been concerned with power
and organization; but rarely in its long history has it acted with
such an arrogant disregard for the conscience of the laity as in the
liturgical changes foisted upon its members after the conclusion
of the last Council. Under a guise of 'liberalism', marvellously sustained by the unsuspecting media, the letter was changed but the
old spirit of Trent prevailed. Worship thus, it commanded, or
detach yourself from the body of the faithful. It was scandalous
enough to banish an ancient and beautiful liturgy with a complete
disregard for the feelings and wishes of ordinary Catholics; but
what was ordained in its place was the culmination of a long and
sometimes sinister historical process.

Since the rise of Christianity there has been a division
between the religion of immediate experience, the religion of

'direct acquaintance with the divine in the world' and 'the religion of symbols, of the imposition of order and meaning upon the world through verbal or non-verbal symbols': in short, the opposition of a highly organized political body to the mystical experience. The 'members of the official religion have tended to look upon the mystics as difficult, trouble-making people'. And finally in our time the civil servants of Rome have succeeded in outlawing any form of quiet prayer where two or more are gathered together.

This is an extremely dangerous move; and it has already led to grave confusion, such as the lack of an inner certainty, a God-given repose. The officials, who are always anxious for a public demonstration, have triumphed. They have always assumed that the ordinary lay person was something of a fool, and needed to be directed on his way from womb to tomb, especially in the manner of his public worship; he must be made to shout and sing at pre-ordained intervals; he has no capacity for anything better. That is the real kernel of modern Church usage.

The patient reader may wonder what all this has to do with a new volume of lectures by the late Aldous Huxley. I make no apology for dwelling on one of those lectures at such a length: the remarkable 'Man and Religion', delivered on 23 November 1959, at the University of California. Religion is, after all, the most important of human experiences; and it is impossible in a review of this length to do justice to Huxley's enormous scope, erudition and humanity. Other readers will find different subjects to stir their imagination and provoke their interest. It is the sort of book that gives off ideas like sparks; it is in the best sense inflammable.

Huxley is not responsible for the remarks above, except where he is directly quoted. But his lecture on religion brought together in my mind very many stray thoughts, which have lain dormant for some time. I have no doubt that his other subjects will have an equal effect on other people.

The Irish Times, 4 February 1978

Tate à Teyte

The Pursuit of Perfection: A Life of Maggie Teyte by Garry O'Connor.
Victor Gollancz, £7.95

Germany is a masculine nation, France is feminine. Spain is masculine, Italy feminine. England is masculine, Ireland feminine. Who has not at some time or another engaged in such like generalizations? They make for a pleasant and not too strenuous parlour game; and they are on the whole quite futile. They remind one of a couple of lines of Dorothy Parker:

> I never said they feed my heart,
> But still they pass my time.

When we come to discuss music, and singers in particular, we are on firmer ground. Musically speaking, there can be little doubt that the Teutonic nations, Germany and Austria, lead the field, or perhaps, one should say, blow the loudest trumpet. Bach, Beethoven, Brahms, Mozart, Schubert – who can deny that these composers are the very foundation of the repertoire? (Haydn might also be included, but it could be argued that he had a Slavonic background.)

And singers? Well here, in the light of the book under review, we might proceed by a process of elimination. Many countries have produced great singers, but Britain rather less than most. In the last century or so she has given only three sopranos of true international stature to the world: Mary Garden, Eva Turner and

Maggie Teyte. (England has fared better with deeper voices: Clara Butt, Kirkby Lunn, Ferrier, Baker.)

Margaret Tate was born in Wolverhampton in 1888. Her family was Scots-Irish and Roman Catholic, and were quite well off. As a young girl she was heard singing in the Catholic Church in Maiden Lane in London by Paul Rubens, a gifted and very rich amateur of music. The Rubenses and a few other influential patrons, including the formidable Marchioness of Ripon, sent the young soprano off to Paris to study under Jean de Reszke, one of the greatest singers of the nineteenth century, and an equally famous teacher. Here she learned a method that was to last her during a public career of nearly fifty years. She also changed her name to Teyte because the French pronunciation of Tate is peculiar.

She made her debut in 1906, and began one of the most extraordinary and unusual singing careers of the century. She became a member of the Opéra Comique, and in a very short time found herself, as a result of the usual sort of opera intrigue, cast as Mélisande in Debussy's new and great opera. Teyte was given the part in order to prevent the return to Paris of Mary Garden, the creator of the character. As a result the young Maggie Teyte found herself being coached in the role by the composer himself, who worked with her on some of his songs as well.

Strangely enough, considering Debussy's reputation with women, he did not become her lover; but there can be little doubt that this strange, violent, mysterious and slightly sinister man was by far the greatest influence in her life. Teyte was to have many lovers of both sexes during her life, but Debussy meant more to her than all of them.

Up to 1919 she led the life of a successful prima donna, singing in France, England, Germany and America. Then she married as her second husband – her first had been a dim French lawyer called Plumon – Walter Sherwin Cottingham, a young American millionaire. For the next decade she more or less retired from public singing. She and Cottingham seem to have been genuinely fond of each other; but I doubt if Maggie Teyte really loved him – or anyone else for that matter during the course of her long life. Also, at the time of her marriage to Plumon, she had undergone an operation, which made it impossible for her to have children – a horrible thing for any woman to do.

She lived to regret it, especially as she had not told Cottingham the truth. Their marriage ended in 1931; and Teyte took up her career again, to find that she had largely been forgotten.

Then her luck turned. In 1936 she was invited to make a series of records of Debussy songs with Cortot at the piano. The project was a tremendous critical and financial success; and from there on Maggie Teyte's career took on something of the quality of a fairy tale. She became a legendary figure; the pupil of de Reszke; the friend of Reynaldo Hahn; the favoured singer of the Belle Époque in Paris; the interpreter who had been coached by Debussy himself, and for whom he had played the accompaniment in public; the only surviving artist with the authentic tradition of French song. (That last claim was not quite true, but it sufficed for America.) In her fifties and sixties, when most singers are either retired or ought to be, this tiny, vivacious woman was performing as well as other artists half her age. She retired in 1955; was created a Chevalier of the Legion d'honneur in 1957; and given a DBE in 1958. She died in 1976.

I heard Maggie Teyte once, at a Sunday night concert at the Victoria and Albert in 1952; and later that year, in November, during Callas's first *Norma* in London, I found myself standing beside a small, elderly lady in the Crush Bar at Covent Garden. It was Maggie Teyte; and she was saying to a group of friends: 'I think she's absolutely wonderful!' Well, they both were, in their different ways: unique and irreplaceable.

Teyte's voice was not large, but it had an extraordinary quality of purity and sensuousness: it was quite unlike any other voice I have ever heard. And of course she was a very great artist indeed. In French song she was not finer than Claire Croiza, a mezzo, whose career was entirely confined to France; but otherwise no female singer was her equal in her chosen repertoire. And her records, most of which I am happy to say I possess, are there to prove it.

As a person? O well, as is generally the case with singers, one would rather listen to them than live with them. Maggie Teyte was intelligent, witty, charming and pretty. She was also selfish, jealous, ungenerous, arrogant and completely self-absorbed. This does not make for happiness; and on the whole, she was not a particularly happy person; but she was an interesting and complex woman, and well worthy of a full-scale biography.

One does not expect any literary merit in biographies of theatrical personages; but this is a rather splendid exception. Garry O'Connor, who is a grand-nephew of the singer, writes with a distinction and grace that one might expect in a biography of, say, Max Beerbohm. He is marvellously good on those great years in Paris before the First World War; and assembles his glittering cast with an artistry that is probably inherited – his father is Cavan O'Connor, the popular tenor.

So interesting and penetrating is Mr O'Connor in his analysis of the great and near-great who formed part of his grand-aunt's world, that one wishes he would deploy his gifts even more in the art of biography. His sketch of Debussy is masterly; and one longs for a more extended treatment of Reynaldo Hahn. It would give Mr O'Connor the opportunity of bringing a whole era to life; a task for which he is clearly fitted; armed with every weapon in the biographer's cache; and gifted with a distinguished prose style. I think we shall hear a great deal more of him.

In the meantime, all lovers of Maggie Teyte's art – of whom I am sure there are fully two or three dozen in Ireland – will rush to buy this book. They are in for a treat.

The Irish Times, 28 April 1979

Roots

Famine by Liam O'Flaherty. Wolfhound Press, £6.30

There are certain books, most of them novels, without which we can have but an imperfect understanding of the country in which they are set. The literature of a nation is far more revealing than all the official histories ever written.

No one who wants to get to know something of Russia and the Russians can hope to do so without reading *The Brothers Kara-mazov* or *Fathers and Sons*. These should be required studies for young people who hope to enter the diplomatic service or do business with the Great Bear. Similarly, the whole of France, in its meanness, its glory and its singlemindedness is to be found in Balzac's *Les Illusions Perdues*.

Germany, with its strange mixture of sentiment and dia-bolism, can only be understood by an acquaintance with the Faust legend, in its many manifestations in prose, poetry and drama; while few novels have ever revealed the soul of a nation as thor-oughly as Robert Musil's *Der Mann ohne Eigenschaften* reveals that of Austria.

If I were asked what book best explains the English charac-ter, I would not recommend Miss Austen, Dickens or even Trol-lope as first choices; that, without any doubt whatsoever, must always be *Tom Jones*: the greatest of all English novels by a very long shot. America? Assuming that that vast affair has a national character, I should imagine *Moby-Dick* would tell us something about it. Americans are forever seeking the Great White Whale, by no means an ignoble pursuit.

Italy and Spain have changed much in recent years, on the surface at any rate; but the novels that still explain them best to us are historical classics, which in itself says something of the Latin character. No novel has ever quite succeeded in ousting Manzoni's *I Promessi Sposi* as the great Italian novel. Its author remains a national hero; and even in death was the inspiration of a masterpiece, Verdi's marvellous *Requiem*. And if the reader does not know the novel that still represents all that is uniquely its own in the Spanish temperament, then he should not be reading this page.

It is in this company that Liam O'Flaherty's *Famine*, first published in 1937, belongs. O'Flaherty is the most heroic of Irish novelists, the one who has always tackled big themes, and in one case, in this great novel, succeeded in writing something imperishable. (What about Joyce, I can hear many readers murmur? But great Joyce is outside the mainstream tradition into which all characteristically national novels fall: they can be understood and loved by the people. Joyce will revert, if he has not already done so, to the universities.)

The Famine of the 1840s was the great watershed of Irish history: before it Ireland was the one sort of a nation and afterwards something entirely different. No political event, even the first arrival of the English, the subsequent tour by Cromwell, the Act of Union, or the establishment of the present State after the Treaty, have had so great an influence on the Irish character as the subject of O'Flaherty's novel.

The Famine itself is of course the greatest character of all in this superb book: one sees it, smells it, touches it, and watches it stalk through the land like some awful, apocalyptic monster. It is in some ways a terrifying experience; but as in all great art, it is also a cleansing one; and, after reading it, many dark corners of the Irish character are revealed to us.

The story itself is concerned with the effect of the potato blight of 1845–6 on the inhabitants of a poor valley in the west; and in particular with the Kilmartin family: the old father, Brian and his wife, Maggie; her clownish brother, Thomsy; and above all the young daughter-in-law of the house, or cabin, Mary Gleeson, who has married Brian and Maggie's son, Martin. Every one of these is a fully realized character, revealed in all their human aspects, good and bad, and ultimately emerging as something very akin to the all-inclusive heroic figures of Shakespeare. Mary Kilmartin in particular has been singled out by two generations of critics as one of the great creations of modern literature. And so she is.

O'Flaherty himself is clearly in love with her, as well he might; but this is a dangerous indulgence for any novelist. It is a measure of this great writer's skill and depth of humanity that she is never made to appear 'glamorous' in the flashy modern sense, although it might be said that the descriptions of her superb beauty remove her from the common mould of her relations and friends. But great good looks were never all that rare in Ireland.

The effects of the Famine turn these simple people into figures of tragedy; and some of them achieve it through an identification with the grotesque. Their privations reduce them to creatures almost, but not quite, on the level of beasts of burden. O'Flaherty has always been unique in this country in his sympathy with animals, and his knowledge of their closeness to people: after all, many of our actions, reactions and physical gestures are evidence of our animal nature. This very delicate theme – it might appear coarse to the unwary, but in fact it is an extremely subtle subject, and is so treated by O'Flaherty – binds all together with nature, under the life-giving and death-appointing sky. It is achieved here with a skill and passionate concern that are breathtaking.

The story itself is simple. Mary survives with her baby, to join her husband on a ship for America. (One can imagine her – so vividly does she come alive – as a very old woman in Boston, telling her grandchildren about the Great Hunger; admonishing them not to forget as they grow up into prosperous citizens of their adopted country.) The old people die; the district is laid waste; and the gombeen men survive to form the backbone of Catholic Ireland down to the present day.

Nothing is shirked in this book. Here we are with all our self-pity, vanity, greed, envy, spite, drunkenness, murderous madness and close-fisted peasant cunning. And so we remain today. But another element entered into the Irish character with the Famine: apathy. And that too remains. Alas. But no one is really a villain in this novel; and the Irish nation is presented also in its courage, its sense of holiness and faith, its kindness and charity, its charm and its magnificent instinct for survival.

Famine is full of unforgettable pictures – it is very much a visual novel; and on its first appearance William Plomer mentioned an affinity with Daumier. I would add Goya. Scene after scene remain branded in the memory, all brilliant, all soil-deep in knowledge and understanding. I would point to the famous description of the beauty of the valley, just before the first appearance of corruption in the potatoes; and old Brian's foolish grin when he uncovers the rotten crop; the flat, listless manner in which the O'Hanlon children report the death of their father – this is one of the finest passages in modern literature; the awful description of the evictions; the passionate restraint with which the love of the young married couple is treated; its depth, and its shyness also. Most moving of all perhaps is the very last chapter, where old Brian dies attempting to dig a grave for his wife in frozen soil with bare feet; and his three-legged dog lies down beside him.

The Wolfhound Press are to be congratulated on making this great novel available again, and at so modest a price. Those who have read it years ago will now want to read it again; younger people will, one hopes, become familiar with it – it is part of their heritage. And finally, it should be required reading for all British politicians who are involved in Ulster. If the Hapsburgs had had the opportunity of reading Musil, they might still be in the Hofburg.

The Irish Times, 13 January 1980

The Ascent to Truth

Merton: *A Biography* by Monica Furlong. Collins, £6.95
The Magician of Lublin by Isaac Bashevis Singer. Penguin, £1.10

The religious sense, like peace, is indivisible. This was brought home to me very forcibly recently when I was reading a book by the Jewish writer, Isaac Singer, who won the Nobel Prize in 1978. *The Magician of Lublin* is set in Poland towards the end of the nineteenth century.

The magician is a circus acrobat, Yasha Mazur, who has a good but childless wife whom he loves, but leaves at home when he goes out on tour. There he is known not only as a superb performer in the ring, but also in the bed. He has numerous affairs, only one of them serious; but he adores women and everything about them, and like most men of that temperament is greatly appreciated in return especially when, like Yasha, he is handsome, supple and kind.

But Yasha is also pursued by the hound of heaven; he feels its breath behind him; and slowly, inexorably, he is hunted down. He reverts to the religion of his fathers, and ends up as a hermit, walled up in a cell in his wife's yard. She feeds him on a tray through a window; he suffers from cold, heat and ill health; and the burden of becoming known as a holy man. People who used to attend his circus performances now arrive in droves to ask for his blessing. The situation is not without irony; but on the whole Singer tells the story of a man with a true and deep-rooted religious sense. One is of course spellbound by the beauty of the writing and the validity of the characters, so brilliantly and lovingly observed; but most of all one is struck by the similarity of Yasha's pilgrimage to those of so many Christian saints, mystics and hermits.

The Jewish religion is one that has always impressed me deeply. Whenever, as sometimes happened in films, I saw part of one of the great Jewish festivals, I have been overcome with a sense of awe and wonder. So very old, unchanging, God-ridden and terrible in its uncompromising faith. I have of course many Jewish friends; but those who are Orthodox do not discuss their observances with me; and the others do not practise their religion. I would give much to attend a prayer meeting at a synagogue; but Jewry is, as it has always been, exclusive.

Of course this sense of discovery and mutual understanding extends also to other religious traditions, and in my case particularly to the Anglican Church. Surely it is not possible for any Roman Catholic to take his religion seriously without experiencing a deeper sense of kinship with his Anglican friends and neighbours? I dislike the word 'Protestant', particularly in Ireland where it carries so many undertones of a purely secular and political nature. Besides, the Church of Ireland is part of the Anglican communion; and therefore, so far as I am concerned, part of the universal Catholic Church.

I have learned much from my Anglican friends; and so might other Irish Catholics if they had any sense. The Anglicans' simplicity and honesty, above all their fearless and direct correspondence with God, are characteristics that are not only admirable in themselves, but a shining example to all Christians of other traditions.

It was therefore with particular delight that I discovered in Monica Furlong's brilliant and revealing biography of Thomas Merton that he had, especially in his later years, the most intense admiration for the Anglican tradition. 'It seems to me that the best of Anglicanism is unexcelled,' he wrote a few years before his death,

> but that there are few who have the refinement of spirit to see and embrace the best, and so many who fall off into the dreariest rationalism. For my part I will try to cling to the best and be

as English a Catholic as one in my position can be. I do think it
is terribly important for Roman Catholics now plunging into
vernacular to have some sense of the Anglican tradition.

By the time he wrote that, Merton had developed into one of
the most formidable religious spirits of our time, the first perhaps
of the truly modern saints. He is also one of the best known in a
general sense, but a great deal less so in the essentials. This beautifully written and intellectually profound biography brings us
very close indeed to the heart and soul of the man.

Thomas Merton was born in France in 1915. His father, who
was born in New Zealand, was a painter of considerable talent.
His mother, Ruth Jenkins, was pure American, and came from a
well-off family; her father was a member of the publishing house
of Grosset & Dunlap of New York. She died when Thomas was
six, and wrote him a letter beforehand to inform him of the event,
which was handed to him after her death. This curious incident
affected him deeply all his life; and he always had a sense of the
loss of feminine affection, which he was to pursue for most of his
youth; and indeed in some ways right through his life. His mother,
though good, kind and dutiful, was not demonstrative.

A younger brother, John Paul, was killed in action during the
Second World War. Owen Merton, the father of the two boys, was
devoted to them, and Thomas in particular came to an understanding of European religious and cultural values as a result of
the wandering life the painter lived. But the elder Merton died in
1931 after a long illness, and Thomas was left alone. All his life he
was haunted by a sense of solitude: his end was in his beginning.

He was educated in England in the normal fashion of the
well-to-do in those days, and eventually went to Cambridge. He
hated it and thought it evil, a not unusual reaction on the part of
many religious people. Not that Merton was even passably pious
during his university days. He was idle and dissipated; and during
his time in Cambridge fathered a child. The mother and child
were killed during the air raids on London during the war. And
that is all Miss Furlong tells us of this episode. Until the age of
twenty-five Merton was mildly dissipated: drinking, making love to

a lot of girls and generally having his fling. But, like Yasha Mazur, the magician of Lublin, he was a marked man. Nothing that he did, or tried to do, satisfied him. He grew to hate the life he was living; and even more significantly the world he was living in.

He became a Catholic, and tried to join the Franciscans, who rejected him on account of his illegitimate child; but they took him on in their school as a teacher. In 1941 he entered the Trappist monastery at Gethsemani, and was ordained a priest in 1949. It is interesting that his three closest friends during the period imme- diately before his entering the monastery were Jews; and they all encouraged his vocation and remained as close to him as it was possible for them to be for the rest of his life.

The outlines of that life are now history. In 1948 he pub- lished the record of his conversion from paganism to Christian- ity; to the silence and rigours of the Cistercian Order. *The Seven Storey Mountain* became a huge bestseller in America, and also in England where it was published in a slightly abridged version called *Elected Silence*. I well remember the furore this book caused; and I also remember my own inability to read it to the end. At the time, and several times since, I supposed this to be due to my own lack of a true religious sense. Now Monica Furlong gives me some reason for hope, for she does not think very highly of it either.

The truth is that this celebrated book is not in essence very original. It is the old story of the rake who reforms, and does so in the most romantic fashion possible by entering a monastery, where all is silence, prayer and physical and mental hardships overcome by the grace of God and the sacrifice of the penitent. The truth is of course somewhat different. *Elected Silence*, as this biographer points out, is a curiously priggish book, and also a wildly inaccurate and romantic one.

It condemns the world and everything in it and lauds the monastic life where, in spite of cold and hunger and hard work, men live aesthetically beautiful lives, full of the joy and peace of those who are chosen and set apart from their fellows.

It may appear so to a few dim-witted monks, but they would have to be very dim indeed. In fact it is a life full of petty jealousy, trivial spite, constant harassment by superiors, and more than its share of religious doubts and despairs. This is particularly true in the case of a man like Thomas Merton, who was an artist and could not, with the best will in the world, cease to be one. He had to write if he was to live; and it is truly extraordinary the amount of writing he managed to do with only two hours a day allowed for it, and the hard work in the fields filling up what remained of the time after the long hours praying in choir.

He came to hate the choir; and one can understand why. The close proximity of all those men for such long hours – in a general unwashed state unmentioned by Miss Furlong – must have been a real trial. Merton began to crave solitude and the life of a hermit; but it was many years before he achieved it, and then only shortly before his death.

Was he a good monk? As the rules went in his early years, yes and no. He was a sociable man, and very egotistical. How he over-came his preoccupation with the self, and grew to accept not only his fellow monks, but also the world outside, with all its human errors, makes this biography a sort of spiritual whodunnit. It is certainly the record of a long and arduous pilgrimage. The Thomas Merton who died so tragically in Bangkok in 1968, of electric shock in an apparently stupid accident, was a very differ-ent and much greater man than the convert of 1940. He had become one of the most influential religious voices of his time, and a man of immense spiritual and intellectual substance.

Merton had some disturbing things to say about the nuclear age. He came to the conclusion that a holocaust could only be avoided by educating the people, all the people everywhere, about the terrible weapon their governments now possessed. Survival was not enough; prevention must be absolute. 'Interior life, asceticism, contemplation, intercessory prayer, above all personal renewal, seemed the only weapons strong enough to stand against the dehu-manisation of man and the crude mass thinking that followed it.' If this seems naive to some people, it might be necessary to remind them that most truths are equally innocent and wide-eyed. It's really all we have.

Father Louis, as he was in religion, also became a great expert on Eastern religions and thought, particularly Zen; and was widely respected in the East for his personal sanctity. He was also one of the first Roman Catholic apologists to recognize clearly the feminine nature of God, who is Mother as well as Father. The Sophia Hagia of the ancients is really 'the feminine, dark, yielding, tender counterpart of the power, justice, creative dynamism of the Father'.

Advanced though this view is, it would hardly have satisfied Rosemary Radford Ruether, the Catholic theologian with whom Merton carried on a remarkable correspondence two years before his death. She was a better theologian than he was; knocked some of his preconceived notions good and hard; and eventually succeeded in clearing his mind of the last shadow of cant. He did not like it at first; but he emerged a far bigger and more accepting person as a result.

He remained a typical American, spontaneous, candid and outgoing; and Monica Furlong has drawn an unforgettable portrait of this greatly gifted human being, who renounced the world, and in doing so gained it in a very modern fashion. I hope this splendid book will be very widely read. If for no other reason than to illustrate the many-sidedness and boundless vitality of the Christian spirit; and the miraculous continuation of its self-renewal.

The Irish Times, 1980 (undated)

The Old Firm

A Guide to Anglo-Irish Literature by Alan Warner. Gill &
Macmillan. No price quoted.

There are two old reliables that British and Irish-American publishers invariably fall back upon, in all and every season, but particularly when there is a crisis or recession in the book trade,
which is nearly always.

In England of course the ace of diamonds is the royal family.
At the moment, the bookshops in Britain are filled with instant
royal biographies. This is the English twentieth-century equivalent of those pious tracts so beloved by Victorian readers. Nothing that is not good and wholesome is ever practised by these
queens, princes, princesses and dukes: and to drive the moral
home they are presented as enjoying all the bliss of a heavenly
existence on this dull earth.

People say that they have a terrible life, and that nobody
would exchange theirs for it for any money in the world; but this
is very largely self-deception. Ordinary persons would not be royal
for the simple reason that they do not think themselves good
enough to lead an existence so plainly divorced from everyday life,
and so clearly blessed by whatever gods there be. The English
royal family are icons, and they know it. So do their subjects. And
the knowledge is a godsend of a slightly different order to hard-
pressed publishers. In America and in Ireland the old reliable firm
is Anglo-Irish literature, on which subject a new book is published

almost as often, month by month, as the royal hagiographies. Professor Warner's publishers list nine other volumes about Anglo-Irish writers, and the movement of which they were a part, on the back of the dust cover of this volume. And that is only a small proportion of the huge output devoted to the subject by other firms in England, Ireland and the United States.

They are not quite as pious as the royal biographies and books of hours; but they do share a certain tone of respectful deference toward the subject under examination. Perhaps it is because these learned professors, high priests of a new religion, are convinced that Yeats, and Synge, and O'Casey and all the rest of them performed deeds that every poor scholar should learn by rote and attempt to emulate, as the monastic students of the Middle Ages pored over ancient manuscripts of the Gospels and the writings of the early fathers. There is nothing new under the sun, and especially so in literature.

There is certainly nothing new in Professor Warner's book. He is an orthodox cleric of the most rigid kind, and has contrived to write a book of 280 pages without once expressing an original idea. Of course the publication is a 'guide' only, and so one cannot expect much straying off the beaten track; still I have read books of this kind before, both devoted to literature and to travel, and the authors have managed to deliver a new idea or two. It convinces me that the modern religion of art has now become dogmatic, and brooks no questions on the subjects of its canonized saints, and the various hierarchical figures who minister to the sacred flame. We live in interesting times certainly; but less so perhaps than when the modern epistles and Gospels were first written. For one thing, in those far-off days the university establishment had not taken the place of the Holy Office.

Professor Warner begins, as is ordained in the rubrics, by defining what Anglo-Irish literature really is. Yes, he does. (I stress this in case anyone might be tempted to take a light view of modern academic criticism: it is in deadly earnest.) He finally decides, after consulting a number of oracles ancient and modern, that it is a mixture of Corkery's dictum that the school is 'literature written in English by Irishmen', and Sean Lucy's notion of 'the Irish experience'. This conclusion is as original as telling us that Queen Elizabeth II is deeply interested in horses, and has a thundering good seat herself.

He dates the 'real starting point' of Anglo-Irish literature as 1800, tying it up with the Act of Union and Maria Edgeworth's *Castle Rackrent*. I disagree with this; but that is beside the point. Students are well advised to stick to the professor's version: he knows the ins and outs of examinations.

He then goes on to give some of the outstanding characteristics of Anglo-Irish writing: the oral tradition, the love of words and wordplay, and a tendency to extravagance and flamboyance, which dates back to Elizabethan times. How this ties up with 1800 is not quite clear; but Holy Writ never is. Then there is the element of fantasy, the historical sense, a curse as well as a strength; the influence of religion, which was until recently almost entirely puritanical; and finally the great Irish talent for improvisation.

This was first noted by Maria Edgeworth in *Ennui*, and later, and remarkably so, by the German writer Heinrich Böll who observed the widespread use of safety pins in Ireland. This is one of Professor Warner's best chapters, although of course he is quoting from 'sources'. Naturally enough, since he is a cautious man, he does not say that improvisation has led to the making of many poets and playwrights in Ireland, but fewer novelists. I give this information myself, gratis.

The learned professor then goes on in Part Two to study six writers: three having views from the Big House, and three from smaller dwellings. These are worthy essays, with some good general information about Maria Edgeworth, Somerville and Ross and George Moore; and a few insights, also second-hand, which may be new to some readers, about Carleton, O'Connor and Kavanagh. The gleam of pure diamond on Carleton's dirty coat, the sentimentality of O'Connor and his high technical skill. His best work is the short story 'In the Train'; while Kavanagh is the poet of common things: 'the frost on the potato-pits, the tracks of cattle ... a green stone ...' All this is like telling us that the Queen Mother is a remarkable old lady for her age, and smiles all the time, whether she feels like it or not.

In Part Three the professor deals with five Dubliners: Joyce, Stephens, O'Casey, Clarke and Flann O'Brien. Like most people with pedantic minds, Warner is strictly truthful. He tells us that he has not read his way through *Finnegans Wake*, which is after all a common bond between students and teachers. Very few people have got through *Finnegans Wake*: academics all, they study keys and guides to it; and apart from records made by famous actors, which make some sense, that is the nearest anyone has ever come to getting to know this extraordinary book. It is full of rare good puns though, which the professor does not mention. He is not the sort of man to describe anyone as a 'son of a bitch'. I am.

So it is quite easy for me to say that James Stephens and Flann O'Brien seem to me largely overrated, desperately stressful in humour and coyly whimsical in fantasy. Needless to say, the professor does not take this view at all. He admits the whimsical in Stephens and contrasts it favourably with Dickens, which I think is overdoing it; but it is the official view as of now.

He finds O'Brien at his best in *At Swim-Two-Birds*. There are, according to Anne Clissman, thirty-six different styles in the book, which in my opinion is a sure sign of paucity of imagination; but naturally Warner concludes that the author is 'lively, witty and funny', and adds that 'at his best he offers us more than witty anarchy and ludic bravura'. Ah, well, maybe he does. What is sure is he is now an 'in' figure in the universities.

Then we get to Yeats. Apart from admitting that his plays do not really play very well, and that he was given to rhetoric, he is clearly the greatest of all Anglo-Irish writers for Professor Warner. A master of words. No one will deny this: but are they worth repeating? He sounds best when he is read aloud by an actor like the late Mícheál MacLiammóir. The sentiments are exactly suited to the romantic stage; in the clear light of day they sound forced, insincere and windy. But Professor Warner does not dwell on these elements. Yeats studies are still important.

He is rather superficial on the modern and living, with nothing new to say about O'Faolain, Mary Lavin, Brian Moore or John McGahern. Indeed the long passage from McGahern's story, 'Getting Through', is one of the best things in the whole book. Joycean, yes; but gloriously comic and dead on mark. Would that academics wrote like this!

Of the poets he gives the palm to Heaney, which is also a present-day trend, with no one apparently able to see the obvious: Heaney is an Irish, rural Rupert Brooke; and Kinsella and Montague are far finer poets.

The rest of the moderns are given short shrift, and many are not mentioned at all. But those who are treated in passing are surely comforted by the fact that since no word of original criticism has appeared in the whole course of the book, it is unlikely to occur in their case. As I finished it, I was again irresistibly reminded of those wholesome royal biographies. Nothing is said, or even suggested, that might disturb the calm surface of the wet prose; we read here only what we want to hear, and this is what we have heard a hundred times before. Does the Queen ever fall off a horse and swear? By God, no!

Just as the royal products are really aimed at the simple-minded and faithful of all ages, so too are these surveys of literary figures who happen to belong to a convenient movement or national culture. Royalty is a great national culture, as pervasive as devotion to various saints in the Middle Ages. The university is the secular wing of this modern theology; and those who have to make their way in the world must take heed of it, if they are to seek employment. Nothing could be safer than Professor Warner's guide; and I would particularly recommend it to pupils at secondary schools between the ages of fourteen and sixteen or seventeen. Having mastered it, they will make few mistakes when examination time comes around. The markers have been brought up on the same twaddle.

The Irish Times (undated). Book published 1981

Herr Doktor Proteus

Dietrich Fischer-Dieskau, Mastersinger by Kenneth S. Whitton.
Oswald Wolff, £15.00

Whenever I am asked how does one become a writer, I sigh and make an effort to change the conversation. Rarely, however, does one escape. When cornered I compare writing to the singing voice; one is either born with it or one is not. The ability to sing is a gift from God. It often takes years to manifest itself; but sooner or later it will declare itself and from there on it is up to the singer to make the best of what he has got: to train it, tame it, husband it and acquire a method that will ensure the longest possible survival of this sometimes noisy talent.

The writer is also born with the gift of expression; and he too must make the most of it, sometimes spending long years learning his craft. Some write easily, like Byron, without apparent effort; others experience extreme difficulty in achieving expression: but again, in either case, the talent is there from the start. No 'creative writing course' can make a writer out of someone who has not a natural means of expression; no singing teacher, no matter how great, can make a singer out of a person born without a voice. And that is the short answer to at least one question that is constantly recurring in the life of anyone who writes in any capacity.

Dietrich Fischer-Dieskau is one of the great singers of the century, and is perhaps the greatest Lieder singer who has ever lived; and he was born with a voice that developed quite effortlessly from a boyish alto into a high baritone. It seems to have been perfectly 'placed' by nature; this most expert of technicians spent little time with teachers, and emerged quite naturally in his early twenties with a voice and style that have changed little with the years, except that the singer has deepened and refined his art, and extended his repertoire to legendary proportions.

I doubt if any singer in the history of music has sung so many songs, and appeared in such a diversity of operas, oratorios, cantatas and various pieces of music for voice and orchestra, several written specially for Fischer-Dieskau. I was about to give myself the pleasure of putting forward my own opinion of the famous baritone's technique; but I find that towards the end of this excellent and very informative biography, the Austrian pianist, Jorg Demus, has done it better than ever I could. 'Even after thirty years,' he writes,

> Fischer-Dieskau's voice shows no tendency to disintegrate into the notorious three registers – the voice is controlled like a cello from the lowest to the highest note of its range. Every sound, every note is possible in every dynamic crescendo or diminuendo and all this is carried by almost inexhaustible reserves of breath which permit a truly sovereign breadth of phrasing.

To this might be added Gerald Moore's superb evaluation of the singer's sense of rhythm, without which even the greatest voice becomes dull. In the theatre it is called 'timing', and again you either have it or you have not. 'Fluctuation of tempo is performed with such subtlety that the listener, while captivated by the life-enhancing buoyancy of it all, is unaware that the musical phrase has lost its fixed mould and now is pliable.' About the actual sound of the voice there are conflicting opinions, as there have been in the past, and always will be in the case of artists with highly individual styles. There are people who found Caruso too beefy and lacking in subtlety; Melba was accused by many of having a pallid, boy-like tone, devoid of expression; McCormack was said to be nasal; Gigli was vulgar, a very beautiful basic sound ruined by mannerisms. And so on and so on.

Fischer-Dieskau has to be heard in the flesh. Nevertheless his records are among the treasures of the gramophone companies, and many of them are already classics unlikely to be superseded in the future. The voice has always seemed to me to have the rare beauty of mellowness and freshness, a combination hardly ever found in baritones, who are often rich, but who nearly always give the impression of maturity, if not ripe middle age. The German baritone's voice has always had, and retains today, an appealing, youthful, almost boyish quality. He may be singing a grave, even frightening song, of which there are many in the Lieder repertoire, when suddenly an upward flick of the voice suggests a lighter, even vulnerable tone. And with it comes the very rare quality of eagerness. Lotte Lehmann had it, McCormack had it, in her great days Elena Gerhardt had it; but few if any of today's singers have it. They are marvellous in various ways; but this small, absurdly effective flicker of eternal youth they do not have.

Dietrich Fischer-Dieskau was born in Berlin as Albert Dietrich Fischer on 28 May 1925. His mother was directly descended from that Kammerherr Carl Heinrich von Dieskau for whom Bach wrote his secular cantata, *Mer hahn en neue Oberkeet*; and his descendant's singing of the passage stating his name is done with great gusto and high spirits (anyone who has this record, which was made with the soprano Lisa Otto in 1960, should cherish it: it is in its way a historical document). The singer's father was a teacher and founded a school in Berlin, where he is remembered by having a laneway in the city named after him.

His son has been singing since he was eighteen and a prisoner of war in Italy. After the war he quickly made his name in opera and recital; and Dr Whitton's book is particularly good on the singer's operatic career. He has sung an enormous number of roles, and is regarded as one of the finest actors of his day with particular genius in make-up, and the ability to transform his enormous frame into a variety of persons, some of whom he can have only an instinctive acquaintance with: but this is what acting is all about. I stress this because most of his career has been spent in opera houses on the Continent: he has never sung opera in the

United States. He is a great Count in *Figaro*, and, I think, a great Don Giovanni also, realizing what Kierkegaard described as 'the immediate erotic' of Mozart's musical expression.

It has been said that if the devil wrote music he would write like Tchaikovsky. This seems to me a superficial view: if the devil composed it would be like Mozart. This is very evident in Fischer-Dieskau's interpretation of Mozart's two famous lechers.

He is also a great Iago, but I don't think a better Rigoletto than Gobbi, although he comes very close to him as Posa in *Don Carlos*. This is a tremendous achievement for a Teutonic singer. He has given great performances in Richard Strauss, particularly in *Arabella*, where his reading of Mandryka will not, I think, be surpassed. He is a famous Amfortas and Wolfram; but he does not really like Wagner, and while acknowledging his greatness, thinks that he does not write with any sympathy for the voice, and goes on for far too long. Oh, how I agree!

Several modern composers have written operas for him, the most notable being Aribert Reimann's *Lear*, in which he gave the great singer a part that one feels only he can sing. Certainly all other singers will be judged by this performance.

However, Fischer-Dieskau is chiefly known here and in America for his Lieder singing. As an interpreter of Schubert, Schumann and Wolff he is never likely to be surpassed; and his achievement in this highly specialized art will, I suspect, be only fully realized when he has ceased to perform in public; and the critics discover that there is no one to take his place.

Dr Whitton is very good on this aspect of the singer, and anyone who loves the German Lied, one of the supreme achievements of Western civilization, will want to have this book, and learn with what care, preparation, and learning allied to his instinctive gifts of timing and phrasing, Fischer-Dieskau approaches these masters. His scope is so wide that it might be said to include the entire range of German song written for the male voice; and the records are there to prove it. Indeed his work is so unceasing and well informed that he is really more like a nineteenth-century man than a citizen of the modern world.

There is something awesome about the dazzling varied career of this shy, erudite man with the radiant voice that seems to express all the eagerness, pain, impulsiveness and sensibility of youth. He is absolutely unique, and will remain so when the musical annals of the century come to be written.

Dr Whitton is of course a fervent admirer of the singer's art; and those, and there are a sad few, who do not delight in all the riches that Fischer-Dieskau has laid before us for so long, will find it too uncritical. Perhaps it is; but it is highly informative on the music that is associated with the subject, and in particular it is in itself an excellent introduction to the Lied; and for that alone may be recommended.

This singer has written three books: one on the Lied in general, a valuable handbook; one on the biographical study of Schubert's songs, a means by which students may get to know all those wonderful songs that were unknown until Fischer-Dieskau discovered and sang them; and a study of Wagner and Nietzsche, a learned book that does not come down on the side of Wagner. No wonder the singer has not been invited to Bayreuth since 1961!

And finally Dr Whitton's book contains a complete and very valuable discography of the enormous number of records made by Fischer-Dieskau. This also will be a source of reference in time to come.

The Irish Times, 30 January 1982

Blood and Gore

Pink Triangle and Yellow Star by Gore Vidal. Heinemann, £10.00

Some time ago I was reading a piece by Mr Malcolm Muggeridge, in which he says that the English essay is now only written in India. No one in England anymore publishes little volumes with titles like *Nostalgia and Other Essays*, which might not be accounted a great loss, were it not for the fact that these fragile compositions are still brought out, in ever-increasing numbers, as books of poetry.

It is Mr Muggeridge who made the point about the Anglo-Indian essay; it is I who have modestly added the information about modern poetry. Needless to say, the Muggeridge argument is to be found in an essay, published in a book of essays, a form which the Great Christian has used all his life. So have many others. Each new article by a political, a foreign or an economics correspondent is written in the essay form. It is only the name that has fallen out of use, having acquired a bad one over those precious little volumes – the precursors, all unknown to their authors, of so much bad present-day verse.

Most of the great essay writers of the last century, and the beginning of this, were first published – very often as book-reviewers – in newspapers and magazines. The authors then collected the best of these pieces and published them in hardback editions every few years. But modern literary journalism is so restricted by space, that it is no longer possible to do this.

93

Some years before his death, I asked Cyril Connolly why it was that he did not collect his articles in *The Sunday Times*, and preserve them in book form. He replied that they were too short, and to attempt to extend them would result in a loss of shape. He then went on to say that not only was he restricted to so many words; but he had only second choice of books, the first going to Raymond Mortimer who was his senior in length of service. Connolly is now emerging as a minor classic – as I always knew he would – while Mortimer is as dead as wet blotting paper.

No such restrictions apply to Mr Gore Vidal, who has become one of the best known, and most widely read essayists of the day. The magazines for which he works give him ample room to extend himself on any subject he chooses. Most of his essays are based on books, but he uses the review as a sort of forum in which to give us his opinion on various matters that interest him. It would be too much to expect that all of these subjects will also interest the reader; but this was always one of the hazards of a volume of essays.

Mr Vidal is at his best when on the attack. His first piece, based on Professor Bruccoli's edition of F. Scott Fitzgerald's stuporously dull *Notebooks*, and the same editor's more interesting *Correspondence of F. Scott Fitzgerald*, is a long overdue assault on that writer's ridiculously inflated reputation. It is his life, and not his novels and stories, which has made him into an American industry. Mr Vidal traces the growth of this commercial enterprise with wit and true malice aforethought. The essay is worthy of Zelda Fitzgerald, who was a finer natural writer than her husband; and one longs to quote her at length. Here she is on Hemingway: 'Bullfighting, bull-slinging and bullshit.' Except for Mr Vidal himself, there are no critics of that calibre around anymore. Pity.

The essay on Edmund Wilson is a fine piece of serious writing; and the great critic emerges with his enormous reputation enhanced. He was never an academic, in the sense that he was never a hack. It is sad to think that the two are now synonymous, as a result of the dark mills of American university labour. Christopher Isherwood's autobiography is the subject of a kindly review; and the very real value of this writer's prose is summed up admirably in a few sentences: 'The verbs are strong. Nouns precise. Adjectives few. The third person startles and seduces, while the first person is a good guide and never coy.' I cannot think of a better model for young writers, especially Irish ones who use the first person so often. Here is the perfect antidote to Joyce.

A review of one of the late Sir Cecil Beaton's diaries brings out the mordant strain in Vidal, as well it might. After dubbing Beaton and all his works 'pretty', which is spot on, he then goes on to pretend that the Truman whom Beaton writes about – the diarist was forever dropping names – is the late, lamented President. Since it is really only little ole Capote, the result is a brilliantly amusing piece of wickedness. This is the sort of thing that gets a writer a *reputation*.

The next two essays did not interest me much. One is a long, and learned treatise on the *Oz* books, all fourteen of them, together with the nineteen written by another hand after L. Frank Baum's death. In this piece Mr Vidal comes too close for comfort to those humourless academics he so rightly condemns. The review of Miss Doris Lessing's science fiction will appeal to those who are interested in them. I am not.

Then there is 'Sciascia's Italy', an essay devoted to the novels of the Sicilian writer. It begins with one of the most brilliant first paragraphs, describing the state of postwar Italy, that I have ever read: and I wish I could quote it in full. This piece is followed by an affectionate and disturbing appreciation of Sir Victor Pritchett as a critic. The English writer finds that American academics do not write well, and proceeds gently to disembowel them: 'Literary criticism does not add to its status by opening an intellectual hardware store.' This naturally fills Mr Vidal with glee; it delighted me too.

An essay on the novels of Thomas Love Peacock gives Vidal an opportunity to deal – with the help of Mary McCarthy, always a glittering ally – with the modern novel. His suggestion that fiction writers should take over the Agatha Christie plot, and use it to express ideas, strikes me as more useful than it appears on first reading. The next essay is about who makes the movies. Since I rarely go to see films I know nothing of this world, and much of the piece is unintelligible to me. But it has one good crack. Mr Vidal worked for a time in films as a scriptwriter, and he invents an old hand, the wise hack, who remarks, when stars began to make their own pictures: 'The lunatics are running the asylum.'

However, I suspect the two essays that will cause this book to sell are concerned with good old sex. In 'Sex Is Politics', Mr Vidal simply emphasizes this in a manner that seems to suggest that most Americans do not believe that politics are affected by sex at all; even more alarmingly, they apparently think that politics are not concerned with the sexual behaviour of the private citizen.

In this and the following piece, which gives the volume its title, I have had the experience of reading, for the first time in my life, an attack on Jews and their way of thinking. Mr Vidal is concerned, as all civilized people are, with the freedom of the individual to behave as nature has made them, in private. An influential section of American Jewry does not agree. A number of well-known writers have let it be known that they hate, detest and abominate homosexuality, male and female. This draws from Mr Vidal a riposte that one can only describe as blood-tipped. Unhappy the Jew or Jewess who falls foul of this deadly marksman.

But it must be admitted that at least two of them, Mr and Mrs Norman Podhoretz, asked for it. Mr Podhoretz fears for the future of Israel because of homosexuality in America. This is the daftest notion I have heard for a long time, and Vidal quite rightly exposes it for the nonsense it is. If in the process Mr Podhoretz gets mauled, and the basis of the Jewish religion's beliefs questioned, then one can only say that they make wonderfully funny targets. Quite as funny as the Imams.

But if Mr Podhoretz is bigoted and uncharitable, he is as sweet music compared to his wife, a lady who writes under the name of Midge Decter. I thought at first that Mr Vidal had invented that one, but it appears that the person in dispute was an editor on *Harper's*, and so must be real, unlikely though it seems. This Ms Midge Decter wrote an ill-judged article called 'The Boys on the Beach', in which she recalls summers she spent at Fire

Island Pines where apparently she came into contact with male and female homosexuals. It is quite clear that she does not know the first thing about the subject, and as a result unburdens herself of every known prejudice about fairies, fags and dykes that has ever been invented. Although her argument is a thoroughly disgusting one, and a shame to American liberal thinking, it is also of course, as all ignorant polemics are, extremely funny. Did you know that male homosexuals all have hairless bodies? And dominate publishing, among a host of other professions? The first remark will come as a surprise to doctors; the second astonished me.

With this kind of thinking Ms Decter – who sounds exactly like a Nancy Mitford American, and I really find it hard to believe that she exists – naturally presents an easy target for Mr Vidal. Never, I believe, in the history of modern letters has a lady and a Jewess been so severely stung by an American WASP. (A bad pun, but the whole subject, and the intellectual Jewish approach to it, is a low one.) Mr Vidal's sense of humour is broad as well as sharp, as the occasion demands.

One feels ashamed of the Podhoretz family; but they are, I fear, very, very funny. Here is Vidal on Mrs Podhoretz's claim that homosexual women show a marked tendency to hang out in the company of large and ferocious dogs: 'Well, if I were a dyke and a pair of Podhoretzes came waddling towards me on the beach, copies of Leviticus and Freud in hand, I'd get in touch with the nearest Alsatian dealer pronto.'

After this Man Miller stuff it must be admitted that the rest of the volume droops a little, in spite of a swingeing attack on the twice-born Christians – who, we are told, now amount to one-third of the population of America. It is of course an evangelical movement, and full of all kinds of weird notions. One, however, is old. They believe in the Pauline injunction that slaves obey their masters, on the grounds that those without money must serve those with money, for money is the most tangible sign of God's specific love. Mr Vidal has a field day with these bigots, who hate the Jews and the blacks as much as the Jews hate the queers. This is a subject that would have delighted Bernard Shaw.

The rest of the book, apart from a review of a book dealing with the children of the rich, which brings out the social side of the essayist, is devoted to politics. He tells us that America is really run by the Chase Manhattan Bank. I think there are a few other financial institutions involved also, but essentially this is true; and again, it comes as something of a surprise that Vidal feels it necessary to write these political pieces at all, since one would assume that most Americans would know by now who their real masters are. Not Carter, not Reagan, but the men in a few discreet, almost anonymous boardrooms.

The real point of these essays, so full of wit, wisdom and righteous indignation, lies in Mr Vidal's grasp of the money principle. He knows it is the modern god, before whose Awful But Hidden Face all must bow. To question it is so obscene as to be mad; indeed this fearful doubt is the only real modern obscenity left. You can put your daughter on the streets, *and* take her money; but you must respect the money.

This, then, is a rich, disturbing and brilliantly witty book. Mr Vidal does not have any particular 'line'; he simply attacks stupidity wherever he sees it. He is neither a liberal nor a reformer, but an aristocrat, who does not give a damn what people say or think of him. His kind have nearly died out; but fortunately this voice and pen are still with us: a bright torch in the gathering darkness.

The Irish Times (undated). Book published 1982

Kate O'Brien: Portrait of a Lady

Kate O'Brien: A Literary Portrait by Lorna Reynolds. Colin Smythe, £9.75

For over a century the Catholic middle class have been the dominant influence in Ireland, and for the past sixty-five years, the ruling class also. Yet, they have been little written about; and compared with the bourgeoisie in France and England, who have produced, with a few exceptions, all the great novelists of the last two centuries, they have been singularly slow in producing creative writers.

It is true that they have given birth to the greatest novelist of the century in Joyce; but he is outside the mainstream of fiction; and of writers to compare with novelists like Mrs Gaskell, Trollope, Galsworthy, Graham Greene and Evelyn Waugh, there have been but few. Of these Kate O'Brien is the best known; and also, I think, the best.

Ms Lorna Reynolds has written a very fine study of this fascinating and greatly gifted novelist, whose works after a period of neglect following her death in 1974 are now being discovered and appreciated by the young.

The world she wrote about is historical: the closed parlours and drawing rooms of the rich haute bourgeoisie, the last years of the nineteenth century and the first thirty years of the twentieth. She also wrote about the Spanish bourgeoisie of the same period. And she was probably the first Irish writer to deal with the problems and anxieties of young women about to go out into the world to earn their living, and 'confront their destiny' in the Jamesian sense.

She naturally knew more about young women than Henry James did; and in particular young ladies of Irish Catholic background and upbringing (about whom he knew nothing).

Kate O'Brien was born in Limerick in 1897, and Professor Reynolds gives us an admirable chapter on the writer's origins and early life. Her father and grandfather bred horses and supplied them to various clients in the UK and throughout Europe, including the British and Austrian armies.

The O'Briens were a numerous and tightly knit clan; and the novelist all her life was very aware of her family and its ties, and never for a moment wanted to break with it. This gave great strength to her books, and was a source of immense comfort to herself.

Her mother died early, and Kate O'Brien was from the age of four brought up by the French nuns at Laurel Hill outside Limerick. This also had an enormous influence on her life: and no other writer has written with such knowledge and sympathy of nuns – in the old Latin Church of course.

The novels are examined in a sensible way in this affectionate and learned study: the five best ones first, and the others in later chapters. Kate O'Brien wrote only nine novels in a writing life of nearly fifty years: not a big output, but among the most distinguished of its time.

Her great themes were the freedom of the individual, the right of women to work as they choose, and to love and marry at their own discretion – a choice by no means open to young girls of her generation.

Since she took a romantic view of love, her stories, with one exception, are tragic. Love is only possible, as in the religious life, when it is ideal and sublimated; profane love is doomed. Yet she pities anyone who has not been through the worldly experience.

Everyone now accepts that *The Ante-Room*, *Mary Lavelle*, *The Land of Spices* and *That Lady* are very nearly great novels in the fullest sense, and only fall short of this when compared with Joyce, Musil and Proust. I think Mauriac was the first novelist of his time, in the mainstream tradition; but he did not write of young women as successfully as Kate O'Brien.

There are excellent chapters here on the novelist's use of time as a technique, her interwoven themes of love and religion, her powerful, if obliquely stated plea for the freedom of women in all spheres of human activity.

Because she was so close to family ties, which are still important in Ireland, she has a profound meaning for the young woman of today, when such ties are weakening: but, as we are all products of two thousand years of Christian civilization, we are not perhaps as free as we think. A reading of Kate O'Brien's novels is still a very necessary part of any educated young woman's experience. Men read her too, of course, when they have the good sense and sensibility to do so.

Kate O'Brien's most famous novel, *Without My Cloak*, is usually regarded as merely a 'good read' and bestseller, and that is all that need be said about it. But Professor Reynolds makes a powerful case for it; and I think she is right to treat it with the four great novels.

Reading her chapter on this much loved book is a very moving experience; a sort of recreation of one's youth; and in her magnificent last paragraphs Lorna Reynolds brought back for me the very voice – a rarely beautiful one – and personality of a great and noble woman, who wrote so movingly and with such grave dignity of the 'holiness of the heart's affections'; and also was not unmindful of that fourteenth-century friar, Jacopone da Todi, who wrote, in theological terms, 'Ordina questro amore, O tu che m'ami'; 'O thou who lovest me, set this love in order.'

I hope this splendid portrait will be widely read; and above all that it will introduce a new generation to the work of one of their great women.

Irish Independent, 17 & 18 April 1987

Edna O'Brien – Still as Fresh as Country Girls' Dream

The Country Girls Trilogy and Epilogue by Edna O'Brien.
Jonathan Cape, £15

Irishwomen have made a distinguished contribution to the novel in English. One only has to think of some of the great names: Marie Edgeworth, Somerville and Ross, Lady Gregory, Elizabeth Bowen, Kate O'Brien, Mary Lavin, Iris Murdoch, while today Jennifer Johnston is of that company.

The other tradition might be said to have been invented by Lady Morgan, who was born in 1775 and died in 1859. She wrote a novel called *The Wild Irish Girl*. That novel is now totally forgotten, but the myth of the wild Irish girl lives on.

Other famous names in their day, who contributed to this essentially romantic idea of Ireland and the Irish, were Caroline Norton, George Egerton (Mrs Golding Bright), Anna Maria Hall, Lady Gilbert and Temple Lane. The tradition is well represented in recent years by Maeve Binchy. It is with these romantic novelists that Edna O'Brien belongs. She is not as bad as the worst of them, nor has she the sheer creative power and high spirits of Maeve Binchy; but it is doubtful if she will last any longer than Lady Morgan or Anna Maria Hall did. They have their place in literary history; and so will Miss O'Brien.

Her first three novels are now collected in one volume and published as a trilogy, with a newly written epilogue. I was perhaps unfortunate that my introduction to the work of Edna O'Brien was through one of her later novels *A Pagan Place*, which I got for review. It was dreadful, and I said so. But these first stories are by far her best work and created a sensation when they first appeared. They were banned, of course; and it is certain that Miss O'Brien was the first Irish woman writer to use a four-letter word in her work.

It is a dubious distinction; but these novels about two very different girls – representing, no doubt, two sides of the author's temperament – and their sentimental education, preserve a certain charm and freshness that have not dated.

The naivety of the writing does now strike one as somewhat knowing, in the way that the Claudine novels of Mme Colette are not really innocent; but Miss O'Brien entirely lacks the great French writer's marvellous sense of style. The whole point of *The Country Girls*, *The Lonely Girl* and *Girls in Their Married Bliss* is that they have no style. While this is perhaps only too true of girls with their background, it is ultimately tedious and self-defeating in literature. The books that are read and reread are those that are written with distinction.

But these stories do give a lively representation of a certain type of young girl in the fifties in Ireland. They are not soaked in self-pity as the author's later novels are; and above all they have a sense of humour totally lacking in Miss O'Brien's subsequent work.

There are some hilarious passages in *Girls in Their Married Bliss*, which is well worth rereading. It is both touching and funny.

The epilogue, which unfortunately Miss O'Brien decided to tack on to these early novels, is sad. Coarse and sad: that is all that one can say about it.

Apart from these three books, Miss O'Brien has written some very fine short stories. Perhaps this is her true metier. It would explain the episodic and improvised nature of her longer work. But this trilogy was well worth reprinting. It was always a mistake to have taken Edna O'Brien seriously. She is really very funny.

Irish Independent, 27 June 1987

Kenneally 'Faction' Goes Awry

The Playmaker by Thomas Kenneally. Hodder and
Stoughton, £10.95

A novelist is occasionally visited by what seems to him a brilliant
idea. It is often for the beginning or end of a story; it is sometimes
a setting; or again a single character who takes on gigantic proportions in his mind. Such ideas have to be treated with great
care, for they have been the greatest single cause of the failure of
many novels that began well, had a good framework, a memorable
character, or a big finale.

The Australian novelist, Thomas Kenneally, was visited by
one such idea that has inspired his new book, *The Playmaker*. Since
it is also the bicentenary of the first landing of convicts from England on Australian soil, it no doubt appeared to him a very suitable time to put his idea into a book. And the framework was
actually a historical fact. In 1787 a group of convicts, male and
female, put on a production of Farquhar's *The Recruiting Officer*,
directed and managed by a Lieutenant Ralph Clark of the Royal
Marines in the Penal Settlement at Sydney Cove.

It would appear to the casual reader that such a project could
not fail, especially since Kenneally is already a celebrated author
with the Booker Prize to his credit. Nevertheless fail it does, and
for two reasons. Given such a perfect setting, Kenneally went to
work to study every available record of the settlement and its
inhabitants, and to check on every item of historical fact he could

unearth. Thus provided with a ready-made cast all he had to do was to breath life into them and provide some fictional, or largely fictional characters to fill out the book. The characters do spring up almost instantly on every page – and there are a very large number of extras – bright, vividly coloured and apparently alive. But they aren't. Turn the pages and most of them fall back dead, never to rise again.

It is possible that there are readers who actually like this sort of thing. In a way it is a bit like television: players appear, make an impression by some trick of the face or body, or are given a piece of dialogue that they repeat on subsequent appearance, thus achieving the status of 'characters'. The reader, or viewer, is not subjected to the strain of following a character as it develops; and of course Mr Kenneally has been provided with a colourful bunch of convicts, whores and sailors to begin with: hardly a page goes by without some vivid piece of business, often sexual, to keep the pot boiling. And at the end there is a grand finale where the author assembles all of his characters under the one tent.

I could not help thinking what a good film or television series this book would make. All those wonderful character parts for Irish and English actors now resting. And what a time they would have with people who are apt to have one eye hanging out, growths on the forehead, half-an-ear or nose and wild hair standing straight up on their heads. Mr Kenneally has the additional advantage of describing these puppets (the above sketch is my own, made up of the sort of humours he describes) complete with smells, which are a great aid to the imagination.

The novel's chief character is the young lieutenant in the Marines, Ralph Clark, who serves as the conscience of the piece. Like so many other young officials in the Marines he is not a very interesting young man, typical, no doubt, but a bit boring; and it is difficult to identify with him. Which brings one to the whole question of Australia and the Australians (Clark is English). Why are they always so boring? Even their greatest artists are boring. The late Victor Gollancz on hearing Joan Sutherland for the first time exclaimed: 'God! She's just as boring as Melba!' I think it is because there is something disproportionate about the country and its inhabitants. They overwhelm, they overpaint, they overkill.

Mr Kenneally has all these characteristics; and he is also a pedant. Great nuggets of accurate information are dropped into this book with all the deftness of a coal-heaver. And while it would not be true to say that this author has no style, the new-minted phrase, the quick wit, the colourful word are not often encountered in his pages. His book is not 'written' as Edmund Wilson used to say; and one can only describe his prose as stodgy.

Others may of course find this novel gripping. I would advise them to have a quick read on the first few pages in the booksellers before they decide. Kenneally is a much praised writer, and is fashionable in England. Nowadays this means nothing in real literary terms. The intelligent reader will form his own opinion. I hope.

Irish Independent, 12 December 1987

Laughter and Tears in the Life of Nora Joyce

Nora: A Biography of Nora Joyce by Brenda Maddox. Hamish Hamilton, £16.95

The wives of famous writers have not on the whole had a good press. They are taken as part of the general background that supports the great man, like his armchair, his pipe and his favourite tipple. At the most they have been praised for their long suffering, their patience and their inability to do anything but provide the usual creature comforts that spouses are supposed to dispense. They must never offer any kind of opposition to the myth of the great man.

There have been, mercifully, exceptions to this hoary belief. Chief among them are the cases where author married author: Harold Nicolson and Vita Sackville-West, Katherine Mansfield and John Middleton Murry, C.P. Snow and Pamela Hansford Johnson, Sean and Eileen O'Faolain, and many more. But the myth of the dim spouse still persists – what was Mrs Anthony Trollope like, for instance?

Of all those supposedly dreary but good wives, James Joyce's partner Nora was thought for years to be one of the most backward. Illiterate, stupid, probably good in bed, but otherwise useless was the impression that many intelligent people had of this remarkable woman. I was lucky in that I knew two men who were intimate friends of the Joyces – Tom McGreevy and Padraic Colum

– and their opinion of Nora Joyce was very different. In fact it was the essential material that Brenda Maddox has now turned into one of the finest biographies to have appeared for some years. Her *Nora* is a triumph of scholarship, wit, sympathy and balance. It is a model of its kind.

Nora Barnacle was born in Galway in 1884. Her father was a baker who had taken to the bottle early in life and ended up as an occasional worker: he would go from bakery to bakery filling in when men were sick or on holiday. As a result the family were very poor. Nora was educated at the local Convent of Mercy, and later found a job as a portress at the Presentation Convent, also in Galway.

She must have been a bright girl of good appearance to be given such a job; and we know now that of course she was both. But she became dissatisfied with Galway, and knew, like many another girl in her position, that the future held nothing for her except the life of her mother. She took a train for Dublin, not informing her family, and travelled straight into literary history.

Joyce met her while she was working in Finn's Hotel in Leinster Street, introduced, it is believed, by one of his friends, Vincent Cosgrave. However they met, the beautiful, red-haired girl from Galway fell in love with the bony young genius and never from that day ever loved anyone else. Joyce, a little cooler, had the same experience. She was the only woman in his life, and he came to rely on her totally as the years passed.

This biography is also the record of a great love story, and one that would make superb fiction. Nevertheless it is true. Nora went away to Trieste with Joyce, unmarried, but full of hope and high spirits. For years they were miserably poor, and at one time she took in washing to pay the bills, while Joyce actually worked as a bank clerk in Rome. Their son Giorgio was born in 1905, their daughter Lucia in 1907. Nora had a miscarriage in 1908; and after that, although Joyce suspected her of deceiving him with other men, which was not the case, the small family was complete until the terrible years of Lucia's madness began in the late twenties. She died, still in an asylum in Northampton, in 1982.

Every detail of Nora Joyce's life and marriage is set down in this book. The most lurid event is probably the series of erotic letters Joyce wrote to her from Dublin in 1909, when he was trying to manage a cinema. Nora responded enthusiastically, but her letters have never come to light, and only her husband's are quoted here. They are much the same sort of letters as Mozart wrote to his wife. In later years Nora turned to religion – long before her husband died – and was reconciled with the Church for many years before her death in 1951. She and Joyce were finally married in 1931; but in truth theirs was a real union from the beginning.

Was she Molly Bloom? The answer is yes and no. Without her Molly would never have existed; but there are several significant differences between the model and the fictional creation, which Brenda Maddox points out. She influenced every aspect of Joyce's work. She gave him the story for 'The Dead'; she is Bertha in 'Exiles'. Her voice, with its distinctive cadences, is that of Molly Bloom, just as her letters foretell the style of that famous monologue. Above all she is Anna Livia, who speaks in Nora Barnacle's voice and no one else's. Nora knew this, and was proud of it, although she never read any of her husband's books. But she knew what she had contributed to them.

She was a woman of great beauty and charm, with a natural ease of manner and a real sense of style. She met many of the most famous men and women of her day and was in no way outshone by any of them. Her intelligence was not a literary one, but it was real. She had her full share of Irish nostalgia; but she was far more inclined to look life in the eye and accept its odd moments of happiness and its terrible burden. Above all she had a wonderful sense of humour, and she and Joyce emerge from this splendid biography as a couple of great comic characters. Nora Joyce had many tragedies in her life, but in the end it is the burble of her laughter that we hear, as we hear it always at the end and the beginning and all through *Finnegans Wake*.

Irish Independent, 18 June 1988

II.

General Journalism

In 1956, *The Irish Times* printed two articles in which John Broderick reflected on his travels in Greece – the first, *'Oedipus* at Epidauros' appeared on 14 August. In the following two years he produced several further travel pieces. Thereafter his 'occasional journalism' ranged far and wide for its subjects. Most of his articles appeared first in *The Irish Times*, often in the Weekend Review section, where he was given space to reflect on his own preoccupations – Athlone, Irish society, the Church, books and writers, human nature – and freedom to write humorously, seriously, sometimes pessimistically, even savagely. Other long articles appeared in *The Fountain*, the magazine of St Joseph's College, Garbally, Co. Galway, where he had been a pupil from January 1938. The final piece in this selection was written in 1985, four years after he had moved from Athlone to Bath, where he was never happy and where he died after a protracted illness in May 1989.

Oedipus at Epidauros

Epidauros began, like everything else in Greece, as a religious centre, the shrine of Aesculapius, the God of Health: a sort of Lourdes of the ancients, to which people travelled from all parts of the Hellenic world. Later, with the decline of the religious significance, it became fashionable as a spa. It is to this period that we owe the huge amphitheatre of Polycletus, which was completed about the middle of the fourth century BC. It is the largest and best preserved in Greece, and there every summer the National Theatre gives a festival of classical plays. It is also the only theatre in which the original Greek circular orchestra is intact. Even the great theatre of Dionysos in Athens, in which the art of the drama was born, has been Romanized: a stone frieze cuts the orchestra into a semicircle.

This year the festival lasted from 23 June to 8 July. Three plays were given two performances each: the *Medea* of Euripides, and *Antigone* and *Oedipus Rex* by Sophocles.

As we know, the classic Greek ideal was the *Kalos Kagathos*, the complete man. The modern Greek has not forgotten this ideal, and has striven in the representation of these great dramas to exploit and coordinate every aspect of art and nature. Outside of ballet, I have not seen so many diverse elements bound together in an artistic whole. First of all, there is the setting, which is superb. The acoustics are so perfect that a match struck in the orchestra can be clearly heard on the top row of the amphitheatre, which can accommodate 14,000 people. It looks out over a cluster of pine trees to low mountains, behind which, in high summer, the sun begins to sink as the drama starts at 7.30 pm. This, too, is part of the whole. The gradual darkening of the mountains from smoke-blue to purple to black, and the cloaking of the trees, provide a magnificently apt background for the mounting horror of Oedipus's tragedy.

This integration of nature is carried over into the costumes, which are all sedge-green or tan: the colours of the earth. Bright hues would have struck a jarring note against the natural background and the sanded orchestra. Nor did the ancients make the mistake of selecting a site of too much grandeur: one never feels, as at some other open-air festivals of Europe, that the scenery is overpowering the performance. At Epidauros it is all part of the splendid whole.

The incidental music for *Oedipus* is by Katina Paxinou, the famous actress who plays Jocasta. It is simple and effective. When the first trumpet notes ring out over the vast amphitheatre, it is not hard to imagine oneself attending a performance of the drama in Sophocles's lifetime. Modern Greeks are proud of their heroic past, and are reared among the great legends of antiquity. I myself had stopped a few days previously at that meeting of the three ways a few miles outside Livadia where, according to tradition, Oedipus slew Laius. It is perhaps the greatest triumph of the Greek National Theatre that the audience participates almost as much as the chorus.

The chorus is very different from anything we have seen in these islands. It is neither scanty nor self-conscious; it participates fully in the action. This is brought about by very simple means. During the first chorus of citizens, a woman moans while the priest is imploring Oedipus to save Thebes from famine. But it is the chorus of fifteen Theban senators that is the chief glory of the performance. From their first entrance, they are onstage in the centre of the orchestra for the remainder of the drama. Their movements are slow and majestic, though never ponderous: one is reminded again and again of a perfectly drilled corps de ballet. During the great monologues they fan out in front of the steps, occasionally taking a half-step forward, inclining rather than moving towards the speaker at certain stressed lines of the speech. Simple and even obvious as this device is, it is enormously effective. Not only does it bring the chorus right into the heart of the drama, which is surely what Sophocles intended, but it also does away with that self-conscious rigidity that is the bane of the chorus as used by producers in English-speaking productions of these plays. With the evening breeze gently stirring the long robes, the illusion of plasticity at Epidauros is complete.

Three of the choruses are sung. This is not the lugubrious drone to which we are accustomed in poetry readings in this country; it is full-blooded Byzantine chanting, which has been compared by one critic to that of the monks of Solesmes. Used so sparingly and in its context, this chanting heightens the dramatic tension to an extraordinary degree, especially as the first chorus sung is that following the first scene between Oedipus and Jocasta, when the net begins to tighten about the doomed king. We begin to understand the true function of the Greek chorus; it does not stand about, it takes part.

Indeed, looking back now, the principal effect of *Oedipus* at Epidauros was a lyric one. This is due not only to the beautiful quality of the voices of the actors and chorus, but to the marvellous acoustics of the place, which might be described in modern jargon as 'high fidelity'. I do not know why the sound in these ancient amphitheatres, built two thousand years ago, should be so wonderful, when the acoustics in so many concert halls built since are so bad. (I carried out the match-striking experiment with a friend in the theatre on the island of Delos, and the tiny sound carried perfectly. Perhaps someone could give us the technical reasons, if they are known? At any rate, the acoustics at Epidauros lend a singing quality to the players' voices.) I have never before in the spoken theatre been so acutely aware of the pitch of an actor's voice. I expect the producer was keenly aware of this also, so that the voices of the various characters were carefully blended: Tiresias was a bass, Creon a baritone, Oedipus a heroic tenor, and Jocasta a contralto; while the chorus was balanced as in opera.

People who have heard Sarah Bernhardt will tell you of the shock they experienced when they first heard her voice; it has been variously likened to the cawing of jackdaws, the cry of a street Arab, and the scraping of sandpaper. It was only on repeated hearings that its marvellous individual timbre became apparent and made all other voices seem insipid. One has something of the same experience with Katina Paxinou. Could this nasal croak be the voice of the actress whom many consider to be the finest tragedienne in Europe? As we know, Jocasta is a comparatively small role; an actress has to make her effect immediately or not at all. Paxinou made it. This actress would, I imagine, create unfavourable comment in a Rattigan dining room; and there is, in fact, something volcanic about her, as there should be about all great players. Her voice is not pretty; it is magnificent. Her face is not beautiful; it is a tragic mask. Her gestures are not refined; they are law-giving. It was the animal vitality she exuded that made her performance so unforgettable: the harsh voice created a mesmeric effect. Her last three lines had the terrible fatalistic sadness of an Attic funeral stela.

Alexis Minotis, who played Oedipus, is a superb actor, splendid in bearing, manly in action and magnificent in utterance. And more than any of the other players, he brought out the ritual character of the performance.

At the end of the tremendous drama the tourist police formed a semicircle about the actors as they took their calls. The audience was not especially vociferous. In Greece the audience applauds the actors, not itself. Passing out by the dressing rooms, the spectators exchanged pleasantries with the members of the chorus, who were washing themselves by a tap outside. One passed down the ramp and through a babble of all the nations, from which this year the clear, distorted English of north Oxford was conspicuously absent, into the great space where the buses were lined up. All along the road to Nauplia, clumps of poplars were graven into silver images by floodlighting. It was all very romantic. I asked my neighbour on the bus what he thought of the performance. He shook his head and shrugged. 'For the tourist it is all right, yes. But it is not what it was. You should have seen it in Gryparis's time, about twenty-five years ago. Then it was really worth seeing.'

One was not, after all, so very far away from home.

The Irish Times, 14 August 1956

The Town at the End of the Appian Way

Niko was small, squat, ugly, and, so he assured me, irresistible to women. He was a sea captain, and a native of the island of Ithaka.

'There is', he said firmly, 'more Greek spoken in Brindisi than in any other port in the world.' He pushed back his chair, murmured an apology in Spanish to a large lady whose statuesque composure had been shaken by his elbow, and gazed happily round the crowded bar. 'And it isn't only Greek,' he rumbled. 'There is more everything spoken in Brindisi.'

One does not idly contradict an experienced sea captain from Ulysses's island; and moreover I was half inclined to believe him. At that hour the bar of the Hotel Internationale in Brindisi was like the ground floor of the tower of Babel. British from Cyprus, from East Africa, Singapore, Ceylon and Hong Kong; Americans from Persia; Egyptians from Paris; Turks from Alexandria; Chinese from Calcutta; drinking, talking, watching, above all waiting. A party of Negro entertainers stranded on the way to Beirut played a gloomy and interminable game of poker in a corner. There, barricaded by whiskey bottles, they had remained for three days and most of two nights.

Everybody waits in Brindisi – for the next boat, the next train, the next plane. Dante described it perfectly in the *Purgatorio*: 'We were alongside the ocean yet, like folk who ponder o'er their road, who in heart do go and in body stay.' The modern world is full of polite purgatories of this kind: air terminals, where the heating is just right, are the best known and the most painless.

Brindisi has performed this function for over two thousand years: it is therefore somewhat less polite, and a great deal more interesting. For one thing, it is the first port of the East.

Europe, like Texas, is a state of mind. The East begins midway down the main thoroughfare of Brindisi, the long predatory street that runs from the railway station to the sea. The first half, the Corso Umberto, is Italian. There is no mistaking the glittering barbershops, the operatic frenzy of the traffic, the huge Mussolini fountain, built apparently of slabs of frozen lard. But halfway down to the sea, where the street veers a little to the left and changes its name to the Corso Garibaldi, one becomes conscious of a subtle variation of tempo, a slowing down, a muffling of sounds almost as if a veil had been thrown over them.

The shops are smaller and less glittering, and the names are spelt in Greek. Behind the beaded curtains of the doorways one hears the sharp yet melancholy plang of bouzoukia. The cafés here are entirely Greek, smelling of aniseed and fried octopus. They are more casual than the Italian cafés; there is more of an air of a private house where one drops in and joins the family. Functional café furniture is interspersed with household effects, a mahogany sideboard, tinted family photographs, a chest of drawers. One curious feature of the Corso Garibaldi is that all the neon signs face away from the sea towards the railway station. One would have thought that the sea would cast up more gullible fish.

The Corso Garibaldi opens onto the quays. And here one comes into contact with the age-old world of the sea, a fraternity as widespread and as parochial as the stage. The great ships at anchor there are always essentially the same ships, and the men who man them have changed little since Ulysses's time. Their world is as deep as the ocean, and as narrow as a plank. They do not wander far; their offshore leave is as circumscribed as a monk's. A few cafés on the Lungo-mare Oriente, the shop windows of the Corso. They walk among these unreal delights with the wary tread of cats picking their way among broken bottles.

Although one knows that life goes on in Brindisi in the same humdrum fashion as it does elsewhere, it is impossible to imagine anybody ever really having roots there. The restless crowds that drift along the Corso are different every night, suspended between one timetable and another. They mingle with an intimacy that is possible only to those who will never meet again; convention being a plant that needs roots. And, on the whole, people do not stay in Brindisi except to die, like Virgil.

Nothing remains of the house where he died except the arch of the courtyard through which he was carried. The young Italian matron who lives on the site is determined to keep visitors at bay, and who can blame her? The cobbled yard filled with children playing at ball cannot have changed very much since the poet's time. Through the open door one catches a glimpse of a shining tiled floor, a huge brass bed, a television set, a statue of the Virgin; after which one is politely but firmly shown out into the street again.

The young woman is, of course, quite right. One has no business indulging in a sentimental journey of this kind. It does not matter very much where Virgil died. He scooped up a handful of time long ago and is feeding on it yet, being, like all great poets, something of a magician. Even the statue crowned with bays, which has been erected to him in the Piazza Victor Emmanuele, and which makes him look like the young Gertrude Stein, can do him no harm.

Modern Brindisi is dominated by two great monuments: one very ancient, the other recent, both elegiac. The huge memorial to Italian seamen was erected in 1933. It is in the form of an immense rudder, 180 feet in height. Seeing it for the first time is a slightly alarming experience: the unusual shape does not at first explain itself – it rears over the harbour like some prehistoric sea-monster. From the top of it there is, however, a magnificent view of the natural harbour, one of the finest in Europe. The inner harbour branches out like the horns of a stag: hence its ancient name of *Brunda*, Latinized as *Brundisium*. There is also an outer harbour, and between the two flows the Pigonati canal where in 49 BC Caesar blockaded Pompey's fleet, as he tells us in his *De Bello Civili*. Facing the opening of this canal across the harbour on the mainland are the two white Roman columns that mark the end of the Appian Way. This is the other great monument of Brindisi, which signifies for all time that it was one of the most important towns in the world.

The Appian was the greatest of all the great Roman roads. Everything that shaped the history of Western Europe came to us along this way. It flung out 350 miles across south-east Italy, which the Romans called a five-day journey. Over it the legions thundered on their way to the east, through towns like Auca, Tarracina, Minturnae, Sinuessa, Beneventum, whose names sound as if they had been beaten out in silver by a sword. We know that essentially the classical toughs who marched this way were not very different from the jackbooted divisions who have thundered across Europe in our time. Yet from the distance of two thousand years they have the imperishable charm of the defeated.

The columns at Brindisi stand at the top of a great sweep of marble steps that lead down to the quayside. Only one of them, sixty feet in height, remains intact, and it is supported by an iron brace. The other, of which only the base remains, was cast down by an earthquake in 1528. These columns are unique: they are at once an end and a beginning, and as such stand a little outside time. And fundamentally nothing has changed in this old port of the East. As the crowd saunters by at the bottom of the great steps, the crowd that renews itself every night, one is reminded of that remark of Shaw's Caesar: 'The crowd in the Appian Way is always the same age.'

Unknown publication, 9 August 1958

Growing Up in Athlone – Or Anywhere Else

When I was a child, I read, as children do, for entertainment. It did not occur to me that the heroes and heroines I admired could ever have existed on land or sea, and I would have been very disappointed indeed if I had met any of them when walking down the street of my native town. When, much later, I discovered that many of the characters of Walter Scott and Dumas were based on historical personages, I felt that I had been cheated.

I was an only child, thrown a great deal upon myself, and ill at ease with people outside my own family circle. It was, therefore, necessary for me to create a world of my own, inhabited by strange romantic creatures who wore shining armour, and performed incredible feats of chivalry and daring against a background of moated castles and fluttering pennants. I was at ease with the Knights of the Round Table, and at odds with the world.

But life breaks in on even the most prolonged adolescence. The enchanted garden of childhood is in many ways an artificial paradise: it can only be maintained when the walls are high, and the gates are bolted fast. Sooner or later they come tumbling down, and the rattle of a passing cart is the tumbril that bears away one's youth. You find yourself in the marketplace, confused, tongue-tied and ashamed of your inexperience.

But although the fall of innocence may be as shattering as it is inevitable, one does not grow up as fast as all that. I don't think anybody can recall the exact moment when they came to a sudden realization of their involvement with humanity. It takes many years before you discover that those hard-faced strangers, so competent, so seemingly successful at the business of life, are also full of fears, and go through the harsh motions of their public existence for the simple reason that they have no alternative.

When you find out that nobody is as tough as they seem, then you have grown up. It took me many years to discover this simple truth; and in the meantime I continued to demand from literature the same sort of escape as I had achieved as a child.

You cannot learn about life from books: but without them you can have no real understanding of life at all. Literature is not a substitute for experience but an extension of it. While I cannot say that all the reading I did as a boy helped me to come to terms with life – if one ever does – I can claim that one book that I read when I was about twenty suddenly made me see that the characters in novels are not necessarily divorced from life, and that the people among whom I lived were just as vital, colourful, strange, and a great deal more imminent than any of the characters I had read about in fiction. The book was *The Return of the Native* by Thomas Hardy.

Like most of Hardy's novels the story is a tragic one. Clym Yeobright, tired of city life, returns from Paris to open a school on Egdon Heath, and marries Eustacia Vye, passionate, splendid, enigmatic, one of the greatest of Hardy's characters, and one of the most fascinating women in the whole of fiction.

Their marriage is not happy, for Eustacia is quite undomesticated, and her strange and terrible death is in the great tradition of tragic heroines. But the plot is the least important thing in the book. Hardy was such a great storyteller, and such is the spell that he casts, that you do not realize until long after finishing his books that his plots are ramshackle enough, and that he never really succeeded in breaking the rigid mould of Victorian convention. Nor is it the superb characterization that makes the book so glorious. Within his range, which was narrow, Hardy could create characters as vivid and poetic as any to be found in Shakespeare.

For the real hero of *The Return of the Native* is not a human being; it is Egdon Heath. Up from the pages of the book it rises, barren, sinister, brooding, dominating the lives of the characters, and compelling the reader to dwell upon its darkened heights. As Sylvia Lynd remarked, 'From the moment that we set foot on Egdon, Hardy has us in his power. We are in the Elf King's country and under a spell.' Egdon in spring, summer, but above all in winter, with the bonfires blazing for the fifth of November.

As I read this strange and terrible book I felt for the first time in my life a complete affinity with its characters and its marvellous setting. I knew Egdon, and I was acquainted with the people who lived upon it. The fact that they were English is irrelevant; for art is international, country people are much the same everywhere, and a novelist as great as Hardy deals with the wellsprings of human action and emotion.

Above all he was a poet; and he saw every character and every situation in a potential glow as vivid and luminous as the fires upon Egdon Heath. But that in itself would not have made me see my own countryside, and my own people so vividly, and almost for the first time, after reading *The Return of the Native*. I saw them because they were there within me, and all about me; but I had not troubled to look for them because I had taken them for granted. In a sense we never see our native place until we leave it. I was lucky to have it suddenly revealed to me in the reflected vision of a great poet.

I am a provincial; and in Ireland that means that although one may have been born in a country town as I was, one is also a countryman. Few Irish towns are big enough to cut one off from the land that surrounds them, and most of the townsmen have their roots in the soil. To the south of Athlone, where I was born and still live, the flat midland meadows stretch out on either side of the river Shannon; and beyond them lies the bog. Here no mountains stand sentinel against the sky, and the great purple plain ends only at the horizon. A figure moving on this vast heath strides across the rim of the world and is etched against the sky.

It is a lonely, secret, and to the stranger, especially in winter, a terrifying place. The people who live there are not, like the traditional Irishman of the stage and the travel book, easy to know.

Just as there is nothing of the soft charm of a Paul Henry picture in that landscape, so too these people do not yield themselves easily to the stranger. But I did not have to get to know them: I was one of them. My forefathers had lived there for more generations than I know, and to this day I cannot throw a stone in the place without hitting a cousin. Nor was I ever lonely on the bog, as I always am in cities. I know its hidden roads, as I have never got to know the streets of Dublin, or Paris, or London, or Rome. And I know most of its houses and the people who live in them. I am not rootless.

And so as I left down Hardy's book at the age of twenty, I knew that its title had a special significance for me. Since then I have seen something of the world, and I have loved one or two corners of it, Ravenna, perhaps, most of all, but not as well as that hidden corner of Ireland whose reflection I first recognized in the sombre magnificence of Egdon Heath.

Undated cutting, probably from the early 1960s

City of the Plain: Some Aspects of Athlone

In his *Irish Sketch Book* of 1842 Thackeray quotes a guidebook of the time that described Athlone as 'old, inconvenient, ill-built and ugly'. The novelist makes no effort to disassociate himself from these remarks, except to say that the improvements then taking place on behalf of the Shannon navigation would doubtless render the place less inconvenient than it was stated to be.

In short, Thackeray hardly left his coach while in the town; and the only remark he passed that might be considered to be original was that a painter would find there 'some good subjects for his sketchbook'.

Today Athlone is of course older still; it remains inconvenient; there are no public or private buildings that might be described as handsome, although many of them are unfortunately all too well built; and its main streets are certainly ugly. But Thackeray, after a hard night in Ballinasloe, and eager to get on to his description of the Maynooth students tanking up with whiskey on the road before going back to 'yonder dismal-looking barracks' of a seminary, might perhaps be forgiven for giving less thought to Athlone than one would expect from a conscientious travel writer.

Yet his attitude is typical. It has long ago been established by writers and travellers that the coastal counties of Ireland are the only beautiful ones; while the midlands are flat, dull and uninteresting. So tourists, driving from Dublin to Galway and the misty delights of Connemara are apt, like Thackeray, to regard Athlone as a sort of combination of eating house and public lavatory on the way to the promised land.

These visitors cannot be blamed: they are the victims of two hundred years of romanticism, which lays it down as a first principle that rocks, mountains, cliffs and stormy seas constitute the most beautiful part of nature, the only aspect that puts man in touch with the sublime. After all, in life it is the obvious that first presents itself to the eye; and most people are too hurried or too idle to search further.

Dorothy Parker once struck a blow at this school of thought, which is still paramount among travel agents, when she remarked of Switzerland that there was less in it than meets the eye. There is more in the midland counties of Ireland than meets the eye; and in these regions Athlone has always been, and remains today, the principal settlement.

It was not built to be beautiful; its first cause and the reason for its existence has always been defensive. Today it has of course become a thriving industrial town, which does not add to its architectural interest, although it has made its character more complex. But essentially it remains what it always was: a garrison town, which has survived a thousand years or so of assaults and batteries, the coming and going of rival factions and the uneasy peace that lay between. It is a singularly wary place. It is, like most Irish towns, of great antiquity. The Shannon is a natural barrier, and in ancient times was the dividing line between the provinces of Leinster and Connaught.

War between the Irish princes swept backwards and forwards over the river with a regularity that was anything but monotonous. The history books are full of gory details like this: 1003, M'Loughlin of Moate and Turlough Mór O'Connor met in battle in Athlone, but a false peace was made between them; 1170, the hostages of Dermot McMurrough were put to death in Athlone by Roderick O'Connor; 1218, the town of Athlone was burned on the Westmeath side; 1227, Hugh O'Connor plundered the market at Athlone, burned the town and killed the constable; 1257, Athlone burned in war between Hugh O'Connor and the

O'Rourke; 1272, Hugh O'Connor plundered Lough Ree and burned Athlone. And so it goes merrily on; the tribes behaving much the same then as they do today. One burning was apparently enough to satisfy the wrath of God in the matter of Sodom and Gomorrah; but Athlone was more resilient. No wonder the inhabitants never became architecturally conscious. With wattle huts and tents going up in flames every few years, there was little opportunity to develop the finer points of domestic style.

The river was, and is, the most important feature in the place. Historians are generally agreed that the fort on the Shannon gave the settlement its name, and about 994 the first attempt to build a bridge was made, another in 1120, yet another in 1210. This was, as might be expected, pulled down by Hugh O'Connor in 1272. Made as it was of wicker and hurdles it cannot have been very difficult to destroy; and no unusual enterprise was needed to throw it up again, although of course it was less fun.

As in the case of so many bridges, barracks and harbours in Ireland, it was the English who succeeded in building something permanent in Athlone. In 1566 Sir Henry Sidney began a new bridge, which was completed in a year, a fact that might amaze some modern contractors. However, it was only twelve feet wide, and passage was further obstructed by three flour mills. Even in those days Athlone had its traffic problems, for on market days and fairs the bridge was described as dangerous. But it lasted until 1844 when the present structure was completed. When I was a boy I knew an old lady, a centenarian, who remembered the Elizabethan bridge; and so, of course did the parents of several of my own relations. It was some yards downstream of the present bridge; and this has resulted in Athlone's Main Street, still so called, being relegated to the background: in the old days it led directly on to the bridge.

The castle, which is by far the most historical building in the town and certainly the ugliest, was built on the site of an earlier fort erected by Turlough O'Connor in 1129. The foundation of the grim, toad-like edifice of today was laid in 1210 by Lord de Grey at the command of King John. During the work a tower fell and killed Lord Richard de Tuite, his chaplain and seven others. This was attributed by the pious natives to the miraculous intervention of Saints Peter and Paul, patrons of the monastery land on which the castle was built. Down the long centuries, I can hear the locals chuckling over their buttermilk and beer at this mishap. Essentially nothing changes.

Athlone reached its greatest prominence during the seventeenth century. During the insurrection of 1641 the townspeople swore to defend the place on behalf of Lord Ranelagh, then Lord President; and proceeded to allow entry to Sir James Dillon and his insurgents. Ranelagh was allowed to leave after a long siege. With the victories of Cromwell the castle was retaken for the Parliamentarians by Sir Charles Coote, and up in flames went Athlone again.

The town's most famous hour came later in the century. The battle of the bridge of Athlone has gone into song and story; but we hear little of yet another burning of the Leinster side of the town by Colonel Grace. He and St Ruth defended the area with the greatest bravery and panache against the forces of King William led by de Ginkel; and we all know how that ended. I heard an interesting sidelight on history a few months ago. A young Athlone man, in the Netherlands with a study group, was received by Queen Juliana. When she heard he was from Athlone, the Queen remarked that a well-known general attached to one of her ancestors had once been Earl of Athlone. It was de Ginkel. A charming and peaceful ending to an old unhappy story.

The town however was not yet finished with fire and brimstone. On 27 October 1697, the castle was struck by lightning that set fire to the magazine; in the explosion that followed, the whole town within the walls went up in flames that could be seen in that flat land for a dozen miles around. It may be supposed that after this experience the inhabitants privately implored Saints Peter and Paul to lay off their combustive activities; certainly since then, except for the burning of the woollen mills in 1941, Athlone has been both peaceful and wet. But all that fire and brimstone, whether from heaven or from invading artillery, has left its mark on the character of the town. The typical Athlone native is inclined to take a back seat, and leave the public affairs of the borough to those settlers from other parts of Ireland and the world who have made their home there.

It was always thus. All down the centuries the town has been accustomed to being occupied by outsiders, mostly military men and their camp-followers. This has led to a certain amount of cynicism on the part of the natives: after all, they have seen and experienced every form of occupation before. If the newcomers want to take the risk of making public fools of themselves, they are welcome to do so; if they prosper and grow rich and influential, that's the luck of the game.

It remains a remarkable fact that most of the public bodies in the town are heavily encumbered with people who have not been born in the area. They seem to have an energy that the natives do not share; or are the locals wiser in their several generations? I have often thought that they are; certainly they are philosophical about the way most of the town's affairs are conducted. What, in the long run, in a life so very short and uncertain, does it matter? And of course they are right. It is hard enough for a man to cultivate his own garden, or his shop or stall or potato patch, without taking on the responsibilities of public affairs. They often wonder, the aborigines, how some of these people lose their heads so easily and pontificate on local politics, industry and general welfare with such a degree of ponderous pomposity; but really, we – for I am one of the troglodytes – can't be bothered.

In time a new bridge will be built, a new road constructed through the old houses that have seen so much of this sort of activity, new factories will be opened, new houses slapped up, new clubs formed, new resolutions passed – by the occupiers. So why should we worry? A heavy-lidded glance, a sceptical smile, and we pass on about our own mysterious business. By our shrugs shall you know us, we Athlonians. And after all these energetic new men spend money, get things done, give employment, we make our living out of them, as we always have. Besides, they are not such bad fellows.

They may not perceive the subtle nuances of local exchanges; they may make some fearful solecisms banging round in an effort to impress themselves, they may even in unguarded moments display a contempt for the indigenous; but it is all no more than an understandable misunderstanding of the greatest of all Athlone qualities: survival. This is no mean talent, given the history of the town, and by its very nature it is self-effacing. In the long tradition of this curious place, possessing as it does all the marks and monuments of those who have come and gone, it is no mean feat to survive to make use of them, and to subject them to a typical, oblique and mildly critical glance.

I have often thought of the first stanza of Kipling's *The Pro-Consuls* in connection with this aspect of my native town:

> They that dig foundations deep
> Fit for realms to rise upon,
> Little honour do they reap
> Of their generation,
> Any more than mountains gain
> Stature till we reach the plain.

The plain is here; miles and miles and miles of it south of the bridge, opening on either side in pleasant, cool and quiet reaches of water meadows; flowing on into the great purple bog that melts into the horizon. One can glimpse something of this vast and very beautiful region standing on the bridge watching the great river flowing south in a slow and splendid arc. There is a wonderful sense of space and limitless sky in this vantage point; all the more impressive because of the narrow and crowded streets that lead onto it. The view is a subtle one, allowing the imagination to range freely, noting the delicate colours, blue and green and silver, that are so striking a part of its composition. In the midlands the mountains are in the sky, ever-changing, shifting and forming and dissolving, trailing long shadows over the quiet land, and sometimes disappearing completely, leaving the river bathed in light.

There are some delightful glimpses of steep narrow lanes running down to the Shannon, which the visitor may or may not notice as he passes through the hellish traffic in the main streets; but if he stays awhile he will find that the most impressive sight of the town, perched upon its little hills, is to be had from one of the narrow roads that skirt the meadows and the bog south of the bridge. Here over the plain, with its hidden paths and half-concealed houses, one can see the roofs and spires etched cleanly and brilliantly against the sky. It is a view that is familiar to travellers in the Netherlands, in southern Lombardy, in the sandy plain of Brandenburg surrounding Berlin, and surprisingly enough, also in some approaches to London.

I have often wondered why painters have not taken Thackeray's advice and brought their sketchbooks with them into these regions. When there are no mountains to distract the eye, the human, the humble, the unpretentious stand out in bolder relief; in those narrow, high-hedged country lanes one comes upon fields, streams, houses and half-concealed gardens that indicate a quiet and deeply entrenched civilization in which people have still time to lean against a wall and study the sky for signs of tomorrow.

At one time such a subject would have been considered to be lacking in interest unless set against a typical romantic background: wild seas to indicate the courage of fisherfolk, rugged mountains to suggest the frugal peasant. But in the landscape around Athlone a man stands up against the sky, his feet planted in the soil, his head in a whirl of light. The great Dutch and Flemish masters were preoccupied with light, as all good painters are; but the human experience in the face of man or child, naked before the heavens, is not easy to capture, and the sense of space, which is such a feature of Russian life, is less easy to portray than a Gothic gorge. Perhaps some day a young and brilliant artist will tackle it. I would like to live to see such work.

It is this feeling of limitless space that the traveller to Athlone and the countryside around it will sense, even if he does not consciously seek it. One of the great modern diseases is claustrophobia; the narrowing confines of cities, the inhumanity of public transport. Space can have a wonderfully soothing effect; a most effective remedy for neurosis. The inhabitants of Athlone may suffer from an increasing frustration in the face of over-crowded streets, and the insidious nullity of housing estates. (Estate: in modern terms a thing always means the opposite of what it is named.) But in the midlands one can escape very easily, and on foot, to a region that lies open and unexploited as far as the eye can see.

This is a most precious possession, and one which only the foolhardy will take for granted. Here, river and lake and gentle hill blend together in a landscape quite unlike any other in western Europe for the quality of its speaking silence and utter lack of dis-cord. It is not to be supposed that people born and reared in such a region ever feel the necessity to hurry. A man who can dominate his fields, standing fixed and immovable on the horizon like a sturdy tree, develops in time a sense of individuality rare even among country people.

One sees them moving slowly along the rim of the horizon, with no impediment to diminish them in that vast and silent place. Nowhere else, except possibly in Russia, does a man walk 'for a while between things ended and things begun'.

The Irish Times, 3 March 1978

Redeeming the Time

What years are the forgotten ones? In nearly all cases they are the recent ones, before time has moulded them into a period, a movement, a school of thought, a war or a peace. The year before last has as little character as yesterday's newspaper.

But there are more forces at work than the hand of history. There are the memories of ordinary men and women everywhere. And it is a curious fact that history seems to move faster than man's private eye. Those who were growing up in the early sixties are not now much inclined to look back upon that particular period, except perhaps for isolated incidents in isolated lives: a birth, a death, a marriage.

Yet those years, from 1960 to 1965, are already written large in the history books. It was the era of John F. Kennedy, Pope John, de Gaulle; while nearer home it was the period that introduced television to Irish homes everywhere, saw the growing political influence of Lemass, and witnessed the first stirrings of enormous change in the Roman Catholic Church.

As we grow older our early years become more vivid to us. In the full flood of life, in our thirties and forties, we are too busy planning ahead and pursuing our careers to indulge in nostalgic memories of our childhood years. That comes with the bending of the bough after we have passed the half-century mark. Twenty years ago I was just as little inclined to look back upon the thirties, the decade in which I grew from childhood to the uncertain dignity of the teenage years. They were also the years of Hitler, Roosevelt, mass unemployment and the talking films; but they had not yet taken their place with any degree of urgency in the theatre of memory. I was not yet old enough to recall those private pieties whose mysterious centre is the rebirth of the world so miraculously granted to every child.

I am old enough now, and to spare; and it was with something of a shock that I realized some time ago that I could remember the Athlone of forty-five years ago quite clearly. And not only that; but the memory was altogether a welcome and curiously comforting one. People, faces, houses, even scraps of conversations that I had thought were vanished forever, fell into place in a more or less orderly fashion in my mind. It was like a blurred film suddenly guided into focus. I suppose it is all part of those uncertain experiences, which we have so often heard of described as the compensations of middle and old age. On the whole it is not to be despised. It is rather like discovering a new dimension of the mind; a drawing-back of curtains on a picture that has long been shrouded and unvisited. It is an interesting picture.

The first thing that strikes one comparing the Athlone of today with the town I remember, is the violent changes that have come upon it. We live in fast-moving times; and are often unaware in our day-to-day preoccupations that the very ground we walk upon is already marked for 'development'. A hundred years ago a man of my age looking back on his childhood in any town in Europe would have found only one innovation – the arrival of the railway. And in 1832 or thereabouts it had still not arrived in settlements of the same size as Athlone. It seems to me that they have come about as a result of the discovery of Things on a scale hitherto unimaginable.

We live in a period that has experienced what might be described as a revolution of the inanimate. It is quite new to humanity; so new that most people have very little idea of what is happening, overwhelmed as they are by an avalanche of washing machines, television sets, tape recorders, refrigerators, synthetic detergents, dry shavers, motor cars, and tinned and packaged foods from the ends of the earth. We have all that and plastic too; and the revolution they have brought about in our lives is a materialistic one, which has its own philosophy, and justifies its existence by the act of being.

A town, like a family, is a microcosm of society. What is happening in the world is happening also in Athlone, in a smaller but no less inevitable way. That the town, as an entity of industrial societies all over the world, is a better place in many ways than it was forty years ago, no one will deny. People are better housed, more prosperous, and most important of all, more numerous than they used to be. This rise in population is one of the great features of large Irish towns in the last half-century. It is no doubt part of the inexorable balance of nature that individuals are in many ways more solitary now than they ever were before.

The Athlone of 1933 was a more compact place than it is today. Baylough, for instance, was almost a country village outside the town; now it is a suburb. In those days the country began at the top of Connaught Street on the other side of the canal bridge. Except for St Peter's Terrace, Forthill – then occupied by Mrs Smith and a huge Airedale – and the Dean Kelly School, the whole of the Batteries was an open space from Shamrock Lodge to the Springwell Road. Even part of the old fort was still lived in by the Brennan family. The top windows were, as I remember, a masterpiece of *trompe l'oeil*. Indeed on the day I arrived at the Dean Kelly School from the convent with a number of other wide-eyed little boys, I was invited by some of the older scholars to jump out of them. The higher education had begun.

The main streets of Athlone have not changed much. (Would that they had, one can hear the motorists muttering.) But the shops have now, nearly all of them, modern vitrolite-and-glass fronts. They gleam like false teeth, and indeed with their new facelifts they have a slightly voracious air. Many of the old names, once proudly painted on elaborate wooden signs, have now vanished from Connaught Street: Huban, Kenny, Doran, Shine, Murray, Jones, Naughton, Craven, O'Brien, O'Meara, Monaghan, Bigley, Hannon, Kirby, Byrne, Watson, Healion. Happily some of these old names are still flourishing in other parts of the town; but not many. The snows of yesteryear have melted fast in that street. Canaries no longer sing in their gilded cages outside Lennons at the top of Patrick Street and the apple trees in Cox's orchard are down.

In such a climate it gives one pleasure to set down the names that still remain. Grenham, Gray, Galvin, Walsh, Egan, Higgins, MacManus, McNeill; to which I can with a certain grim satisfaction add my own name; the name of one who still remembers the days of open fires in the shops.

How wonderful they were on long, dark, cold winter evenings. And how pleasant it was for a customer to be invited to come behind the counter and warm himself. Shopping in those days was a very leisurely business; and sometimes even included the drinking of tea in a snug, cosy, heavily upholstered room behind the shop. How is it that in an age in which communication has become faster and faster, we have less and less time to dawdle? It is certainly curious.

Another feature that has almost entirely disappeared is the step into a shop. For some reason, steps down were considered good for business; steps up were bad. Certainly to descend from street level gave one a cosier feeling; and to look out and see a procession of giants go by on the footpath added to the wonder of being a child. I think perhaps that the reason for the popular 'step down' was that it usually belonged to an older established shop, outside which the level of the modern street had risen. This meant a more solid and more faithful clientele. In those days people did not shop around as frantically as they do today.

The Athlone child of the late seventies takes the wireless and television for granted; they are part of life, like jeans and plastic cups and bombs in the North. But in the early thirties broadcasting was still a great novelty. Few houses possessed a wireless; and no doubt it is because of that that I can remember vividly listening to the abdication speech of King Edward VIII in 1936. But on the whole, families in those days had to rely on their own talents to entertain themselves.

Nor were telephones general in the thirties. I doubt if there were more than fifty or sixty in the whole town. Professional men and the larger business houses had installed them; but they were decidedly uncommon in private houses. Motor cars were not of course a novelty; nevertheless a new one was a source of very considerable interest to the neighbours.

These may seem trivial things to mention nowadays, so completely have we assimilated the marvels of science. But in fact they are not unimportant; for without them the structure of society as a whole was different. We were not deluged with things and we were not subjected to the influence of mass communication, which, catering as it must for as wide an audience as possible, always settles for the lowest common denominator.

The culture that is disseminated with the greatest vigour is essentially a vulgar one, in the Latin sense of the word; and it is a depressing fact that no great art has ever arisen out of popular traditions. *Porgy and Bess* is not really in the same league as *Cosi fan tutte*. In those far-off days no one associated loud noises with a way of life.

This island, cut off from the mainstream of British and European development, has always been about twenty years behind the times. Today, as a result of television, we are not more than three or four years behind the latest fads. But in the thirties, Ireland, particularly in the provinces, was a whole generation late in the march of technology. It was possible for a child growing up in those days to be influenced by the spirit of an older, more leisurely, more individualistic Ireland. Round many an old corner one could still catch an echo of the eighteenth century; a dying fall, hardly more than the footstep of a ghost. But it was there. Old women still combed their hair with racks, mirrors were glasses, a recipe was a receipt, and leisure was lees-ure.

What was there also in those days was a very definite sense of involvement with the town, and with one's neighbours. Even I, who was a shy child, and have never become a really sociable person, was aware of it. But it was of course a local, almost a street loyalty. I was born and brought up in Connaught Street and it is significant that my memories do not include the Leinster side of the town. The fact is that until I went to the Marist Brothers school at the age of eleven and a half, I simply did not know that part of the town. But in our own very limited and parochial way we were all very close. We did not have to attend seminars about community spirit: it was there, as naturally as the air we breathed.

Nowadays, with the speed and efficiency of mechanical communications, people have become reliant on them, with the result that the individual finds himself more and more cut off from his fellows. This is already a serious problem in cities. The world of gadgets is the world of disassociation. The fact that Athlone today has over eighty clubs of one kind or another seems to suggest that people are aware of this danger. In my young days we had no need of them; one had one's family and relations. Nowadays even families have to struggle to preserve their identities in a computer society. The organization man is just around the corner, and he drives a very fast car in the service of Big Brother. I am grateful to have been brought up in a more static and more self-assured society.

There are so many memories. Ass carts in Connaught Street and herds of sheep on the Batteries. An old-fashioned gramophone in Walsh's out of which, after much strenuous winding, the voice of John McCormack would float through a horn. The slow tramp of four police feet on the street at night. The crowing of cocks in backyards behind the shops. A whole volume might be written about these hidden spaces, a feature of every Irish town.

A friend of mine, settling in Banagher to write a biography of Anthony Trollope, noticed this and remarked upon it in his book. All such houses in small Irish towns have an unexpected and very long garden (or 'yard') at the back; one of those in this lower region of Banagher has a great arched carriage gateway and, behind it, four acres of orchards and fields (*Anthony Trollope* by James Pope-Hennessy, London 1971).

I have mentioned Cox's orchard. It was the largest garden in Connaught Street, full of delectable apple trees, and a rambling rose twining round an old-fashioned summer house, where Miss Mizie Cox sat on a summer's day, quietly knitting. The silence was such that one could almost hear the click of the needles across the poppies in the long grass. Galsworthy, a much maligned author, has left us a perfect little word picture of just such a scene: 'Summer, summer, summer, and the soundless footsteps on the grass.'

I wonder if any of our children today will bear such a memory of a quiet childhood when they grow up. I doubt it. It seems to me that everyone spoke softly in my childhood, and amused themselves in a very tranquil manner, they did not raise their voices while walking sedately along the canal banks, or taking tea in the yacht club, or sitting in their windows watching the neighbours go by, an occupation that never seemed to tire them. One has a memory of voices of course, but on the whole they are quiet ones, and hardly ever raised in anger or amazement.

It is not now possible to stand at an open doorway, or sit in a raised window anywhere in the main streets of Athlone without being deafened by noise, poisoned by oil fumes, irritated by passing transistors and maddened by the shrieks of playful infants hurling four letter words at one another as they go about their innocent ways. No wonder that privacy and quiet are two of the most expensive commodities in today's world: one has to be very fortunate indeed to enjoy what was a commonplace in my youth.

It is not possible to end any reminiscence of the Athlone – the Connaught side of it – of forty years ago without a reference to the old church of St Peter's in Chapel Street, now the Dean Crowe Hall. One remembers the Dean himself ambling through the streets wrapped in his long black Spanish cloak. I remember being surprised, growing up, to discover that all priests did not wear such splendid garb. But of course Dean Crowe was a law unto himself; kindly, humorous, tolerant, wise and witty, he was also what the Irish admiringly call a terrible rogue. Those who do not understand just exactly what that means are missing a great deal in life.

The old Dean was an institution, and deserves a whole book to himself. So does that old church, or chapel, as it was called by the older people, a reminder of the days when the Catholic Church was not the Church by law established. This old building served the parish of St Peter's from the end of the eighteenth century until 1937, when the magnificent new edifice in the square was completed. I served at the first Mass said there.

I expect that several learned papers have already been written about the old building in Chapel Street. If not there ought to be, for it was by far the most interesting and unusual religious structure in Athlone.

The small porch always engaged my attention, hung round as it was with black-framed memorial notices of dead parishioners. My own father was commemorated there, together with the departed relatives of many a friend and neighbour. I have not seen this feature in any other church; and of course it has entirely disappeared today. I often wonder what has happened to those hopeful little notices with their black-edged borders, all so kindly and so devoutly meant. Many years later I remembered this porch with its solidly hung wall, and transferred it, in a book, to the new church, where it has no cause to be. Such are the devious ways of novelists.

The inside of this old building was most unusual; and in many ways pre-dated today's idea of gathering a congregation close about an altar. In St Peter's this was achieved by means of galleries. The altar, raised high with some eight or ten steps leading to it, was placed against the wall in the middle of the church instead of the end. The seats were arranged in three sections, in front and at both sides of the altar; and over these were the galleries. They were famous; and it is sad to think that there are thousands of people in the town today who have never heard of them. They were known as the organ gallery, the old men's gallery and the grand gallery.

This latter had something of the air of the royal enclosure at Ascot. It was heavily patronized by the more fashionable female section of the parish, and was a brave sight at Easter, full as it was of new hats of a herbaceous variety. No new outfit could possibly be worn without first being displayed in the grand gallery of old St Peter's. The ladies said that they put on their new things so as to invoke the blessing of God; and perhaps they did.

The two other galleries were less fashionable. The organ gallery housed the choir, presided over by the famous Dinkie Donnelly. This was rather a mixed section, much in favour with the young bloods and the more advanced maidens of the town, who indulged in a certain amount of giggling and pinching under cover of the organ music. All in all, rather a racy set.

The old men's gallery was exactly that; although it also housed several old women who had reached that time of life when common humanity overtakes the idea of sex. A great deal of coughing, blowing of noses and clearing of throats from this gallery; and once or twice, I was told in an excited whisper by another altar boy, an old person had been removed from the place on Monday, having been dead since the previous day.

It would be nice to think of some modern architect modelling a new church on the style of this old chapel. It would save a great deal of ground space, and give some variety to the horrid sameness of modern church architecture.

But one must not be too sentimental about the past. It had one great advantage over the present in the minds of my generation: we were young. It has been ever thus. In Victorian times we read of fond parents and grandparents in novels, bemoaning the behaviour of the younger generation, and harking back to brave days of old. Two thousand years ago the poet Horace, a wise and worldly man, was denouncing the vices and follies of the age in the third book of his *Odes*:

> Our generations, fertile in vice, defiled
> First marriage, first the family and the home;
> From that defilement foul corruption flowed.

Have these lines a familiar ring? They have. The truth is that in every age something is lost and something gained from generation to generation. I am very well aware that these fleeting recollections of mine are those of someone who was brought up in comfortable circumstances. To children growing up in the poor and overcrowded lanes just off Connaught Street, the age cannot have appeared so golden.

But I still think that the unhurried pace of those years before the war created a better climate for humans to live in. If, with the greatly improved social conditions of today, we could achieve a way of life as tranquil and assured for everyone, then we would have gained something wonderful indeed.

The Irish Times, 12 January 1980

God Save the Queen

Every schoolboy knows the epigram that Wilde lifted from the great French aphorist La Rochefoucauld: hypocrisy is the homage that vice pays to virtue. If we assume that there is some truth in that saying, and I think there is a great deal, we are forced to the conclusion that there is a great deal of virtue in Ireland.

The writer must always be studied in relation to the society that gave him birth; and by society I mean our community as a whole. We are all products of it whether we like it or not; in revolt or in acceptance we are part of it.

It is therefore necessary, before discussing writers and such, to examine the claims of this society of ours. They are considerable; and perhaps the simplest way to conduct this enquiry would be to consider what our society expects a young man to be. Many of the rules that our establishment has laid down for our guidance apply also of course to young Irish women; but I can't speak about them with the same authority because I've never been a girl.

The conditioning of our young man will begin long before he is born, even before he is conceived. Since ours is a Christian republican society, it will be assumed, if he is expected to be a normal member of that community, that his family before him should also be Christian and republican. If his family are monarchical Moslems he would be regarded as somewhat unusual, and therefore not typical enough for the purpose of our study.

At one time it would be essential for our young man to be born a Catholic; but of recent years we have become rather more liberal in this matter: Protestants are now generally accepted as more or less thoroughly Irish but not perhaps quite as Irish as some. Born then into a Catholic, Christian legitimate family, our young man will be exposed from his earliest years to the atmosphere which prevails in such families. As likely as not he will be one of many; for in our society large families are looked upon as a gift from God. The atmosphere will be pious. All Irish families are deeply religious. They attend to their duties joyously and often, they contribute spontaneously but according to their means to the support of their pastors. They are honest, hard-working, frugal, virtuous and sober.

Coming from such a background it will be expected that our man will inherit all of those admirable qualities. If for instance at the age of fifteen he commits incest this cannot be held to be the fault of the family unit; but must be something evil and un-Irish in himself. Typically, he will love his parents and his brothers and sisters, as brothers and sisters and fathers and mothers ought to be loved: that is deeply but with restraint.

He will have a sense of religion. He will learn his prayers at his mother's knee; and afterwards more thoroughly at the feet of the nuns. His education will be a special concern of his family, and of society at large. If he is to be really typical he will be educated by the Christian Brothers. But here again there is a large measure of tolerance today. We don't very much care anymore if he is educated by the Jesuits, so long as he applies himself diligently and honestly to the curriculum laid down for him by his elders and betters. No need for us to examine the pros and cons of this system of education, which is the product of a society dedicated to high moral principles and practical virtues. Our young man will not question it either; but buckle down, make the most of it, and pass his examinations on merit. If he does he will meet with the approval of everyone.

Meanwhile his social life outside the family will have been taking shape. He will come into contact with other products of Christian republicanism; and he will know exactly what is required of him. He will be courteous, quiet, modest and interested in games, which he will have learned from his earliest youth are calculated to preserve a healthy mind in a healthy body. If any other young man questions this he will not hit him a puck on the gob; but will attempt to reason with him and show him the error of his ways. For it is well known that a lack of interest in games, and even worse a tendency to criticize their great and beneficial role in our society, is a sure way to lose one's virtue; and our young man will preserve this by every means at his disposal, including prayer. However, if he plays games hard enough and enthusiastically enough, his virtue will take care of itself. Cynics may scoff; but it is a cardinal rule of our society that there is nothing purer and more upright than a good all-round athlete.

Our young Irishman will banish all dark notions from his mind as vigorously and as successfully as Sir Christopher Wren banished swearing from the site of St Paul's Cathedral. This is a notion that should be hung on every Irish school as a portent of things to come. Indeed so admirable and realistic is this sentence that it might well have been written by an Irishman.

> Whereas, among labourers and others, that ungodly custom of swearing is too frequently heard, to the dishonour of God and contempt of authority; and to the end that such impiety may be utterly banished from these works, which are intended for the service of God, and the honour of religion, it is ordered that profane swearing shall be a sufficient crime to dismiss any labourer.

But this is a digression, touched upon mainly to indicate that our Irish ideas of right and wrong are not entirely insular. Besides, Wren flourished in the seventeenth century; and attitudes have changed somewhat since then, even in this country. That is not to say that swearing is encouraged on building sites, or anywhere else. Our young man will be aware of this; and will swear nothing but good oaths – like the temperance pledge. If he takes this loudly enough and abides by it, he will meet with the unreserved approval of our society. For we place a great deal of emphasis on sobriety in this country. Only the climate has the moral right to be wet at all times.

Sober then, chaste in mind and body, studious and well informed on matters of importance, such as the opinions of his immediate superiors, he will be prepared to go out into the world and earn his living. It is assumed that he will be able to do this in Ireland; for strangely enough our society has evolved no definite opinions as to the code of behaviour a man should adopt if he has to emigrate. A warning perhaps will be sounded; for it is generally held in this country that all foreigners are immoral, un-Christian, and much given to suicide and lunacy. But as I have said, things have changed a little since the seventeenth century: it is common knowledge that unspeakable things go on in England, and not only on building sites. Our young man, having secured a job in his native country, on merit, will thank God in private and in public that he has been spared from such contamination.

What job is he likely to hold down? It really doesn't matter. Such as it is he will be duly grateful for it. Society frowns upon an agitator; and reserves its best smiles for those who quietly blend with their neighbours and friends in a spirit of community effort. Thus if he is a teacher he will teach what everybody else teaches, and evolve no disturbing theories of his own; indeed if he has absorbed all the facets of our culture in the way that society would wish him to do so, he will not be aware that any such theories exist. He will be much too occupied saving his money in order to get married, settle down and bring up a family as virtuous and typical as himself.

This is simple. Hard-working and restrained as he is, he will not throw his money around. He will put it in the bank or the post office and watch it grow; and with every pound the approval of society will swell also. He will know, of course, from his education and his spiritual reading and his observations that we are not a money-grubbing people; our values are not as superficial as that. However, one must pay one's way; that is only realistic; and besides it is part of the general attitude of our society to the question of honesty. An honest day's work for an honest day's pay leads to an honest night's sleep.

And so the happy picture goes on, gentle and peaceful and law-abiding and God-fearing, into another generation. And our little fiction ends. For fiction it is, of course, and restricted on the whole to one mythical young man. I haven't the space to touch upon the claims of society with regard to political probity, religious sincerity, war or social justice.

Indeed, these claims are not very practical. They are ideals, which one may or may not agree with; set up out of a mixture of self-interest, fear and self-protection. They vary from country to country, according to religion and climate and the average prosperity of the individual citizen. What is frowned upon in Cork is often OK in Cairo. The old adage, when in Rome do as Rome does is an admittance of this truth. But one must not stress the contrasts between one culture and another too heavily: all organized societies have their taboos, myths and ideals. What I think we have to realize is that no one ever lives up to them all the time or for the right reason.

In our own society we lay great stress upon virtue; which we have interpreted in our own way as applying almost exclusively to sexual morality. We have sometimes forgotten that virtue consists of a great deal more than that. The seven principal virtues are faith, hope, charity, justice, prudence, temperance and fortitude: the first three are theological, the last four moral. The finer spirits in every civilization have upheld these as ideals, and rightly so, for we are not apes. But few people in any society have lived up to them all the time. Is that any reason why we should throw them overboard? I don't think so. But simply to agree with them in public and consistently disregard them in private is not enough. Neither is it enough for an individual or for a community to lay stress on one of them at the expense of the others.

But where does the writer come into all this? Is he supposed to be possessed of all those virtues, while everybody else is bereft of them? By no means. Like everybody else he is born into a society that upholds certain values. As he grows older and matures he realizes that these ideals are not generally put into practice. So do a lot of other people. But the writer has a special kind of temperament; a special talent, which by its nature requires him, indeed forces him, to speak out. If he is an Irish writer he will in all likelihood have been brought up in an atmosphere at once pious and narrow-minded. There are exceptions to this rule, but at the moment, strangely enough, I can't think of any.

From his earliest youth he will have heard a great deal of talk about religion, and perhaps also about patriotism; for the two things unfortunately have always been closely connected in this country. I think they are now growing apart; for patriotism has given way to politics, and religion is becoming increasingly private, which is what it should always have been. It will be interesting to see what effect this development has on a new generation of writers; but speculation along such lines is idle, and one can only deal with the situation as it is at present, and especially what it has been in the recent past, when writers now active were growing up and coming to grips with the society that gave them birth.

The picture is not a happy one. In all cases writers who seek for the truth below the surface of things find themselves at odds with their own people. They are banned, or they are distrusted, or they are forced for economic reasons to leave the country. The idea has grown up and is generally accepted here that a serious writer must expect to be regarded as an outsider; a stranger not in a strange land, but in a land all too familiar; a rebel, an agitator and a person of dubious morals. This is the pattern, formulated long ago, and repeated to this very day. A barrier exists between the creative writer and his own people, the very people who inspire him in the first place.

I have already remarked that we are all products of this society of ours; in revolt or in acceptance we are part of it. And that is the whole trouble; for this country, while producing an unusually high proportion of creative artists, is not on the whole sympathetic towards literature. It might be asked why a community of this sort, deeply suspicious and wary of any highly individual talent, should in fact produce such a large number of poets, novelists and dramatists.

Is society in this country attempting to be something that it isn't; or are our writers simply inexplicable sports, by-blows, freaks? The truth surely lies somewhere between these two extremes. For one thing artists have always existed in some shape or form in all societies. They are just as natural as bank managers; indeed a great deal more so, since artists are thrown up by an act of God, and bankers are produced by an act of parliament. The one is the product of a particular social system; the other is a child of nature, as old as humanity itself.

Now it cannot be doubted that we have a great deal more respect for bank managers in this country than we have for writers. I think if we follow this line of reasoning we shall discover why it is that we produce so many artists, and why we distrust them so much. The bank manager stands for respectability, solidity and caution; the artist is a product of the national subconscious that nourishes the roots of poetry, vision and recklessness: he is in his own way a kind of prophet. But in this country he is even more than that. He is a throwback to something that we have deliberately suppressed in our society during the last hundred years or so.

The Irish are not by nature a respectable people in the Victorian sense of the word. Parliamentary manners and Emily Post refinement have never been more than skin-deep in this country. A passing acquaintance with our history, and particularly with our Gaelic literature, should be enough to convince even the most sceptical that we are in fact a rowdy lot. But the circumstances of history and politics have conspired in the past century to superimpose an alien culture upon us. This is largely due, I think, to the rise of a Catholic middle class in the century following emancipation. After many generations of dispossession, we began to acquire some property again; and unfortunately for us this great social change took place at a time when the morality of property was inextricably associated with Victorian respectability. What price St Brigid, or O'Bruadair or Merriman, when all that was safe and profitable and virtuous was represented by a dumpy, ill-favoured and narrow-minded German lady known to history as Queen Victoria?

There we were, coming in from the small acres, setting up our little shops and our little factories and our little banks, and anxious very naturally to succeed. And there right in front of us was the greatest success story that the world had seen since the heyday of the Roman Empire – nineteenth-century England in all its copperplated philistine glory. Is it any wonder that we said to ourselves: we must be like these people if we are to succeed. It was very natural. In this country we have seen the rise of the American empire; and all over the world, from Tokyo to Tubbercurry, people are scrambling to acquire the habits and manners of a nation whose chief concern, according to the late Evelyn Waugh, seems to be the frustration of the processes of nature.

How much more vulnerable was our position. We were occupied by England. We saw at first hand, and not from television screens or visiting marines or itinerant GIs, the profit that patient merit of the unworthy takes. Success must be solid; it must be thrifty; it must be cautious; it must above all be respectable. There is nothing wrong with being respectable – some of my best friends are highly respectable people – and those other Victorian virtues were in themselves admirable, in business. But they are not the sort of qualities that encourage arts and crafts that are not profitable. In our case the assumption of a public code of Victorian morality was disastrous; because it was never more than a veneer. It is well known that there is nothing more soul-destroying than a mask that hardens: the personality trapped within grows twisted, suspicious and resentful. Above all it cannot bear to be told that it is wearing a mask. I think that something like this has happened to our society. There is a dichotomy, of course, between the public and private morality in all communities. But in ours the gap is deeper and wider than in most, chiefly because of the very strong emphasis we lay on religious observance. When all the public virtues of restraint and caution and fear of scandal are associated with an established Church, as was the case in Victorian England, and has been the case here, there is a frightful danger of hypocrisy. You are confusing religion with the civic guards; and in all likelihood you will end up with the same creed that Bertrand Russell put forward in his *Outline of Philosophy*, that good is mainly a social concept.

The writer growing up in this atmosphere will sense that

behind the facade of respectability in which he will doubtless pass his youth, many things go on that would not have amused Queen Victoria. He will see people who profess loudly and often their faith in Christian ideals acting in a way that would seem to suggest that they do not put these principles into practice. From there it is very easy to jump to the conclusion that the whole thing is a fraud; that we are all hypocrites, and that our little Christian republic is a whited sepulchre, where purest faith is unhappily forsworn, and gilded honour shamefully misplaced, and art made tongue-tied by authority, and simple truth miscalled simplicity, and captive Good attending Captain Ill.

But I don't think that any Irish writer of quality really believes that this is the whole story; and of course it is not. Irish writers do not attack their country, as they are often accused of doing. They reveal, which is a very different thing. And what do they reveal? That we are neither more chaste nor more honourable than the citizens of any other country. That is all. And when that is written down and published, the public, or a certain section of it, carry on in exactly the same manner as a leading citizen in a provincial town might be expected to behave if the bank manager published his overdraft in the local newspaper. So uneasily do we wear our mantle of respectability that when anyone suggests that there may be a hole or two in it, we immediately jump to the conclusion that he is accusing us of walking about, like the emperor in the fairytale, stark naked.

It all boils down to the fact that the public does not like to have its sacred cows milked; and our sacred cows are for the most part very sensitive, and do not like being confused with Irish bulls. Most of them carry on as if they had never heard of a bull; and their milk, according to themselves, is the milk of paradise. They are very refined indeed.

They rather remind me of a mythical family, which I shall call the O'Shennanigans. The O'Shennanigans are very polite. They are not very far removed from the soil; but they prefer to forget about that. They are well off. They might be in business, or trading in one of the professions: it doesn't really matter – they have got on. Mr O'Shennanigan plays golf; and his wife plays bridge; they holiday abroad, preferably in Spain or Portugal – 'so law-abiding you know' – while their eldest son Master Howard O'Shennanigan is being put up on a horse. They have a fine suburban villa with central heating; and are toying with the idea of putting in a swimming pool, like the O'Looneys down the road in 'Innisfree'.

Both these families are high Tories; and for a long time they have had the run of the mill, as it were; but now they are sometimes confused because trade unionists have taken to quoting tracts emanating from that hotbed of socialism, the Vatican. Nevertheless, by and large things are still pretty cosy, and utterly removed from any kind of contact with sordid reality.

Now, let us suppose that into this citadel of appalling refinement there bursts a wild-eyed stranger with straw in his hair, and dung on his boots and country matters on his mind. You can imagine the high drama of consternation that ensues when it is discovered that this lunatic is Mrs O'Shennanigan's long-lost cousin from the outer bog. He swears, scratches, tells bawdy stories about his neighbours, neglects to crook his little finger when drinking his tea and reminds his cousin of that old uncle of theirs who had fourteen illegitimate children in three parishes. The O'Shennanigans are disgusted.

A bit far-fetched? Perhaps. But that is the way many people in Ireland react when one of their writers reminds them that they are made of flesh and blood, and not plastic. In a society sure of itself, in touch with its past, and unafraid of the facts of life, books that have been banned here during the past forty years would appear very mild representations of life as it really is. Far from being traitors in the pay of English publishers, our writers, like the creative artists in every country, are a reminder of something far more ancient in our national consciousness than tea-party ethics. And it isn't necessary for writers to go about, like Mrs O'Shennanigan's cousin, with straw in their hair and dung on their boots. Few of them do; although some of them undoubtedly have country matters on their minds. It is enough for them to be representatives of a very ancient tradition to get them into trouble with a society whose values are largely second-hand, and whose attitudes are a bit shaky. Novelists, poets and dramatists in this country are forever being accused of being bawdy, dirty-minded and obsessed by sex. If they are, and I don't think this charge is true, it is because we have deliberately suppressed many of our most deeply rooted national characteristics in the interests of a soul-destroying and largely fake refinement.

This is the reason why the relations between Irish writers and their own people are so often abrasive. We don't fit into the O'Shennanigan's 'lounge'; and neither do the O'Shennanigans. Which is the whole point. It seems to me that this situation accounts for the fact that there are so many short, sharp exchanges between our writers and the self-appointed guardians of the cult of Victoria. Make no mistake about it, she and not St Brigid is our national saint. Pray for us O Victoria, that we may not be amused by the truth; and forgive us our trespasses in 1916. We didn't really mean it. Nor did we.

The writer on the other hand reveals a society that is heir to all the sins of the flesh, which is, in short, human; and the guardians respond by accusing the writers of being immoral persons. 'Who do those people think they are?' the cry goes out. 'They have their nerve', and so on, and so on. As if all immoral activities were confined to artistic circles!

But this situation of the writer representing something ancient and almost forgotten in our national personality also accounts for the surprising degree of private encouragement that he receives. 'But, don't quote me.' I was once asked at a meeting in my native town what positive characteristics I would apply to the Irish people; and I think I surprised the gathering, a collection of pious businessmen, by replying – tolerance. I think that individually Irish people are broad-minded and inclined to live and let live; and they have a sense of fair play. It is the public image in this country that is wrong. We're the greatest propagandists since the Jews – they've beaten us to it because they have the Bible – and some of us are idiots enough to believe our own publicity. There are people in this country who have convinced themselves that they are not like the rest of men, and that all immorality resides on the other side of the Irish Sea, and should be kept there, along with our millions of Irish exiles. Much in the same way as Queen Victoria – God save her – once described Monte Carlo as a hotbed of turpitude. The inference being, of course, that London was the New Jerusalem.

I wonder does any intelligent person in this country really believe this nonsense? Surely this is the reason for the sort of love–hate relationship that exists between the nation and its writers. Rows there are certainly, and bannings; but I think it will be observed that a writer, no matter how controversial he may be at the beginning of his career, is usually accepted in the end, if he sticks to his guns, does not lose his nerve and refuses to sell out and become a yes-man.

This happens a great deal quicker of course if he dies. We love death in this country. No lover ever was more excited at the prospect of joining his beloved than the Irish nation with a big funeral in view. And as for statues ...

Take the case of Joyce. Forty years ago, when he was being lionized in Paris, he was considered so depraved here that our censors would not sully their chaste lips by uttering his name, or contaminate Irish printing presses by having the titles of his books printed on the lists of banned publications. Now I understand that clerical students are studying him like blazes. If you can't lick 'em, join 'em. And perhaps if he were alive today we would probably be honouring him, and ourselves, by making him a doctor of one of our diploma mills.

For I do believe that the average person in this country has a certain respect and even admiration for the artist who is not afraid to be himself, to discover his own instincts, and to tell the truth as he sees it. In every Irish heart there lurks more than a little of Molly Bloom and Blazes Boylan. And a very good thing too.

The Fountain, 1968

John McCormack: The Technique Behind the Legend

On the Sunday following the singer's death on 16 September, 1945, Ernest Newman, the biographer of Wagner and Hugo Wolf, and the most influential as well as the most feared English music critic of his time, wrote an obituary notice of John McCormack in *The Sunday Times*. It is well worth reprinting, since it says everything that need be said about the singer who became a myth in his own lifetime:

> Of the millions who enjoyed the singing of John McCormack, few realized how great an artist he was, and why? To the multitude he was the unrivalled singer of simple things expressed in a simple musical way, with a special gift for clear enunciation and clean-cut, melodic line drawing.
>
> But these gifts, admirable as they were in themselves and in his use of them, were only part of a much larger whole. He was so perfect in small things because he was steeped in greater ones, was subtly intimate with them, and had attained complete mastery of the expression of them.
>
> What he did was to carry over into his performance of simple songs an art based on, and subtilized by, the most intensive study of the masterpieces of song from Handel and Mozart to Hugo Wolf. He was a supreme example of the art that conceals art, the sheer hard work that becomes manifest only in its results, not in the revolving of the machinery that has produced them. He never stooped to small and modest things; he invariably raised them, and with them the most unsophisticated listener, to his own high level.

This is a remarkable tribute from one of the most exacting critics of the century. I know of no other tenor who could have drawn such words from Ernest Newman. Few will deny that most of the songs by which McCormack is remembered, and which caused him to be one of the greatest public idols of his day in America, were sheer, unadulterated slush. As songs, 'Mother Machree', 'Little Boy Blue' and 'I Hear You Calling Me', among many others, are enough to turn the stomach of a self-respecting horse. Musically speaking there is nothing to be said for them at all; as anyone who has heard them sung by any other singer will immediately realize. But McCormack got away with it; and not because, as has been so often repeated by his fanatical admirers, he really believed in the nauseous sentiments expressed in these songs. I don't think McCormack was deceived by them for a moment; they were largely forced upon him by the insatiable demands of his Irish-American audiences whose love of the auld sod has always been expressed in an orgy of what Saul Bellow has described as 'potato love'. McCormack, great showman that he was, gave them what they wanted and, like Liberace, cried all the way to the bank.

But it cannot be denied that he sang with a difference. He brought to them the same technical mastery, polish and sophistication that he lavished on Italian arias and the better sort of art-songs. His diction and phrasing were so good that he was able to give point and meaning to the most banal words and the most obvious melodies. This gift was not, as some imagine, altogether spontaneous. Anyone who has listened to John McCormack's earliest records will realize that his diction in the beginning of his career was far from perfect. His singing was crude, his phrasing haphazard, and the voice itself nasal and raucous. How hard he worked in the few years between 1905 and 1910 only God will ever know. The raw boy from Athlone emerged in the latter year as a master of the art of bel canto; and the greatest lyric tenor of his time. But it was no accident. It was, as Ernest Newman indicated, all the result of hard unrelenting study. The voice itself was transformed into a free supple instrument capable of every demand made upon it, and with a quality of tone that was unique in its beauty. It would never have become so if he had not learned how to develop it properly; and learning the mastery of any art is altogether unromantic. When McCormack moved the hearts of millions by his rendering of simple songs, he did it entirely by technical means.

In the last ten years of his public career, particularly after he came out of retirement to sing for the Red Cross, he had very little voice left. But such was his power of handling words, that one forgot the lack of voice and was conscious only of the extraordinary interpretative quality that he displayed. Ageing, tired, having lived through all the banal sentiments of his youth and aware of their hollowness, he had nothing but technique to fall back upon; and it did not fail him. Some of his last recordings are among the most loving he ever made.

Some of his sentimental admirers may disagree; many others will feel that I am being heartless: but I feel sure that when I describe him as the greatest professional singer of his time, John McCormack, if he were still alive, would be the first to agree. There is nothing romantic about great art.

Athlone Tourist Gazette, July 1970

An Immodest Proposal

A few years ago a new economic theory was proposed; and received a certain amount of publicity at the time. Since then little has been heard of it, so far as I know, and I suppose this is not surprising, since it attacked the very foundation on which the business of society is conducted. It concerned itself with the supply and demand of labour; and it seems to me that what it suggested is so simple, obvious and effective that sooner or later it will have to be adopted by the governments of all those countries that describe themselves as 'democratic'.

The theory advanced the idea that no one should be required to work at anything that did not interest them. There is nothing new in this, since artists have been practising it since the world began. Writers write, painters paint, singers sing and dancers dance because they are responding to an inner impulse, which makes the idea of any other occupation abhorrent to them.

As a result people engaged in the arts are not taken very seriously by governments, since they seem to represent an outlook on life that is neither real nor earnest. It does not, for instance, correspond with the finest principles and absolute dedication to hard work and unrelenting concentration of such bodies as the civil service. They, we are always given to understand, are overwhelmed with responsibility; and their labours for the benefit of their fellow citizens are onerous in the extreme. They are literally slaves to duty.

So successful has this piece of propaganda been for so long now, with all the authority of the State to back it up, that most people actually believe it. Yet on the whole, it has been an abject failure, for the simple reason that no sane person would take up a job as clerical officer in any government department in any country for any other reason except to save themselves from unemployment and penury.

That is, and always has been the great threat, which has intimidated millions, has created great misery and frustration and is now collapsing. Unless people enjoy their work, it is absolutely unreasonable to expect them to perform it efficiently.

Nowhere is this more evident than in Ireland. For years, young people, encouraged by anxious parents who remembered the days when living was hard and precarious, have actually competed frantically with one another for jobs that may be safe, but are usually boring, empty and unfulfilling. (The younger generation being as conditioned and victimized as their parents and grandparents.) A job 'with a pension' has caused untold millions to waste the best years of their lives chained to desks, at which they do very little except stare at files, and glance at the clock to check the hour of their deliverance.

Well, obviously, they are now getting beyond ulcers and premature heart attacks. They are simply walking out of their boring situations in greater and greater numbers and taking to the streets in protest at the boredom and futility of their employment. It seems to me that it is this reaction that is the true cause of all the strikes and general labour unrest in this country at the moment. People are often not quite sure why they are on strike; in most cases it is not because they are badly paid, or exploited; it is simply because they are bored and frustrated. And no wage increase, no change in working conditions, no sonorous appeals to patriotism and responsibility are going to make any difference. After all, politicians are in politics because they like power and public life; most workers in most factories and government agencies are there because they have no other choice. How many people, I wonder, realize this?

Now it is well known that the Irish excel in four particular activities: talking, drinking, fighting and gambling. Surely a national effort could be made to harness the energies wasted at the moment in these pursuits, and turn them into something profitable to the exchequer, and popular with the great mass of the people.

For years now, and in particular since the long period in power of the late Sean Lemass, most people in the country have been labouring under the misapprehension that the Irish can in some mysterious way be transformed into productive ants; capable of sustained industrial action, like the Germans and the Japanese. Nothing could be further from the truth; or more alien to the Irish character. This country, or at least the southern part of it, will never be made into an industrial society that can compete with nations whose inclinations, heritage and achievements have made them proud of producing more nuts and bolts than anyone else.

We are not like that; and never have been. And it is foolish and short-sighted of any government to assume that we are. The whole world – insofar as it takes any heed of us at all – is aghast at the state of labour relations in this country. Strike follows strike with relentless predictability, often for reasons that are obscure to the strikers themselves; but which are very obvious to any think-ing person. The workers have been told over and over again that their future lies in industry, and in particular in those projects lured into the country by tax reliefs; and which are run for the most part by Americans and Japanese. Neither of these two nations have the faintest understanding of the Irish character. And neither has the Irish government.

All sorts of theories are put forward for our deplorable indus-trial record of disputes and stoppages; and everyone, including the workers, is quite naturally bemused by them. Which is not sur-prising, since they are all ill-founded and psychologically wrong. Workers strike in this country because they are bored to death with the ridiculous effort to transform a nation of bummers, bowsies, betters and bruisers into something economically respectable and diligent.

When this sort of abominable human misconception of the potential of the Irish nation is abandoned, we might get on with the real work of actually achieving something, instead of drawing up useless blueprints for projects that never get off the ground; and would be scrapped in any case as a result of the sheer weight of boredom and apathy of the population. For Irish workers are, together with some of the highest in the land, ready and willing to turn this country into a paradise of prosperity, almost overnight, if they are given the opportunity.

Obviously the first thing to do is cash in on the national addiction to alcohol. There are few, if any, nations who can beat us at this game. If the consumption of malt were made a feature of the Olympic Games, we should leave even the Russians standing – or falling: no mean feat in this field.

The government must, and very soon at that, legalize poteen: 100 per cent proof. Anything else is simply a waste of time. It should also issue licences to everyone who applies for the making of this celebrated national beverage. In this way thousands would be instantly transformed into enthusiastic entrepreneurs, anxious and concerned to push their own products, and thus benefit the country as a whole. It is safe to predict that there would be no apathy among workers in these small, intimate but intense industries. County would vie against county, even parish against parish, in the manufacture of the best and most lethal concoction. The spirit of the nation would take on something of the frantic enthusiasm of an All-Ireland final at Croke Park. Surely the first duty of any government is to convert this mass of energy into productive channels. Poteen will do the trick.

It is generally accepted that the consumption of alcohol in all societies is connected in the minds of the populace with the idea of virility and strength of character. No one has any respect for a man who cannot hold his liquor. An alcoholic is a sick person; and that is that.

If then it became known to the world outside that the strongest booze to be had anywhere on earth was freely available in Ireland, think of the rush of tourists that would bring. No more pathetic advertisements about the soft charms of Ireland, which no one believes any longer; just the invitation: come to where the real hard stuff is. Quite apart from getting drunk, which relieves

161

the mind of the necessity of facing harsh reality, most men everywhere are particularly anxious at all times to prove their virility to themselves as well as to others. This is especially true today, when male supremacy is everywhere threatened by female competition. Who, even twenty years ago, would have dreamed that the UK would one day have a woman prime minister?

Today women are challenging men at the liquor stakes. So the tourist invasion that would follow the public availability of poteen would by no means be confined to men. The ladies would follow in equal if not greater numbers; and joy would be unconfined.

Nor would this consumption be limited to poteen. Here the national genius would feel itself put to the test, as it has never been by industry. Who cares who invented the internal combustion engine? It's a bloody bore; and other races are welcome to the manufacture and refining of it, in its various manifestations. Our talents can be put to better use so far as internal combustion is concerned. A nation that can produce a formula for an earthly paradise out of a heap of rotting potatoes can surely go on to better and higher things.

We could, for one thing, immediately solve the terrible national problem of litter and waste, which at the moment pollute every street and hedgerow in the country. Fermentation is the secret of alcohol. All that rotting rubbish, debris, orts and drast could be turned into some peculiarly Irish and generally exotic spirit. It might be called 'stews'; and give the virgin customer the same kind of delicious shock experienced by many a stern teetotaller when introduced to Irish coffee. And if the stews contain a few dead rats and minced cats or dogs, what of it? Modern chemicals can do wonders; and in any case people have been dining off such fare, suitably sauced, in expensive Dublin restaurants for years now without any apparent ill effects.

It might be asked how all this is going to be financed, if the entire nation is to be given up to the manufacture of various stews. This is easy to answer. By gambling, of course. Casinos might be opened in every town, and licensed to remain open all night as well as all day. I don't think that any Irishman, living in such a well-ordered society, would grudge 10 per cent of the loot going to the government to keep a few public representatives in their jobs. But we should not need a full-time cabinet as we do now, beset as we are with economic troubles of all kinds. Take industry and all its boring side effects away; and the government would find itself with little to do. Besides, most of the politicians, even those who are filling the jobs they so carefully planned for themselves in Brussels – a dull and expensive dump – might be tempted to return and join in the fun.

It would be very much to their taste. For, of course, the talk would be unconfined. Kept afloat on native brews and stews from morning to night to morning, Irishmen could babble their heads off, on all and every subject, without sitting through unwitty debates on the Continent, like the representatives of other and less gifted countries. For how often do our men in Europe get a chance to express themselves at any great length in their traditional Irish witty and sparkling way?

Industry does of course at the moment provide one safety valve for the Irish that would have to be provided in the new Constitution. At the moment all the aggressive instincts, which are not given their natural outlet running back and forward across the Border blowing people up, are worked off in strikes.

But this could easily be altered. Think of regional rivalry. It is well known that this is strong and often bloody here.

What with casinos and public houses in competition with private residences where poteen and gambling are equally available, there would be no lack of competition in the land. Publican – for an honoured name and profession dies hard – would be set against privateer; and casino against gambling school. In this way a perpetual ferment, in every sense of the word, would be ensured; and heads broken every hour of the day. The boys would be down from the North like shot – especially like shot – to join in the new industry. For could it be said that a pub in Ballyfechim in Clare is providing stronger brew than an enterprising entrepreneur in Ballymechim in Limerick? It could not; and strong men would arise in great numbers to prove it.

How the tourists would stare, having first of all taken cover. For naturally, such high spirits would flood the country with sight-seers; unlike the trickle who now arrive to watch our strikes and listen to the soft voice and the diamond wit. Cosy shelters could be provided in every town and village where these goggling visitors could sit in comfort and safety to watch the natives having it out. Nothing as large, of course, as the bullrings in Spain; but the general principle is sound. Not everybody loves to take part in a fight, especially if it involves knives and broken bottles, not to mention shots in the back; but practically everyone likes to watch such goings-on, as is proved every day by the television news. We have a priceless asset in this country; and no one is making the slightest effort to profit from it. It is a crying, bloody shame.

Nor could humanitarians be outraged by what is after all merely an expression of natural instincts: for the Irish also possess two other very positive attributes widely scattered among the community. We possess the best nurses in the world, as anyone who has had occasion to stay in hospital will know. I had always taken this for granted, until I was taken ill in a foreign country, when the difference was startlingly revealed to me. The nurses there were competent; but compared with their Irish sisters they were like amateur actors competing with a West End cast.

Nor are our Irish doctors very far behind. Their brilliance is not sufficiently appreciated; and it is distressing to read how many of them are abused for being too highly paid. Nothing could be further from the truth. Our doctors are dedicated men, completely devoted to their vocation, which is a high and sacred one, and the idea of money hardly ever enters their minds. Naturally they might be expected to welcome the new Ireland with real humility and profound joy. For is it not their mission to help in any way they can to make their fellow citizens happier and better adjusted men and women?

It is now generally recognized that the stress and strain of the life most people live at the moment is caused by their being caught up in an economic rat race that is not of their making, and that is driving some of our best citizens to an early grave, and putting their widows on a diet of pills and rich foods, calculated to destroy not only their waists, but also their minds. Doctors are well aware of this, and also of the high rate of suicide in the country. Even among the medical profession one hears of sudden deaths and twanging nerves brought about by overwork, and worry over the appalling unhappiness of their patients, as they work on and on at jobs that were clearly designed for machines, not men.

When, therefore, the rate of liver disease rises under the new dispensation that I am proposing, who better qualified to deal with it than our doctors? For one thing, it is something they really know about; and since it is in all cases brought about by leading one's own life as one would wish, and dying in the same manner, it cannot cause doctors the distress they experience at the moment, faced as they are with a waiting room full for hours and hours every day with neurotics who don't know what is the matter with them; and expect the harassed doctor to tell them how to cope with life.

The obvious answer is to encourage them to leave their boring jobs, take to the bottle, queue up at the bookie's office, and hit their neighbour over the head with the bottle – when it is empty, of course. A full bottle used in this way sometimes softens the blow, causes little injury and is a sinful waste of precious alcohol.

No, we need have no worry about the ability of our medical men to cope with the new Ireland. Most of them will take to it enthusiastically themselves; and those with more than usual dedication will rejoice at the number of rotten livers in the dissecting rooms. It will afford the scientifically minded a superb opportunity of studying this distressing national complaint; and perhaps coming up with a total cure for cirrhosis. What a benefit to mankind in general this would be. And in particular to us, since it is absolutely essential to the new order that no one should be forced to give up drinking to save his liver.

More will die, but in the end science will benefit by an increased opportunity for the study of diseased organs. The balance of nature will adjust itself; and in the end our national liver will be preserved impervious to alcohol: a highly moral development.

Nor should we tolerate anything less. After all, the health, wealth and happiness of the nation are at stake.

There remains the question of the law, and some sort of order, always, fittingly, last on the agenda of any Irish scheme of things. No trouble should be experienced from that quarter, as we embark on our natural and long-delayed experiment with legalized drinking, fighting and gambling destiny. After all, none of this is new to the guardians of our peace. I should not be at all surprised if they would also welcome the total abolition of the laws of libel. What is the use of talking all day and night, if you cannot slander your neighbour? And, after all, in the new dispensation anyone who feels affronted can always hit his verbal assailant on the head with the nearest heavy object; thus closing the case without recourse to boring legal detail and expensive court procedures.

We have one of the most benign police forces in the world; perhaps *the* most benign. Crime really does distress and upset them; and whenever they can in all humanity they look the other way. Getting involved with hardened and dangerous criminals is the very last thing they want. Why should an unarmed policeman get his head shot off for political reasons? The people who should undergo such risks are the politicians, who are responsible for the present state of the country in the first place. No one will be sorry to see them out of a job in the new Ireland that I am proposing. Least of all, I suspect, the police force.

What they are really good at, and always have been, is social work; and it is the sort of thing that they also particularly enjoy. People in trouble of a purely human kind will know just how good the Guards are in a case of a sudden death, or a lost relation, or an injury in the home. The force is superb in humanitarian work, and has never received anything like its due in this respect.

In the new Ireland, the police can be relied upon to enter into the spirit of the thing with enthusiasm and tolerance. Talking, fighting, drinking, gambling: these are human activities that they well understand, and look upon with a benevolent eye. And if the two parishes in dispute over the quality of their liquor have to be dug out of one another, the Guards can be trusted to cover the spadework with efficiency and a decent respect for human frailty. No, we need expect little opposition from the police to these modest proposals; for they are heartily sick of the humbug that for so long now has tried, sometimes with a measure of success, to get us to think of ourselves as sober, diligent, hard-working and productive, when we are manifestly the opposite. This delusion has led to all manner of evils in the bodies politic and private.

When therefore some of us have to be rushed to hospital as a result of overdrinking, or a too-serious preoccupation with our local poteen or gambling room, the police will transport us with the greatest expedition and sympathy. Once there, our gifted nurses will fulfil their natural function and native genius for looking after us in their own inimitable way. And they will have more time to give to us, for the wards at present filled with victims of the various stress diseases – among which I have always numbered cancer – will be empty. We shall all be happy doing our own things; instead of the prefabricated social ants that modern science has, through the influence of the multinational business cooks, and our own supine public representatives, urged us to become.

The proposal that I have put forward seems so obvious that it has always seemed incredible to me that no one has ever yet even attempted to put it into practice. What has prevented them? I can think of one good reason; one that reveals the secret of modern government in every so-called 'advanced' country. It is too simple. And the first tenet of present-day tyranny, especially when, in the case of the 'democracies', it is the soft and especially corrupting kind, is to make everything appear more complicated than it is. The Irish character is simple, even obvious. What on earth would the civil service do if the majority of the people discovered this truth about themselves?

Perhaps this proposal will help them to start thinking about it. For after all, civil servants are the principal people who would benefit under the new order. Can it be that they don't want freedom? Old Mother Ireland's chickens? Truly, we have made ourselves a cockeyed country in which to live.

The Irish Times, 23 August 1980

A Curate's Egg at Easter

During the last conclave in Rome, a Jewish friend of mine in London remarked, not entirely facetiously, that he supposed the cardinals might be considered to be rabbis of a later dispensation. This is not quite so far from the truth as one might think. The tension that has always existed between Christians and Jews arises from the similarity between the two ways of life, and not otherwise as so many people imagine.

Easter, perhaps more than in any other religious feast in the calendar year, emphasizes this intertwining of ritual roots. Without the Jewish festival of the Passover it is unlikely that Easter, as we know it, would have developed as it has. It might not indeed have come to be celebrated at all, when one begins to think about it in any serious manner.

When I was a boy, the religious significance of Easter hardly impinged upon my consciousness at all. It meant chocolate eggs, simnel cake and holidays. The ceremony that really captured my imagination was the Tenebrae ritual of Holy Week: the purple-shrouded statues; the darkening of the church lights; the knocking of prayer books against the altar steps, so very reminiscent of the thud of earth on a coffin at a burial; the terrifying chants; the empty tabernacle. *Domine, audivi auditum tuum, et timui: consideravi opera tua, et expavi.* 'I have considered Thy works and trembled.' That was the ticket for Easter, as I recollect it.

After all this heavy theatre it is not surprising that Easter Sunday and the week that followed were something of an anticlimax. It was so typical of Irish Catholicism to lean heavily on the gloom and doom of Holy Week, and hand the celebration that followed it over to Padraig Pearse and the other heroes of the Post Office.

How many children growing up thirty or forty years ago confused the risen Christ with the Easter Rising of 1916? And the Church made no great effort that I can remember to redress the balance. Now of course, it is somewhat different: more and more people have come to think of Pearse and his men, if they think of them at all, as pretty dim figures; and how many nominal Christians now really believe in the resurrection of Jesus Christ? Given the circumstances in which so many middle-aged people like myself were brought up, it is surprising that we believe in anything at all.

I must have been at least fourteen when I heard an old Franciscan friar, who was a friend of my family, declare that Easter was by far the greatest and most important feast in the Christian year. 'If Christ be not risen again, your faith is vain', came as a complete surprise to me. In those days Christmas was quite obviously the most important day of the year; and even yet, after some study and rethinking on my part, in my bones I still think of Easter as in some way a second-class occasion; particularly as I am not politically minded. I can see St Paul's point very clearly: the whole fantastic edifice of the Christian establishment amounts to nothing more than one of the most lasting and majestic of European institutions, if its Founder be not risen at Eastertide.

It seems to me that this cornerstone of Christian belief must have been a great deal easier to accept in the early years of the Church. For one thing there was the ancient tradition of the Passover, dating, according to tradition, to a command given by God to Moses. The Jews were a pastoral people, and it was perfectly natural for them to sacrifice a lamb to propitiate the somewhat choleric deity of their time. So as to make quite sure that this awesome personage did not overlook their little gift, they sprinkled the blood of the lamb on the lintels and side-posts of their habitations, so that the Lord should pass over them when he set out to give hell to the Egyptians.

It did not seem to occur to the Jews that this ritual was not entirely confined to their own race, the chosen one. It has been traced back to Babylonian usage; and what is even more interesting, given the nature of recent history, it was also a part of Arab custom. Perhaps the two peoples will be able to celebrate the feast together some day. Stranger things have happened, especially during the rise of Christianity.

For of course Easter was observed as a spring festival from the earliest times of which we have knowledge. Just as the early fathers of the Church, shrewd old birds that they were – and not overscrupulous – fixed the birth of Christ to coincide with the pagan festival of the winter solstice, the Roman Saturnalia, so also they adapted the resurrection of Christ to that time of the year when pagans celebrated the rebirth of nature and the return of the sun.

The Passover lamb of the Jews became the true Lamb of God in the new dispensation. It was, one supposes, inevitable, considering the large number of Jewish Christians in the early Church. As might also be expected, the Gentile converts eventually had their way as to what day of the week Easter should be celebrated.

What is really interesting is the fact that the name of the feast is neither Jewish nor Roman, but Teutonic. When Christianity reached the semi-barbarous German tribes it immediately incorporated, in its celebration of the most important event in the history of the new religion, the heathen rites and customs that accompanied the observance of the spring festival. Germans being Germans, these rites laid heavy stress on the symbols of fertility. Truly, our great Christian feasts are a strange mixture of the agricultural, the mystical and the magical.

Nearly all of the customs and symbols that are associated with Easter are pre-Christian. The egg, an obvious symbol of fertility and new life, dates back to the ancient Egyptians and Persians. The Easter hare, never very popular at Eastertide, also dates back to ancients: the Egyptian word for the animal is associated with human fertility. And so it goes on. The myth of the sun dancing on Easter morning goes back to the ancient capers in honour of the sun. The Easter kiss is not, as one might expect, Christian, but pagan; so are the traditions of lighting new fires and wearing new clothes with the advent of spring. The Easter bonnet is as old as woman herself.

It is obvious that the very idea of Easter and the celebrations that accompany it are the products of a pastoral people, living in close communion with the earth and its seasons. Most of the people who rush out to buy up large and expensive eggs, or small and equally expensive hats, are completely out of touch with the way of life that made the spring festival of rebirth and renewal such an important event in the lives of the ancients. We live in a consumer society that is nominally Christian, but actually half-pagan. To most of us nowadays Easter means a bank holiday, some tedious Church services and racing on Monday. Pagan and urban; no wonder there is confusion.

It is constantly being claimed, especially by popular prophets of the mass media, that modern society is restless, neurotic and anguished because it has turned away from religion. In these islands that means Christianity. I have always been sceptical about claims of this kind. Christianity does not necessarily make people happy: that is not what it is all about. Why should we assume that God is a thoroughly nice old boy, whose chief aim in eternity is that we should all be as gay as larks, if only we abide by the rules supposed to have been laid down for our instruction and enlightenment?

Nor is it correct to claim that people who cannot or will not accept the idea of personal immortality live a life of despair. I have known a goodly number of ageing hedonists, and all of them were quite as cheerful as Christians, and reconciled to the idea of eventual extinction. Naturally they regretted the fact that they had to die; but then, so do Christians.

Easter is a time when the emphasis on an afterlife is particularly strong. I wonder how many people, even among those who think of themselves as true believers, really accept this idea without reservations? When I was growing up, we were given to understand that the resurrection of the body was to be taken literally; and one must remember that for many centuries it would have been a highly dangerous thing to question it. Now we are told that we shall all arise and shine in a sort of spiritual body.

The truth is that nobody has any very clear idea of what, if anything, is going to happen after death. It would surely be a far more honest thing for the Church to admit this once and for all. It might help to clear up the confusion that exists in the minds of many genuinely religious persons today. But the Church, as always, remains ambiguous; and priests are no help at all. Were they ever? With two honourable exceptions, I have never in my life succeeded in getting a straight answer from any of them on an important theological question. If evasion were a prerequisite of entry into the kingdom of Heaven, then the clergy would most certainly make it.

Of course, no one really understands anything about an afterlife. Extinction we can understand, but eternity is outside our range. Here again we find little honesty among religious professionals. Take it or leave it has always been their policy; and today, in spite of many public professions of liberalism, that is still fundamentally their attitude. Since Easter is completely associated with the person of Jesus Christ, the Church has always assumed that anyone coming into contact with the Gospels must immediately, if they are in good faith, fall under the influence of the Perfect Man. After this, any doubts they might have on the subject of the resurrection must be completely assuaged.

There are people whose whole life has been taken up with a study of His personality, which apparently yields them a more than normal satisfaction. Every moment is lived, insofar as is humanly possible, in an awareness of His presence; and for that they count the world well lost. And they have hope. It is all there is.

But what of those who do not fall completely under the spell? I suspect their numbers are larger than we are prepared to admit. When I first read the New Testament I was amazed to find myself disappointed; the character of Jesus is very sketchy, and not always as admirable as I had been led to suppose. Why had one not been prepared for this? Why indeed? I was brought up in the days of blind faith. Is it any clearer-eyed today? I wonder.

It seems to me that Cyril Connolly put many of my own thoughts into words in his *Unquiet Grave*. He finds Christ petulant,

and far from Christian in His attitude to the Pharisees. Such incidents as the violence used on the man without a wedding gar-
ment, or the praise of usury in the parable of the talents, strike
Connolly as arrogant and bad-tempered.

He then goes on to say:

> Impatient, ironical and short-tempered, he was a true faith
> healer, inspired by his sublime belief in himself and tragically
> betrayed by it. I can't believe in his divinity, yet it is impossible
> not to admire his greatness, his majesty, his fatalistic intuition
> and that mixture of practical wisdom with sublime vision
> which alone can save the world. His faith carried him through
> to the end, then wavered ... About the miracles I suspend judg-
> ment. But not about the Sermon on the Mount. Those loving,
> dazzling, teasing-tender promises are like the lifting of the
> human horror, the bursting of a great dam.

If the children of my generation had been exposed to that
sort of comment, together with Bernard Shaw's preface to *Andro-
cles and the Lion*, instead of the pious pap we were served, it would
have saved many of us the long, slow and sometimes anguished
journey towards the acceptance of a very human man, with all the
faults of His humanity, as the Son of God. Cyril Connolly, who did
not claim to be a believer (how can anyone be sure of that about
anyone?) was in fact a better guide than Maritain or Pope Pius XII.

And this Easter, all the old platitudes will be taken out once
again and delivered from a thousand altars. If that were not bad
enough, we now have to suffer an extension of those ham performances at the lectern during the very celebration of the Mass
itself. It is a sore trial; and anyone who has been subjected to the
reading of the scriptures and the Canon of the Mass by the average Irish priest has no need to believe in Purgatory; he will have
had it all over by the time he gives up the ghost.

It is a notable fact that nearly all priests are failed, or perhaps
one should say, frustrated actors. Unfortunately few of them have
the high degree of polish and natural ability of the present pope,
who is a brilliant performer. In the old days, the murmur of Latin
and the ancient ritualistic gestures saved many a person with a

knowledge of what good theatre should be, from distracting thoughts of suicide or murder, or both. This is no longer the case. Encouraged now to do his own thing, more or less, the average priest, intoxicated by the presence of a captive audience, and drunk with the power of the charismatic idea, loses no opportunity to express his ego, which is usually an inflated one.

This is not good for any minister of religion; and it is, or should be, a source of scandal to his congregation. No parishioner should be obliged to put up with boring and ill-prepared services. They should let their priest know this and in no uncertain terms; but alas, the Irish will put up with anything, once inside the door of a church. We suffer the apathy of indifference.

It is intolerable that this Easter the same old congregations will kneel and sit through the same ceremonies, conducted in pidgin English by clergymen who for the most part can neither walk, talk, nor remain silent in a manner befitting the solemnity of the occasion. As for liturgical music, it is now quite clear that the clergy are prepared, either through ignorance or self-indulgence, to play down to the worst instincts of the people. We are told that pop Masses appeal to the young, which is like saying that Barbara Cartland should be encouraged because she appeals to more readers than Jane Austen.

Of course the translations of the various offices and prayers are banal. But bad as they are, and lacking any sense of poetical rhythm, which might help to enlighten congregations exposed to the trite language of television, they could be worse. They might, for instance, be translated into Americanese. In his diary, Evelyn Waugh has a vernacular version of the salvation suggested by a correspondent in the *Catholic Herald*: 'Hiya Moll, you're the tops. You've got everything it takes, baby, and that goes for junior too. Look Moll, you put in a word for us slobs right now and then we konk out.' It is strange that rock and punk should be accepted as OK in churches; whereas the above translation of the Hail Mary is not used even in America. As far as I know.

In our modern consumer society, I don't really think that Easter in the religious sense has any great relevance anymore.

After all, our way of life, our ambitions and achievements, are purely worldly. How many of us offered a certain chance of a deal that would make a return of 200 per cent, but which would entail the missing of the Easter Mass, would choose the latter?

Christianity, as Bernard Shaw pointed out in 1915, has always in its purest form been a minority religion. The world, as he put it, 'consists of a huge mass of worldly people, and a small percentage of persons deeply interested in religion and concerned about their own souls and other people's'.

So this year, and for some years to come, the Easter dues will continue to be paid by respectable members of society; Easter duty will trouble the minds of others; and the Christian message of the feast in the Pauline sense will impinge itself on a small minority. For the rest it will be chocolate eggs of various degrees of size and price; it will be a jolly weekend with lots to eat and drink; it will mean some travelling to the sun; it will mean more or less what it used to mean since man first stood up on his hind legs and bellowed at the moon. After a long hard winter, the cutting edge of spring. Time to replenish the stock of condoms and make sure the pills are in the overnight case; time for that new silver mink stole and those heavenly Italian shoes; time to try out that new cocktail and buy an antique chamber pot in which to plant the begonias. Time for fun. And pray for us, Midas, Prince of Light.

Does anyone really want an eternity, which can only be described in the vaguest, wishy-washy terms, after all those pleasures? Not bloody likely.

The Irish Times, 14 April 1979

A Man for all Seasons: Pope John XXIII

During the fifties I was often in Venice, usually in the late spring or early summer. Autumn is the 'season' there, when café society from all over the world gathers in the ancient city to make it hideous with peacocking; and it is a sensible man who absents himself during these vulgar displays.

Naturally one spends a lot of time in the Piazza San Marco; after walking the narrow lanes and crossing half a hundred bridges, it is pleasant to sit in one of the two cafés, in sun or shade according as one wishes. But Venice really begins in the great basilica of San Marco, which dominates the piazza. It never struck me as a place of prayer, anymore than St Peter's in Rome is; but as a sumptuous tribute to the deity, expressed in marble and mosaic, it is undoubtedly impressive, if not overwhelming. One hopes that God has catholic taste in the secular sense of the word. It would be awkward if He disapproved of the Byzantine.

It has always fascinated me, and whenever I was in Venice I found myself wandering in and out of it quite a lot. One day in 1956, I was in the centre of the basilica when I noticed a small crowd gathered before the high altar, as if they were waiting for some service to begin. This was a highly unlikely sight – the crowd, I mean, not the Mass, which took place there several times each day, without anyone noticing that anything in particular was going on.

But that day was rather different. For one thing, it was the feast of Corpus Christi, the Thursday after Trinity Sunday. Turning around, I saw a small procession entering the basilica through the central door from the atrium. It was led by a number of clergy and choirboys; and last of all came the Patriarch. He was flanked on either side by two tiny boys who held up his scarlet soutane as he mounted the steps of the great bronze door; and behind him, two equally tiny tots were struggling under the weight of the immensely long cappa magna that prelates wore at that time.

The Patriarch was very short and very fat, and as he waddled past me, I had an impression of a great Borgia nose, brilliant dark eyes and a very unhealthy pallor of the skin, dark yellow, blotched with age, and gleaming with perspiration. I asked an Italian as we left the church to avoid the Mass who the Patriarch was. 'A man named Roncalli,' he replied. 'Used to be nuncio in Paris.' He then shrugged his shoulders and screwed up his mouth in that typical Italian gesture, which means that they've seen everything and nothing really impresses them anymore. Another fat, old Italian cleric, I noted to myself as I made my way out and across to Quadri's to refresh myself.

How wrong we were, that cynical Italian and myself. How very, very wrong. Later, but before I had left the café, the Patriarch carried the monstrance under a golden canopy in a short procession from one side door of the basilica, across the top of the square, and around the side to the left. The traditional Corpus Christi profession of faith. I thought of the old French song, set to music by César Franck, 'Dieu avance à travers les champs'. There were no fields here; but the spirit was the same; and I was profoundly moved.

And at that very moment two American women of a certain age, but uncertain vintage, began to make ribald remarks about the ridiculous pagan rite they were watching. Although I was not at that time, nor for many years afterwards, a practising member of the Church, my Irish stomach was turned by the remarks of these semi-barbaric women, painted like Red Indians, and speaking in hoarse, wild accents. I took a long ice-cream spoon, and rapped one of them hard on the knuckles, telling both of them in a furious tone to shut up. Clearly no male creature had ever addressed them in such a manner in the whole course of their lives, and they were stunned. But they shut up.

The next time I saw Cardinal Roncalli, he was Pope John XXIII. We were received in what was then called a semi-private audience, in the Hall of Benedictions in the Vatican. It is from here that the Pope steps onto the balcony of St Peter's to give his blessing at Christmas and Easter.

I well remember waiting at the great bronze door of the Apostolic palace on a fine February morning in 1959. The present Bishop of Elphin, Dr Conway, then spiritual director of the Irish College in Rome, was there with a group of seminarians.

The doors opened, and the great marble stairs rose before us, and at the entrance to the hall we were met by another Irishman, Mgr Ryan, now Bishop of Clonfert, who told us to give the Pope a good hand. It seems strange now to recall in the light of after-events that Vatican officials were not at all sure of the reaction of the public to this curious old man, who had only three months before been elected to the Chair of Peter.

There was an interminable wait, during which I got into conversation with two Florentine priests, who told me that the new pope was late for everything. The crowd was not large, perhaps 200 in that vast marble chamber, and I retired to a corner with the Florentines, who passed the time by regaling me with the latest Vatican scandal. This provoked much chuckling among the three of us; and also roused the ire of an inexorably corseted Irish matron, who bore down upon me, rebuked me for such a display of levity in a sacred place; and, giving the Florentine clerics a piercing look, added: 'And as for the Italians, my son, who was ordained here, tells me that they never mix with them. An inferior race.'

One of the priests spoke very good English, and we were convulsed with laughter at this sally, but at that moment the leather curtain over the entrance was drawn aside, and the Pope was borne in on his chair. A moment later, the pious matron was loudly applauding the most eminent living member of this 'inferior race'.

He looked even worse than I remembered him in Venice. His colour was darker and yellower; and in the white papal garments he looked flaccid and obese. He had not yet taken to wearing the large, wide stole that did something to disguise his girth. His hand was raised in a small, almost tentative blessing, very far removed from the superb balletic gestures of Pius XII; and also unlike his predecessor, he seemed to be acutely uncomfortable in the swaying desia gestatoria. When it was lowered to the ground at the foot of the throne, he clung to it like a drowning man. The subtle Florentines looked at me and raised their eyebrows.

Pope John mounted the few shallow steps to his throne, settled himself comfortably in it, kicked aside a footrest, gave a more relaxed wave of his hand, smiled; and then launched into the business for which he had clearly been born.

He began to speak to us as though he was on easy, familiar terms with each one. He possessed the rare gift of making every occasion, no matter how solemn, seem informal and relaxed. He welcomed us to Rome, and sounded as if he really meant it. I think he did. He reminded us that all roads lead there; and that no matter where we came from, what our business or beliefs were, he was there to welcome us. Welcome, welcome.

He cracked jokes; and at one point a young Swiss Guard was so overcome with merriment that he had to hang onto his pike, while he doubled up with laughter. The Pope looked at him with a benign eye, and smiled. It was an expression of such warm and natural paternal solicitude that one did not feel anxious for the young soldier: one envied him.

And so it went on; and gradually for some, immediately for others, we realized that we were in the presence of someone so extraordinary, that few of us could hope ever to meet his like again. I do not remember the rest of his discourse, except that he made a joke about the firemen of Rome making a retreat, and having the waters of salvation turned on them for a change; but it really did not matter what he said, on that occasion at any rate. He made us welcome, he bade us be easy, and invited us to return.

What flowed from him was the force of a rare and supremely warm personality. He radiated goodwill, confidence, and hope. I could feel the impact of that personality in a purely physical way: it flashed out like an electric current. I had never experienced anything like it before, and while in his presence could feel only a sort of heightened sense of being alive and well, and wanting to cry out with joy. I am not easily moved in this way.

The facile sentiments of instant awe and general well being are fairly easily aroused by personages occupying great historical positions. After all, the papacy has been part of European history since the mid-dawn of our civilization; and the Pope is first in precedence among European sovereigns. His situation must often seem, even to non-believers and indifferent Catholics, as being almost halfway between earth and heaven. He is a sacred personage; and naturally his slightest gesture is apt to produce an effect out of all proportion to its meaning.

Pope John had of course all this tremendous heritage, this vast accumulation of myth, legend and prestige behind him. But so had Pope Pius XII, who had in addition a presence that was full of grace, dignity and aristocratic charm. Yet he had left me unmoved. I felt that I was watching a superb performance by a very famous actor against a setting of unequalled pomp and circumstance. This is unfair to the memory of a great pontiff, who most certainly was not acting out his role. But he lacked warmth; and his humanity was of a very special and rather rarified kind. I could watch him with one part of me unmoved; cool, watchful and in full control of whatever critical faculty I have.

Pope John took immediate possession of all one's faculties, emotions and prejudices, and transformed them into something so fully alive and pulsing that one felt, for a while at any rate, a sense of humanity reaching out, its burden of flesh and blood suddenly made clearer and more significant in the light of this radiant personality. He was a life-giver, a bringer of good tidings, a messenger of hope.

This above all is what Pope John achieved as the sixties began; and he, more than any other single person, gave the decade, or at least the beginning of it, its sense of renewal and hope. He believed in humanity; he went straight to the essential goodness that is the mark of God in every creature; and his simple and direct faith and joy were felt by all, even those who had never had the privilege of meeting him. This is a good man, they thought; the world is not such a bad place after all.

He had the same effect on the Church over which he was elected to preside. Seventy-eight at the time of his election, he seemed to many merely a holy old man put there to prepare the way for a younger and more vigorous pope. Instead, he revolutionized the Roman Catholic Church in little more than four years; and died the most famous and best-loved pontiff since the Reformation. The decade that produced such a man must have been a remarkable one. The Church that nurtured him was, and remains, surely even more remarkable.

Apart from his tremendous personality and obvious sanctity, Pope John XXIII will be chiefly remembered by history for his convening of the Second Vatican Council. Why did he do it? And why did he find it necessary to call it together in the first place?

Quite recently a correspondent drew attention to something I had written in a review of Mr Bill McSweeney's book on Roman Catholicism, in which I said that I had my own theory as to why Pope John acted in the way he did. The correspondent complained that I did not then give my theory. In fact I did give it. But as I do not think that my explanation can be of any importance either one way or the other, I merely included it in passing in the last paragraph of the notice. I wrote: 'The Council was meant to test the faith of Roman Catholics who were bogged down in ritual.'

I believe that this is precisely what Pope John was sent to do; and did it with surpassing courage and foresight. He found the Church hidebound by ritual and legalism. In his later years, Pius XII, attempting to run the Church on his own, unwittingly played into the hands of the Curia, who saw to it that any opinion even slightly at variance with a rigid and reactionary attitude to Church matters was silenced quickly and quietly. Things went on – or seemed to, for it was partly an illusion – in their preordained way; the same answers, the same prayers, the same daily round, the same ceremonies, the same elaborate exchanges, the same insistence on outward forms and hieratic gestures. No questions. There is no doubt that such a Church has many attractions for many people; and it is by no means to be deplored utterly. But it could only lead to stalemate, a hardening of the arteries of faith and a gradual withering of the great virtue of charity. Pope John changed all this, simply by being himself.

He was a human being on a grand scale; and he saw the Church's problems as essentially human and fallible ones. He opened the windows to let in some fresh air through the fusty halls of the Vatican palace; and if the wind blew up into a storm that swept away much that was good in the old dispensation, together with the deadwood, that was not Pope John's fault. He provided the spirit, the paternal care, the constant concern that any institution must possess if it is to flourish: and after that he was content to leave it to God. He knew that in time all would be well again; that a good shaking up does no one any harm, and that the Church had to go out and live in the market place with the modern world.

It has often been asked how Pope John would have reacted to the changes brought about by his Council. Well, I think it can be safely surmised that he would have been deeply saddened by the wholesale defection of priests and nuns that began in the late sixties. He would certainly have been shocked by the movement that for a time sought to play down traditional Roman Catholic devotions to the Mother of God, including the recitation of the rosary.

He just might have approved of the changes in the liturgy; but he would almost certainly have insisted that the Latin Mass be also available to those who want it – as indeed is stated very clearly in the Conciliar documents. He would have deplored the total banishment of the great heritage of polyphonic church music, which has been kept alive largely through the dedication of the Benedictines, who have now lived through that phase as they have so many others down the centuries.

Yes, I think there are a lot of things that happened after the Council that Pope John would not have approved. Many of them were merely change for the sake of change; more were the result of that Roman arrogance that Pope John did so much to assuage. The attitude of forcing change and a particular brand of liberal-

ism on the laity was really the same old Curial method put behind
a different policy.

What he would have approved was the new openness to the
beliefs and traditions of other Christian Churches. This saintly
old man did more for ecumenism in four years than had been
achieved in the six decades before. I think it must be admitted
that he probably hoped the new spirit of understanding and tolerance would lead in the end to a return of the Reformed
Churches to the primatial see of Rome. Yet, he was a great realist.
He must have known that this was very unlikely to happen; and
his open-mindedness towards other communions was certainly
genuine. He could not, of course, say so in public, but he must
surely have recognized the fact that Christianity probably
demands several traditions; and that the real ecumenism lies in a
growing respect of one for another. This, I think, he achieved; and
perhaps in the fullness of time all will be one; but not absolutely
on Roman terms.

Pope Roncalli was a man of considerable sophistication and
worldly wisdom. As nuncio to Paris, all doors were open to him.
There are drawing rooms in the Faubourg, which Proust may have
heard about, but could never hope to penetrate. Even the Duke of
Windsor could hardly expect to be admitted there; and nor was
he. Here the papal nuncio met the old and immensely reserved
Catholic ruling class of Europe. He knew their views. But he also
knew how the small farmers of Sotto il Monte felt about things.
His experience of men and events was, if not vast, certainly wide.

Yet ultimately it is his own personality that transcends everything; and it is a more complex one than might at first be supposed. His public life is well documented, but we have also a
unique record of his private thoughts and spiritual pilgrimage.
Few popes have left such a revealing record of their inner
thoughts as Pope John did in his *Journal of a Soul*.

It is a surprising book. It is the diary of a man reared and
formed and fully committed to the very special and rather narrow piety of the post-Tridentine Church. Every single rule in the
book concerning poverty, chastity and obedience is noted here,

and followed with the gravest intent. In a 'meditation' at the beginning, Fr Giulio Bevilacquo notes that Pope John's spirituality was founded upon a technique. 'Every technique degenerates if it remains purely mechanical, that is, isolated from all noble inspiration. On the other hand no great conception can be realized without a rule, without a discipline.'

Here we come very near, I think, to the secret of Pope John. He was a man of great humility who knew that in order to achieve the spiritual goal he had set for himself, he must regulate his life and his thinking with very great care. All the little exercises, the constant reiteration of simple prayers, the preoccupation with the fifteen decades of the daily rosary, the scrupulous attention to his breviary, the apparent obsession with age and death, the little confessions of human errors. In 1961 we find him, at the age of eighty, writing: 'Everyone calls me "Holy Father", and holy I must and will be.' Well, he made it.

But right to the very end the exercises were kept up with unflagging dedication. In his review of the *Journal* when it first appeared, Graham Greene said something about a barrack square, and the daily marching of it, round and round, up and down, until at the end the recruit was fully equipped for the most rigorous tasks that duty demands. Something like that. The good old Pope would have understood the analogy. He was the supreme example of the necessity for a strict rule of life; and the spiritual freedom to rise above it. One cannot exist without the other.

What then of his influence, his effect upon the Church? I think he came at a time of great decisions for the Roman communion. It could go along the way laid down by Pope Pius and his predecessors; change little; close up the drawbridges, and disregard the modern world and all its frantic restlessness and impatience with age-old ritual and ancient traditions. Many people, including myself, would have preferred such a course; but any institution is apt to become mechanical and ritualistic to a degree which ultimately dulls the spirit.

Any Church that deliberately made an attempt to shake itself free of the accumulation of the centuries must first of all be absolutely sure of divine guidance. Members of the Church were shaken out of the torpor of the years; their whole way of life jolted and disturbed. What Pope John brought about was a sort of sacred gamble, which proved the vitality and resilience of Catholicism. Only a man of absolute faith could have risked it; and this Papa Roncalli had. Not for an instant did he doubt the influence of the Holy Spirit; and the reliance of his Church upon the mercy and wisdom of God. And he made his people think.

The deposit of faith remains, and cannot be altered. The faithful have passed through a difficult and traumatic experience, which by and large has made them sit up and take notice of the events taking place in the religious world about them. And in the end, the Church has come through its self-imposed ordeal. The rules remain; but generally speaking they are now applied with a more sympathetic and widely human touch. And in the present Pope we have a man with a personality as strong and vivid as Pope John; and a heritage of paternal concern for his flock, which his marvellously warm and human predecessor would surely have admired and commended.

The sixties opened with a tremendous surge of hope and simple joy brought about by the goodness of one supremely kind and holy old man. The enthusiasm waned after his death; but his spirit must always remain an inspiration to all men and women of goodwill. When the history of the twentieth century comes to be written, Pope John XXIII will take his place among the greatest men of his time; one who opened up the Church to the whole world and who personified in his own life the teaching of Christ and His apostles. His memory is a precious one indeed.

The Irish Times, 15 November 1980

Letter from Rome

There has always, I feel, been some confusion about the nature of ecumenism. A worldwide movement has been launched with the best of intentions by clergy and laymen, to reconcile the doctrinal disagreements that have existed for so long between the various Christian communions. This has led to a very considerable opening up of purely social contacts among Christians; and also, to a certain extent, the opportunity to worship together under the same roof has been afforded people whose parents would never have dreamed of such an extraordinary happening. What it boiled down to was that Roman Catholics were allowed to venture into Reformed churches and graveyards – the dead were divided too, even more than the living – and members of the various congregations once lumped together as 'Protestant', came into churches highly and colourfully decorated with all the seductive art of the ancient dispensation of Rome.

All this was to the good; and considering the essentially dogmatic and dictatorial character of the century, it was also a marvellous achievement. At least now Christians were learning to live together; and above all to appreciate one another's beliefs. This process has even gone on in Northern Ireland, in spite of a very real ordeal of 'dungeon, fire and sword'; and such a living movement there cannot, I think, be too often mentioned and spoken of with the admiration, and indeed awe, which it deserves.

But, and it is a very big but, has any one Church made any really fundamental doctrinal concession towards another? And if they had, would it necessarily be a good thing?

Religion is after all a social art; an aspect of it that is rarely appreciated, and hardly ever mentioned. It cannot exist outside of a social order, however primitive; and usually achieves its highest expression when a civilization has reached some degree of sophistication. One thinks of the great Anglican divines of the late-seventeenth and early-eighteenth centuries; the Irish monks of the seventh and eighth centuries who drew a remarkable tribute from that uncompromising atheist, Bertrand Russell; and the high degree of religious awareness so characteristic of the best minds of the nineteenth century.

We do not live today at a time when civilization is self-evidently flourishing: it is a time of violence, restlessness of soul and body, and great moral confusion. Yet, one of the most remarkable aspects of the period is the continued vitality of Christianity against, it would sometimes appear, every conceivable disorder, both outside and inside the Churches. But, it seems to me, that in its struggle to survive – Christianity has become in recent years a little blurred at the edges, as it were.

And so is ecumenism. What exactly does it mean – what are its aims and where is it all leading? Many people must have asked themselves these questions more than once at the present time: and received on the whole a dusty answer. Socially, ecumenism is, and one must hope will remain, a great success. Indeed, what other alternative has it? Hardly any at all, in my opinion.

It may be that there are some ultra Roman Catholics who expect that in time all those other Christians will meekly submit, and, filled with the Holy Spirit, wend their way humbly and contritely down the long road to Rome. Well, of course, it *may* happen; anything is possible: but somehow I don't see it ever taking place in my lifetime, or in the span of any infant just born and destined to become a centenarian.

On the other hand, there are those who seem to imagine the development of Christianity as a kind of worldwide movement with a Billy Graham tone, complexion and general deportment. In short as something good, mild, undemanding and generally vague. I don't think that will happen either; and furthermore I believe it would be a tragedy if it did. What I think will happen is that, with goodwill, the various Christian denominations will continue on their present ecumenical course; growing in understanding and sympathy with one another's points of view; and learning to live and let live. This needs a greater effort than is generally supposed.

It would, I think, be a pity if the Christian traditions were to give up, or water down their firmly held, and in nearly all cases, hard-earned acceptance of the Christian message. It may not be a very ecumenical thing to say, but surely it is a good thing that there should be more than one Christian tradition; it gives variety and vitality to a religion that is inextricably associated with our European heritage. This includes some of the most shameful acts and periods known to history; but it also expresses the highest point of civilization yet reached by man. And through it all, the many coloured banners of the various Christian communities, in and out of communion with the primatial see of Rome, have added their own peculiar artistry and grace to a teeming scene of unending human activity.

Ecumenism as a social phenomenon is then, as I see it, a very good thing. It may also be constrained to *remain* a social activity and I hope a no less tolerant one – if Christians of all denominations become aware in time, as they surely must, of the implications of the recent *Letter* of Pope John Paul II to the bishops of the Church, issued to coincide with this year's Holy Thursday. It is devoted to the Eucharist; and it makes clear, in no uncertain terms, the traditional attitude of the Roman Catholic Church to the doctrine of transubstantiation.

It is a remarkable document, and a very important one indeed. As I suspect that it will not be widely distributed in this country – where verbal ecumenism is all the rage – I think it a good idea to examine it at some length, and point out a few implications that have not been mentioned in the carefully edited versions released to the press.

The Pope begins by stressing the Eucharist as the principal and central raison d'être of the sacrament of the priesthood, which 'effectively came into being at the moment of the institution of the Eucharist, and together with it'. This was defined, as is stated in a footnote, at the Council of Trent. It seems self-evident to me; but there are those, much involved in ecumenical work, who may not necessarily agree. For one thing there were no women at the Last Supper.

Bishops and priests are also in a special way 'responsible' for the 'Great Mystery of Faith' through their ordination; and while it is given to the whole People of God, to all believers in Christ, it is the especial trust of those who are anointed to celebrate it. 'The priest fulfils his principal mission and is manifested in all his fullness when he celebrates the Eucharist ... This is the supreme exercise of the "kingly priesthood", the source and summit of all Christian life.'

I seem to remember at one time a great deal of talk about the 'royal priesthood' of the laity; and much confusion ensuing as a result. Pope John Paul II seems determined to retain the priest as 'the one real professional', as Evelyn Waugh once insisted he was, at the time of the first liturgical changes. It was not the happiest of descriptions; but one can see, and appreciate, what Waugh – and most other people – meant at the time. And still mean, in spite of all the experiments, good and bad, indulged in since.

The Pope then goes on to say that the worship given to the Trinity in the Eucharist at Mass, must be present at all other occasions. 'It must fill our churches also outside the timetable of Masses.' This is a very significant point, especially as the Pope continues: 'Adoration of Christ in this sacrament of love must also find expression in various forms of Eucharistic devotion: personal prayer before the Blessed Sacrament, hours of adoration, periods of exposition – short, prolonged and annual – (forty hours) – Eucharistic Benediction, Eucharistic processions, Eucharistic Congresses.' He then writes: 'All this therefore corresponds to the general principles and particular norms already long in existence but newly formulated during or after the Second Vatican Council.'

The latter statement will come as a considerable surprise to most Catholics, who have not seen or heard the old and much loved ceremony of Benediction for at least ten years. When I asked a young priest about the dropping of it, he explained airily: 'Oh, the charismatics have taken the place of that.' Admittedly he was a very silly young man; but why give up the rite, if it *had* to be replaced by something so very different? However, in true papal style, John Paul II blandly gives the impression that all those traditional devotions are still being held as if nothing had happened. No doubt they are in Poland; and this is the only instance of what might be construed as deviousness in a document that is remarkable for its plain speaking and genuine fervour. Of course, it may be that this most subtle of men is telling the bishops to set to and get working, without causing them to lose face. I think they will get the message.

In a remarkable section devoted to the Eucharist and Christian life he points out that as the Eucharist was first constituted as a supreme act of love, it should manifest itself, through those who share it, in a deeper awareness of the dignity of each person. 'The awareness of that dignity becomes the deepest motive of our relationship with our neighbour.' This is a profound and moving passage; and believers in the extraordinary sacramental nature of the Eucharist will understand exactly what is meant here. So very simple a concept; so very difficult to put into practice. Yet Catholics must do it, or perish.

Rarely can a Supreme Pontiff have communicated such an urgent and powerful sense of brotherhood to his flock as Pope John Paul does here.

He proceeds to explain the links between the Eucharist and other sacraments, baptism and confirmation, and after another profoundly spiritual and moving passage on the sacramental style of the Christian life, he comes, as one might expect, to the question of penance. 'It is not only that penance leads to the Eucharist, but that the Eucharist also leads to penance. For when we realize who it is that we receive in Eucharistic Communion, there springs up in us almost spontaneously a sense of unworthiness, together with sorrow for our sins and an interior need for purification.'

For most Catholics over thirty-five this will seem quite right and natural; and a very lucid exposition of the Church's position.

If we believe in the Christian Revelation, then we must have also a sense of awe and unworthiness. But of recent years, in what was, I am sure, an honest and very well-meant effort to correct the strictness of the traditional confessional box, which was truly awful, less and less emphasis has been laid on the sacrament of penance. It is certainly a bad thing to be obsessed with a sense of sin, it is no less unbalanced to play it down. For it is very easy, in a society largely pagan in many aspects of its daily life, to lose the sense of guilt completely. If we can cheat our neighbours by short-changing and overcharging, by dishonest work, and a national system of passing the buck, then it is inevitable that this slackness of conscience will extend into other and more intimate aspects of our lives. It is surprising how easy it is to deaden one's conscience; easier, and cheaper by far than killing one's neighbour; and we all know how little effect it produces. Sin is cheap in every sense of the word.

The Pope is aware of this. 'We must always take care,' he writes,

> that this great meeting with Christ in the Eucharist does not become a mere habit, and that we do not receive Him unworthily, that is to say in a state of mortal sin. The practice of the virtue of penance and the sacrament of penance are essential for sustaining in us and continually deepening that spirit of veneration which man owes to God Himself and to His love so marvellously revealed.

No doubt these words are aimed at various trends in America and the Netherlands, where the practice of auricular confession has been much discounted of recent years. But I think it applies generally to all Catholics; and it would be a mistake to suppose that we are in some curious way more 'regular' in this country than elsewhere. Confession has now been made an act of reconciliation in every sense of the word; but it would be a mistake to suppose that evil no longer exists, or is somehow less evident that it once was. Evil, like sex, is here to stay. It is certainly better to lean towards presumption rather than despair; the former leads to suicide, mental or physical; the latter encourages fatuousness. But, really, I'd rather be suicidal than silly.

The Pope concludes the first section of his *Letter* with the remark that his general reflections will be followed by detailed 'indications' from the Sacred Congregation for the Sacraments and Divine Worship. A nice little touch, this.

He then goes on to deal with the sacred character of the Eucharist and Sacrifice. He begins, as one might expect, by stressing that in spite of certain changes down the centuries, there has been no change in the essence of the 'Mysterium' instituted by the Redeemer of the world at the Last Supper. Certainly the Pope does at all times in this *Letter* keep to essentials. It is the work of a quite exceptionally lucid and well-balanced mind; but there is nothing in it to bring any great joy to those ecumenists who feel that the Roman Catholic Church should turn from its traditional doctrines, and age-long usages. For this reason it is also quite the most honest and straightforward statement of a given position published by a Church leader for a very long time. After reading it we know exactly how we stand.

This is an unusual and most refreshing characteristic in papal pronouncements; and should be welcomed by all, whether they agree with what is said or not. He has much to say about the mysterious and sacred nature of the Eucharist, in a passage that might appear at first reading to be redundant; but that in fact is leading directly to what follows, and is calculated to give it strength. It seems surprising that a pope should find it necessary to declare of the Mass that:

> It admits of no 'profane' imitation, an imitation that would very easily (indeed regularly) become a profanation. This must always be remembered, perhaps above all in our own time, when we see a tendency to do away with the distinction between the 'sacred' and 'profane', given the widespread tendency, at least in some places, to desacralize everything.

I honestly don't think that this rebuke applies in any great measure to the clergy and laity in this country. There have been 'experiments' to be sure; but they tended to be clumsy and lacking in style rather than corrupt. But without such a man as Pope John Paul II to draw attention to this very serious matter – to

Christians only, of course – it is possible that the example of overzealous reformers in other countries might make itself felt here as the way things should be done. We have an unfortunate tendency to copy the worst elements in other societies, while overlooking the best and most traditional in our own. It is surprising that the Irish should suffer from a lack of imagination in so many areas; it would be comforting to think that this is due to simplicity. Alas, it is the result of ignorance.

But no bishop, however simple or ignorant, or both, could at this point in the papal letter fail to understand where all this careful and measured reasoning is leading to: 'The Eucharist is above all else a sacrifice,' says the Pope; and goes on to quote a statement made in the ancient Greek Church linking 'today's sacrifice' with that 'offered once by the only-begotten Incarnate Word: it is offered by Him (now as then), since it is one and the same sacrifice'.

The Pope goes on to emphasize the role of the priest; and a distinct line is drawn between his function, which exists by virtue of his ordination, and participation on the part of the laity. They do, of course, share in the sacrifice, especially in the offering of the bread and wine, and also naturally by communicating. But it seems clear to me here that the Pope is taking care that the distinction between the ordained priest and his congregation is maintained. There will be no more dancing round the altar on the part of semi-skilled ballet dancers, as happened in many churches in France and the US. For this relief, much thanks are due to this most sensible of pontiffs.

Having firmly stated the sacrificial nature of the Mass, the Pope now proceeds to deal with what is perhaps the single most important point in the whole *Letter*. It is not new; simply a reiteration of traditional Catholic doctrine. The only surprising thing about it is that the Pope should feel it necessary to write about it with such uncompromising firmness:

> For the bread and wine presented at the altar and accompanied by the devotion and the spiritual sacrifices of the participants are finally consecrated, so as to become *truly, really and substantially* Christ's own body that is given up and His blood that is

shed. Thus, by virtue of the consecration, the species of bread and wine represent in a sacramental unbloody manner the bloody propitiatory sacrifice offered by Him on the Cross to His Father for the salvation of the world.

This passage carries a footnote, associating it with a decree of the Council of Trent. There have been several attempts since the last Vatican Council to play down, or subtly change the actual meaning and claim of this ancient doctrine of transubstantiation. The Eucharist was a symbol of Christ's death and risen body; the presence of God accompanied the consecration; the act was one repeated only in memory of the Last Supper. And so on. All these views are in themselves valid and most precious to those who hold them; and no one should lose sight of this for a moment. But they do not represent the traditional and enormously important Catholic belief in transubstantiation. If one does not accept this, then one is not a Roman Catholic; and it seems quite clear to me that the Pope is stating this in unequivocal terms. It may be regretted by many, who were prepared to water down or change the ancient teaching of the Church in the interests of a misguided sense of ecumenism. It is not by bending with the wind that people make themselves open to the minds and hearts of others; but by holding firmly to their own beliefs – which in all Christian communions embody above all the practice of charity – and respecting those of their neighbours. This, it has always seemed to me, is the true ecumenism; the sort that receives and gives respect.

Nothing is more heartening than this firm and honest declaration by the Pope. Now people know exactly where they stand, what they are required – or not required – to believe; and John Paul II has once again, and not for the first time in a short reign, shown the way forward.

He also makes a thoroughly sensible and easy reference to the new liturgy. 'It has given', he writes, 'greater visibility to the Eucharistic sacrifice. One factor contributing to this is that the words of the Eucharistic prayer are said aloud by the celebrant, particularly the words of consecration, with the acclamation by the assembly after the elevation.' This is certainly true; but it does call for a much greater effort on the part of the congregation; and I was delighted to read that the Pope is well aware of this. It has been one of the chief difficulties of our time; especially to those with any real sense of reverence. They have for some years now been aware of the dangerous burden that the new rites have so suddenly and without preparation, laid upon the laity, who have not been accustomed to such a serious responsibility before. Why should this generation be expected to respond in such a manner never demanded of their forefathers? It is not only a fairly terrifying exercise in humility; it is a further extension of the Christian mystery, already overwhelming enough in all conscience.

And so the Pope writes: 'All this should fill us with joy, but we should also remember that these changes demand new spiritual awareness and maturity, both on the part of the celebrant – especially now that he celebrates "facing the people" – and by the faithful.' That is putting it mildly; but how else could he put it? He knows what he is about; and that as head of the Church he must proceed with delicacy, and that kind of gentleness that is only possible in the very strong.

In the next section of his *Letter*, bearing in mind all this new and abrupt maturity so increasingly demanded, he goes on to state something that has already been laid down in four separate instructions and decrees by the Sacred Congregation of Rites and the Sacred Congregation for Divine Worship between 1965 and 1971. And this is that there are also those people who, having been educated on the basis of the old liturgy in Latin, experience the lack of this 'one language', which in all the world was an expression of the unity of the Church, and through its dignified character elicited a profound sense of the Eucharistic Mystery.

> It is therefore necessary to show not only understanding but also full respect towards these sentiments and desires. As far as possible these sentiments and desires are to be accommodated, as is moreover provided for in the new disposition. The Roman Church has special obligations towards Latin, the splendid language of ancient Rome, and she must manifest them whenever the occasion presents itself.

These are the words of the Pope himself; and it is he himself who uses, in its particular context, the term 'Roman Church'. I do not know what diabolical fury possessed so many priests and bishops after the ending of the Second Vatican Council concerning the question of Latin. For many years it was enough merely to mention it to be met with ribald remarks and sarcastic references to an 'elite' attitude; and this from people who should have known better. Perhaps after so many centuries they felt ready for change; and change with no holds barred. Little charity was extended to those who felt acutely embarrassed by the vernacular rite; often for the very reason that the Pope has now expressed. They did not feel either prepared or worthy to participate in such a sacred occasion almost, it sometimes appeared, on a level with the celebrant. The word got about that anyone who asked, however timidly and hopefully, for a Latin Mass was in some way a dangerous reactionary, if not a fascist. Those who do not often practise humility are all too ready to accuse others of a lack of it also. The Mass had become an ego trip; and so had the gutting and redecoration and rearrangements of churches on the part of those in authority. Most of these efforts are painful to contemplate, and an affront to elementary good taste; and as usual the people, silent, uncomplaining, perhaps apathetic, certainly long-suffering, paid up for something the nature of which was not even communicated to them. Truly their faith was great – and their patience even greater.

But it is idle to recriminate. Now that the Pope has spoken, and is evidently prepared to follow up this *Letter* with specific instructions, perhaps the timid wishes of those who would have preferred a less violent break with the past will be taken into account. After all, it is in many ways merely a matter of courtesy; which is also a Christian virtue. Certainly I look forward to a Latin Mass being said in each parish at least once a week. That, surely, is not asking too much.

For those who ask more, the Pope has also some words of encouragement – and warning. He speaks of the increase of the number of people taking an active part in the celebration of Mass.

Groups of readers and cantors, and still more often choirs of men and women, are being set up and are devoting themselves with great enthusiasm to this aspect. The word of God, sacred scripture, is beginning to take on new life in many Christian communities. The faithful gathered for the liturgy prepared with song for listening to the Gospel, which is proclaimed with the devotion and love due to it.

Well ... all this is, of course very admirable, in itself; and one wishes that the makeshift choirs that one so often hears nowadays, and above all the singing – if such it may be called – of the congregations were more in tune, not with heaven, but with the accepted system of musical notation. I am blessed – and cursed – with an acute sense of pitch, which makes it extremely uncomfortable for me to listen to singing that is not properly in tune. As this also applies to voices – it is not generally understood that many people have speaking tones that are sharp or flat – and listening to them, after a head-on clash with an enthusiastic but ill-equipped singing congregation, is a real headache. I do not suffer in silence; but from the lack of it.

However, the Pope gives one some cause for hope here also. 'The same sense of responsibility also involves the performance of the corresponding liturgical actions (reading or singing), which must accord with the principles of art.' Unfortunately he does not specify what 'art' he is referring to. Is pop 'an art'? How many guitarists play like Segovia, John Williams or Julian Bream? Is the Pope encouraging popular art, which has its own disciplines, or classical? One assumes that he is suggesting that whatever form Church music takes, it should have some shape, meaning and sense of pitch. At present all that can be said is that standards of singing and playing in church are, in this country at any rate, deplorable. This does not mean that they are unacceptable to God; and we all know that it is the spirit that counts; but there are limits; and the yowls that I have heard in some churches in recent years would not be tolerated in any well managed music hall; except, of course, for the comic acts. We can only hope and pray very hard indeed that harmony in every sense will return to the churches. Better still that, at times at least, the peace that passes all understanding will once more reign there during some portions of sacred ceremonies.

The Pope then leaves this somewhat difficult area, and addresses himself to a very important interior subject indeed. This is the question of those who, as he puts it 'could participate in Eucharistic Communion and do not, even though they have no serious sin on their conscience as an obstacle'. He puts this down to 'a lack of interior willingness' rather than a feeling of unworthiness: 'a lack of Eucharistic "hunger" and "thirst", which is also a sign of lack of adequate sensitivity towards the great sacrament of love and a lack of understanding of its nature'.

Here I find myself rebuked. I was brought up in an era when great emphasis was laid on the sense of sin; and with all the goodwill in the world it is difficult to shake this off. Nor, I think, would it be advisable to do so. But the Pope's words do give us here great ground for hope; and a wonderful breadth of vision and tenderness towards the members of his flock. What he is proposing is an ideal, as indeed is the whole of the Christian message, and one can but listen and read with gratitude and reverence.

However, he does not neglect to point out the contrary impediment: a taking for granted of the reception of the Eucharist. He mentions that 'there has not been due care to approach the sacrament of penance so as to purify one's conscience'. And then he unleashes a bombshell. Speaking of those who can find nothing on their conscience to prevent them approaching the Lord's Table, he writes:

> But there can also be, at least at times, another idea behind this: the idea of the Mass as *only* a banquet, in which one shares by receiving the Body of Christ in order to manifest, above all else, fraternal communion. It is not hard to add to these reasons a certain human respect and mere 'conformity'.

I think it is a pity that the old system of Masses without Communion should have been abandoned. I know that the new order is supposed to represent a deepening of our involvement with the Sacrificial Victim; but it cannot be denied that the present Mass does, by reason of the attitude of its congregation who are, after all, only human, exercise a considerable moral pressure on those who suffer from a conscience more, perhaps, aware of sin and its implications than is healthy. The attitude of people, which is inherited from generations of ancestors of a similar cast of mind and spirit, cannot be changed overnight, or even in one generation. A case could, I think, be put for such a Mass, together with the Latin rite. Otherwise we shall all have to achieve a very high degree of spirituality; and as I have said, we are but human.

The Pope then deals with the newly revived custom of receiving Communion in the hand; and mentions a 'deplorable lack of respect' reported in some cases; and the unfortunate case of those who were refused the Eucharist on the tongue. This may strike many people as a minor matter; insofar as anything concerning the Eucharist can be so described. But I think no one in this country has yet given one of the reasons why Communion in the hand was discontinued by the Church. *One* reason, I repeat, among many others less sensational.

There has been in several countries, and in particular France, and in more particular there, in Paris and Lyons, a long and horrible tradition of Black Masses. There is one church in Paris where the crypt, always kept locked, is opened again and again, and a Black Mass said there. It is very easy for some unfortunate person, filled with devilish urgency, to take the Sacred Species in the hand, secrete it in a handbag or pocket, and take it out of the church in order to pay homage to the Prince of Darkness. Let no one imagine that this custom is either rare or on the wane. So long as evil exists, so will this horrible rite be made available for those who crave it. And there are enough ordained priests, out of the Church, who are prepared to go through these obscene practices for money. It may seem far-fetched; but then so was Auschwitz. I don't think there is much danger of devil worship gaining a following in this country; but to dismiss it as an impossibility is as fatuous as declaring that man is essentially good, and his misdeeds entirely the result of circumstances.

I doubt, however, if the Pope had anything as extreme as Black Masses in his mind when in the latter part of this *Letter* he exhorts priests to bear themselves with dignity and simplicity, one naturally following the other. We have, I think, seen enough 'creative' interpreters of the Mass, dashing backwards and forwards across an altar, like operatic tenors with a 'frog' in the throat; waving their arms, wagging their heads, throwing back their long locks – if they possess any – and generally behaving in a most alarming, and thoroughly undisciplined manner. The Pope has news for them.

> He (the priest) cannot consider himself a 'proprietor' who can make free use of the liturgical text and of the sacred rite as if it were his own property, in such a way as to stamp it with his own arbitrary personal style. At times this latter might seem more effective, and it may better correspond to subjective piety; nevertheless, objectively it is always a betrayal of that union which should find its proper expression in the sacrament of unity.

And finally the Pope ends his *Letter* with what must be a unique statement on the part of a Sovereign Pontiff. He asks for forgiveness, in his own name and in the name of the episcopate, for everything that 'for whatever reason, through whatever human weakness, impatience or negligence, and also through the at times partial, one-sided and erroneous application of the directives of the Second Vatican Council, may have caused scandal and disturbance concerning the interpretation of the doctrine and veneration due to this great sacrament'. And in conclusion he again lays particular emphasis on the problems of the liturgy. It must never, he writes, be an occasion for dividing Catholics, and for threatening the unity of the Church.

Thus ends one of the most remarkable spiritual documents of our time. Its clarity, single-mindedness, and breadth of vision are evident on every page. Its profound religious wisdom and knowledge of human nature are perhaps only to be expected. Yet how often do we come upon them in such a concentrated form in these turbulent times?

The *Letter* is simple and easy to read; written with grace and lucidity not often associated with papal documents; and the translation is beautifully done. Whatever unknown hand is responsible for it deserves an acknowledgment and a salute.

One would have to be singularly mean of spirit not to respond to the fervour and warmth that inform this *Letter*. And its humility is an example to all. I hope that it will be widely read by the laity. It would be a pity to think of it ending up among the dusty files of some episcopal office. Besides, why should the bishops have all the good tunes?

A response to '*The Holy Eucharist*' *Letter of the Supreme Pontiff Pope John Paul II, to all the Bishops of the Church.*
The Irish Times, 19 April 1980

The Novel from the Novelist's Point of View

It will be necessary for me during the course of this talk to resurrect a corpse. This will present no difficulty to me, but whether you of little faith will accept it as a fait accompli is of course quite another matter. I hasten to assure you that I don't think I'm God, well not yet anyway, and the corpse that I want to breathe some life into is not Gilles de Rais or the Marquis de Sade with whom some of you might associate me as familiars. No, I don't want to produce somebody like that, interesting though it might be: I want to resurrect somebody even worse – the novelist.

For some time now it has been fashionable to say that the novel is dead. This claim is usually made, I've noticed, by theatrical critics, political commentators, historians, biographers, travel writers and people of that sort. How many of them have in their time tried their hand at writing novels and failed is something that none of us will ever know. The most recent explanation that these critics give for the death of the novel, is that its place as a form of social commentary and analysis has been taken over by television, radio and films. They have a point here, and an important one. Their message is not so much that the medium is the message but the medium is the messiah.

However, like all false prophets their theories while immediately attractive are essentially superficial, appealing largely to the eye; and they evade one very important point, and that is that interpretation is not the same as creation. Before I try to point out the differences between the novel and the various forms of mass communication, I think it is necessary to make some attempt to define just exactly what the novel is. Various definitions have, of course, been given over the years by many eminent writers, and one of the most interesting things about this is that all of them are different; in fact there are as many opinions about the meaning and value of creative writing as there are thinking human beings. Some of you may think that this doesn't throw open the area of discussion very wide; nevertheless there is considerable disagreement about it; whereas there are no two opinions about the function of a washing machine or a television interviewer: both are there to mangle dirty linen.

But the novel is a very open form. There are no strict rules for writing a work of fiction; and it cannot be taught even in seminars presided over by the newly emancipated Knights of Columbanus. It is the most personal, the most secret of arts; and in the last analysis it is the fruit of individual instinct, experience and reflection. It can be romantic, picturesque, picaresque, ironic, tragic, comic, religious, irreligious, realistic, fantastic, obscure, obscene or high-minded; or a mixture of all these elements. In short it can be anything and everything, so long as it is not produced by a committee. That is its great strength; and that is why the novelist is always distrusted by all those birds of a feather who flock together. The writer is the last free man, for he is essentially a private person, and no one ever knows what he is going to say next. For this he has to pay a price, often a terrible one, because the impulses of the creative temperament are always directly opposed to the static attitude of organized society in every country.

At the moment these attitudes are almost entirely directed towards the manipulation of the new and powerful methods of mass communication. And this is where the pundits who claim that television and radio have taken the place of the novel make their great mistake. No one can say that these mass media, whatever their other merits may be, are the reflection of a personal vision. Indeed they are essentially impersonal; and their comments on the social scene are always suspect because they are nearly always the product of a committee as distinct from one man's personal vision of the world as he sees it – and this is exactly what the novel is. Now, it can be said that many novels and plays are adapted for television and radio; but I don't think we need concern ourselves with these, for such productions are second-hand material, rather like a tape recording of a voice, and very often an edited tape at that. Of course there are original plays written for television and radio; but I've never heard of an original novel written for the media for the simple reason that the detailed psychological analysis of character and situation that the novelist can develop in his form of expression, are quite unsuited to the visual character of television and films. Where the eye is involved and seduced by a series of images the process of thought is somewhat diminished; and certainly the imagination is dulled. And this is the great danger to the freedom of the individual artist. The moment he begins to think in terms of collaboration with others such as technicians, cameramen, continuity girls, producers, directors and backers, he is in effect serving on a committee; and I have never heard of a chorus of storytellers.

For the novel is based on that most ancient and primitive of human impulses – the desire to tell stories. This I will freely admit is a collective urge, but in a very different sense from the pallid spirit of compromise that prevails in television studios and film sets. Jung, in his essay on psychology and literature, has put it like this: the artist is not a person endowed with free will who seeks his own ends, but one who allows art to realize its purposes through him. As a human being he may have moods and a will and personal aims, but as an artist he is a man in a higher sense – he is 'collective man' – one who carries and shapes the unconscious, psychic life of mankind.

Now, the urge to tell stories is deeply embedded in humanity. But in modern times it has fallen somewhat into disrepute. To quote Max Beerbohm in another context, it has been cosmopolitanized, commercialized, mechanized, standardized, vulgarized to such an extent by the mass media, that sometimes practising this ancient, delicate and profoundly human art, one feels rather as Virgil may have felt in showing hell to Dante. Yet it survives. And here again those critics who claim that the novel is dead make another fundamental mistake. The forms that this storytelling impulse takes certainly change from generation to generation: the epic poem would now seem to be obsolete. Can you imagine anybody sitting down in his right mind to write an epic poem? Yet people go on writing novels and people go on reading them; and this would not happen if this ancient instinct were now dead.

It might be interesting to trace this back. The novel is a development of the epic that belonged to a more primitive stage of civilization when there was a magical sense of harmony between man, nature and the gods. Thus the subject matter of most epics was legendary and its narrative methods laid little emphasis on literal authenticity. But in later times as society became more complex and class distinctions developed, the novel emerged as a sort of commentary on the tensions inherent in an urban bourgeois way of life. As people became more conscious of the manners and morals evolved by communities increasingly preoccupied by economic affairs, than which nothing is less poetic, they demanded an equally increasing sense of realism in literature so that they could recognize themselves in a world that had become smaller and less heroic. Hegel, the German philosopher, has put this very well when he said that modern civilization being inexorably prosaic, the novel's typical theme had to be the division between the poetic and spiritual aspirations of the individual and the commonplace realities of his existence. Hence the novel is essentially a bourgeois form.

Here again we come up against one of the objections to its continuing existence. For instance, in the nineteenth century when there were very clearly defined class distinctions, the various tensions, which were constantly fermenting under the surface of manners and morals, provided a wonderfully fertile field for the storyteller's particular gifts. All kinds of ready-made plots were easily available, and the novel fulfilling its role as a social art reached its highest point. In those days it was important both politically and morally if the duchess ran off with the footman, because the very foundations on which a very elaborate social hierarchy had been constructed would collapse if such goings-on were allowed to continue. Nowadays such an occurrence would be almost impossible for the simple reason that the few duchesses that remain can't get their hands on a footman. And more important still, it would no longer be regarded as a moral issue because the social structure has changed. From this some critics infer that an art form so inextricably connected with the analysis of social behaviour has outlived its usefulness. This is a very superficial view; and I suspect that the people who hold it have never got beyond Jane Austen and Henry James.

The novelist is chiefly concerned with the problem of appearance and reality. At one time the reality of power and influence was very closely connected with an elaborate code of manners. In order to get at the truth behind those manners the novelist had to concern himself with a tremendous variety of social niceties; and it is quite true that some writers gave the impression of being preoccupied with manners to the exclusion of all else. But the great novelists always knew that manners indicate the largest intentions of men's souls as well as the smallest, and they were perpetually concerned to catch the meaning of every outward nuance. The greater the gulf between human pretensions and the reality that lies behind them – a notion of reality that changes as quickly as manners – the richer the material for the novelist.

Lionel Trilling, one of the few sane American critics that I know of, has a fine passage about this in his *The Liberal Imagination*. The characteristic work of the novel, he writes, is to record the illusion that snobbery generates and to try to penetrate to the truth that, as the novel assumes, lies hidden beneath all the false appearances. Money, snobbery, the ideal of status, these become in themselves the objects of fantasy, the support of the fantasies of love, freedom, charm, power, as in *Madame Bovary*, whose heroine is the sister, at a three-centuries remove, of *Don Quixote*. The greatness of *Great Expectations* begins with its title: modern society bases itself on great expectations which, if ever they are realized, are found to exist by reason of a sordid, hidden reality. The real thing is not the gentility of Pip's life but the hulks and the murder and the rats and decay in the cellarage of the novel. This is all very well; but it brings us bang up against the problem of reality. I have said just now that this changes as quickly as manners. Nowadays we assume that reality consists of all the unpleasant things in life: blood, murder, greed, rape, envy, spite and realpolitik.

If this is the case then there is indeed no need for the novelist to concern himself any further with human behaviour, for reality according to his definition is to be encountered every evening on the television news. The innumerable acts of daily kindnesses and ordinary human civility are not recorded; but if an old lady is burned to death in a tenement we hear about it. That is reality. At one time I became so fascinated by this macabre spectacle that I thought of keeping a little black notebook to make a tally of all the people who are burned alive every evening on Telefís Éireann. But I gave it up. The wrong people always seem to escape the flames.

I think that reality lies somewhat deeper than this. Certainly behind all the posturings and pretensions there are in all societies less pleasant aspects of human behaviour with which it is right that the novelist should concern himself. Otherwise he will fall a victim to the pornography of pudicity, thus giving his readers an altogether false impression of what life is really like. And this is something that the novelist must constantly ask himself: what is life really like? We are sometimes accused of turning up stones for the sensational purpose of revealing the maggots underneath. This is perhaps better than pretending that life is as smooth as a stone; but either way it gives a somewhat distorted view; and forces one to give some sort of definition of appearance and reality.

We can be more sure of the former than of the latter. The ease with which people imagine they can recognize appearances, and the difficulty in trying to discover the reality behind them, has led to a great deal of dualism on this subject. Appearance is looked upon as one thing, and reality as something quite different; whereas in fact the two are inseparable. In his *Ethics*, Spinoza writes that self-preservation is the fundamental motive of the passions; but self-preservation alters its character when we realize that what is real and positive in us is what unites us to the whole, and not what preserves the appearance of separateness.

Life as we know is composed of good and evil; and it is sometimes difficult enough to separate them. But without pointing out the less attractive aspects of mankind – its cruelty, greed, selfishness and so on – it would be impossible to discover the good. This I think is the great error that those zealots who fulminate about immoral literature make: so many of them are Manichees at heart. The world for them is neatly divided into good and evil; and needless to say they are always on the side of the angels. They have done more harm in their time than all the pornographers of New York put together.

This then is what the novelist is fundamentally concerned with: the outward manners, actions and conventions of human beings as opposed to their inner thoughts, passions and animal instincts. So long as people live together in organized societies with their differing customs, rituals and multifarious tribal rites, so long will it be necessary for the creative artist to point out that appearance and reality are in fact one and the same thing.

So it doesn't matter in the least that the elaborate manners and rigid class structures of former times have now largely vanished. They provided rich material for the novelist in their day; but we need not regret them. In a sense, the novelist has always been outside society anyhow. With the rise of a complex modern way of life he adapted himself to it; made use of it for his own peculiar ends; and succeeded in creating a new art form called the novel. But he himself is an heir to a much older tradition, a manifestation of the human spirit as old as mankind itself. Bourgeois society did not create the novelist; and if it passes away the creative impulses will survive in some other form. That time is not yet; and I do not think it will arrive for a long time to come. Instead of becoming simpler and more inevitable, society today, contrary to all the hopes of the political reformers, has become ever more complicated, even more mannered, and in many ways a great deal more pretentious that it was when the jolly old duchess eloped with the footman. The insistence today is not so much on

class distinctions as on the absence of them – and this in the face
of the most blatant evidence to the contrary. In Victorian times
the middle and upper classes believed it was their divine right to
civilize the natives of darkest Africa by clothing them in Lan-
cashire cotton, and to keep the working classes in the place to
which it had pleased God to call them. Nowadays it is as good as
your life is worth to suggest that a trade union official might have
the same morals as a duke – unless the duke happened to be a particularly stuffy one. People do not really believe that they are just
as good as one another; only that they are better. The scope for
social comedy is, I assure you, wider than ever. Man is still a bundle of contradictions, which he is frantically trying to tie together
with the ragged rope of social conventions.

The novelist is particularly conscious of these contradictions;
largely in relation to himself. He knows that he is not all of a
piece, that he cannot say at any particular time that he is a particular type of person. Large claims have been made for the novelist's temperament, mostly, I need hardly add, by novelists themselves. D.H. Lawrence proclaimed: 'Being a novelist, I consider
myself superior to the saint, the scientist, the philosopher and the
poet. The novel is the one bright book of life.'

Now, this is bunkum. The novelist is not superior to anybody;
indeed by many reasonable, if conventional, standards, he is distinctly inferior. Just as the novel is, as I have said, a very loose
form of art, so too the novelist is a very loose sort of person in the
sense that he identifies himself with the characters and backgrounds of other people in a way that is sometimes appalling. I
have a theory for instance that Shakespeare didn't have any character at all of his own: that he was a human sponge who soaked up
the personalities of others and found in every one some respon-
sive chord in his own make-up. All creative writers are a little like
that; and that is what makes them so disturbing. They are elusive,
changeable, unreliable, ungrateful, vain, egotistical, lecherous,
opinionated, cunning, cruel, restless, mercurial, sadistic, cowardly,
hypochondriacal, vicious, vindictive, violent, and to cap it all, full
of self-pity. They can also be courageous, loyal, honest, noble,

hopeful and kind. Some of them are charming and some of them are not. If you are one of those people who like others to be direct, simple and uncomplicated I would advise you to keep away from writers, because from your point of view they are nothing more than a mess. But they are a sentient mess; and sometimes, although not always – it is not necessary for a novelist at all – intelligent as well.

Is it his awareness of the contradictory elements in his nature that drives the novelist, sometimes unconsciously, to put them in some kind of order? It can be said, I think without much fear of dispute, that there is an inexorable balance in nature – a kind of compensation. The most obvious example of this is perhaps the heightened sense of smell and touch that the blind develop. The creative artist is flawed as a human being, I think there can be no doubt about that. The fluidity of his nature makes him singularly unfitted for ordinary human intercourse, which is usually based on the assumption that people can adapt themselves to certain clearly designed rules of behaviour. But the artist, being very often tormented by indecision and the chaotic fever of the imagination, finds it difficult to accept any code that limits his freedom of expression. Here again Jung puts this well: The artist's life', he writes,

> cannot be otherwise than full of conflicts, for two forces are
> at war within him – on the one hand the common human
> longing for happiness, satisfaction and security in life, and on
> the other a ruthless passion for creation which may go so far
> as to override every personal desire. The lives of artists are as
> a rule so highly unsatisfactory – not to say tragic – because of
> their inferiority on the human and personal side, and not
> because of a sinister dispensation. There are hardly any excep-
> tions to the rule that a person must pay dearly for the gift of
> the creative fire.

As I said, this is well put; but it still presents us with the problem of why. Why? Why should some people have this creative fire and others not? Well, the short answer to that one is that we simply don't know, anymore than we know why some people should have good singing voices. We can, however, trace back the manifestations of this creative gift and perhaps arrive at some tentative conclusions as to why some people feel the need to tell stories. I am assuming of course that the story is the basis of the novel. This has been disputed, especially in recent times, but I feel that these arguments are largely a question of philology. Even the most advanced of modern technical experiments in the novel all have some sort of arrangements nonetheless. *Ulysses*, regarded in its day as the last word in technical daring, has, as you know, a pretty elaborate ground plan. The newest thing is the publication of unbound chapters in a box, which the reader is expected to arrange for himself. Even this involves some sort of order on the part of somebody: a kind of a literary jigsaw puzzle.

The fundamental basis of the story is the arrangement of dramatic events calculated to inspire interest and, if possible, wonder. In this way people are taken out of themselves, both the writer and the reader; and we can imagine our ancestors, having shed their tails and come down from the trees, huddling about a flickering fire in a cave listening to the tribal storyteller, and for a little while forgetting the fear of the unknown that lurked outside. They who listened must have had some dim idea that life was unsatisfactory in almost every possible way, and that only in imagination could it be made to correspond with their own longing for something greater, more orderly, and more easily understandable than the savage world of nature by which they were surrounded. It isn't very different today. Nature has to a very large extent been tamed; but the longings of mankind have not. At one time they felt that the world was too large for them; now they feel that it is too small. The storytellers, I suspect, have always felt that it was too small, even back there in that cave with the unknown outside. Surely there was something else, somewhere, since one could imagine it. And this sense of searching for something outside ourselves continues, perhaps behind the social fabric, perhaps not anywhere except in our own minds; but a dim feeling of something greater, more dramatic, more interesting and more coherent than ourselves. Carrying within himself something of the ferment and the chaos out of which our little planet evolved, the primitive storyteller and his descendant, the novelist, felt instinctively that these conflicting forces would destroy him, tear him apart, if he did not attempt to draw them together and make some creative use out of them. And I think this is the real basis of the novelist's particular gifts and peculiar temperament.

Life, I suppose, is a continual quest for something, largely a muddled thrashing about for love, for certitude, for survival. It must be dynamic, otherwise it has no meaning. The storyteller does not provide us with answers, that is not his function. 'Oh, what a dusty answer gets the soul, when hot for certainties in this our life,' exclaimed Meredith. What the storyteller does, I think, make plain is that there is a continuing quest for certainties. That certainly is his function, if he has any at all apart from being an entertainer.

This role is beautifully exemplified in a little story that I'll tell you now. In older and perhaps more sensible civilizations than our own, the ancient oral storyteller still persists. And the best known place where he can now be seen – a little vulgarized by tourism to be sure – is in the great square in Marrakech in Morocco. There in the evening the storytellers sit in their booths, surrounded by listeners and smells. They have their repertoires, and one of their most famous stories is called 'Tea in the Sahara'.

> There were once three girls from the mountains. They were called Outka, Mimouna and Aicha. They go to seek their fortune in a town called M'Zab. Most girls from the mountains go to Algiers, but these three girls want one thing more than everything else. They want to drink tea in the Sahara. So, many months pass and they are still in M'Zab, and they are very, very sad now because the men are all so ugly. Shockingly ugly, like pigs. And, what is more, they don't pay enough money to the poor girls so that they can go and have tea in the Sahara. But one day a Targui comes – a tribesman from the desert – and he is tall and handsome on a beautiful Arab horse. He talks to Outka, Mimouna and Aicha, he tells them about the desert, down there where he lives, and they listen and their eyes are big. Then he says: 'Dance for me' (and they dance). Then he makes love with all three, he gives a silver piece to Outka, a sil-

ver piece to Mimouna, and a silver piece to Aicha. At daybreak he gets on his horse and goes away to the south. After that they are very sad; and the men of M'Zab look uglier than ever to them, and they are only thinking of the tall Targui who lives in the Sahara.

Many months go by, and still they can't earn enough money to go to the Sahara. They have kept the silver pieces because all three are in love with the Targui. And they are always sad. One day they say: 'We are going to finish like this – always sad, without ever having tea in the Sahara – so now we must go anyway, even without money.' And they put all their money together, even the three silver pieces, and they buy a teapot and a tray and three glasses, and they buy bus tickets to El Golea. And there they have only a little money left, and they give it all to a bachhamer who is taking his caravan south to the Sahara. So he lets them ride with his caravan. And one night, when the sun is going down, they come to the great dunes of sand, and they think: 'Ah, now we are in the Sahara; we are going to make tea.' The moon comes up, all the men are sleeping except the guard, who is sitting with the camels playing a flute. The three girls go away from the caravan quietly with their tray and their teapot and their glasses. They are going to look for the highest dune so that they can see all the Sahara. Then they are going to make tea.

They walk a long time. Outka says: 'I see a high dune,' and they go to it and climb up to the top. Then Mimouna says: 'I see a dune over there. It's much higher.' So they go to it and it is much higher. But when they get to the top, Aicha says: 'Look! There's the highest dune of all. We can see to Tamanrasset. That's where the Targui lives.' The sun came up and they kept walking. At noon they were very hot. But they came to the dune and they climbed and climbed. When they got to the top they were very tired and they said: 'We'll rest a little and then make tea.' But first they set out the tray and the teapot and the glasses. Then they lay down and slept. And then – many days later another caravan was passing and a man saw something on top of the highest dune there. And when they went up to see, they found Outka, Mimouna and Aicha: they were still there, lying the same way as when they had gone to sleep. And all three of the glasses were full of sand. That was how they had their tea in the Sahara.

All storytelling is like that. Whether the author is determined to get behind appearances to reality as he sees it, and this can be done without very much movement of the characters, or whether he sets his characters going at a cracking pace, the impulse behind it all is essentially a quest for something. Perhaps none of us deserve better than a glassful of sand at the end of a long journey; that is not the point really from the storyteller's angle: it is that we set out to make the journey in the first place. The voyage out: that is the impulse behind all storytelling. And that is what so often gets him into trouble with the moralists whose vision of the world is so often static. Yet in many ways they are not so far apart – that is often the real cause of the trouble. Both of them are concerned with seeking some kind of order in the chaos that one – the moralist – usually discovers to be all about him, and the other – the creative artist – knows is within him.

E.M. Forster has a very good passage on this subject of order in connection with art. In passing I might refer to the beginning of this talk when I was discussing the question of the reported takeover from the novelist, on the part of television and film producers. It is sometimes said that films have outpaced the novel technically: their impact is swifter, and their vision more immediate. Certainly they are, compared with the Victorian novelists who were, to put it mildly, leisurely in their approach to telling a story and developing character. Films, we are told, changed all that and exercised a considerable influence on the novel. Historically speaking, this simply is not true. The naturalistic dialogue, the swift action and the rapid succession of images usually associated with films were, in fact, introduced into the novel in 1905 by Forster in a book rather aptly called *Where Angels Fear to Tread*. Whatever you might think of his novels – I think they are bloodless in the main – he is an important figure in the development of the novel.

But to get back to order. In a lecture, which Forster delivered to the American Academy of Arts and Letters in New York in 1949, he had this to say:

> In the world of daily life, the world which we perforce inhabit, there is much talk about order, particularly from statesmen

and politicians. They tend, however, to confuse order with orders, just as they confuse creation with regulations. Order, I suggest, is something evolved from within, not something imposed from without; it is an internal stability, a vital harmony, and in the social and political category it has never existed except for the convenience of historians.

Where is it attainable? In the entire universe there seems to be only two possibilities for it. The first of them is the divine order, the mystic harmony, which according to all religions is available for those who can contemplate it. We must admit its possibility, on the evidence of the adepts, and we must believe them when they say that it is attained, if attainable, by prayer. 'Ordina questro amore, o tu che m'ami', said one of its poets. 'O thou who lovest me, set this love in order.' The existence of a divine order, though it cannot be tested, has never been disproved.

The second possibility for order lies in the aesthetic category; the order which an artist can create in his own work. A work of art, we are all agreed, is a unique product. But why? It is unique not because it is clever or noble or beautiful or enlightened or original or sincere or idealistic or useful or educational – it may embody any of those qualities – but because it is the only material object in the universe which may possess internal harmony. All the others have been pressed into shape from outside, and when their mould is removed, they collapse.

I don't agree with absolutely everything that Forster says here. If you examine his line of argument throughout the essay you will see that it is really a defence of art for art's sake. And this attitude leads to a certain sense of isolation on the part of the artist; and inevitably to a feeling of superiority. I don't see how you can escape from this implication in any glorification of art. Certainly the artist is often – too often – regarded as an outsider by society; and certainly he himself sometimes anticipates this judgment. In this, I think, he is wrong. Although his gifts are undoubtedly rare, and particularly the gift of invention, his temperament is one that is largely shared by humanity as a whole. He is a man like any other. If he has vices, he is not alone in this. If he possesses noble qualities of heart and mind, that is not unusual either. We are all a mixture of good and bad. If there is a difference between the artist, and what is known as the ordinary man – if there is such a thing – it is that the artist is more acutely aware of the conflict within him, and the many personae which exist in him. In this he is rather like the actor; and indeed many writers have been great actors – Dickens is the supreme example of this. But it is an analogy that can be carried too far. The actor is an interpreter, and is not usually creative. His emotions very often are no more than skin-deep. It used to be said of Sarah Bernhardt that when she was moving the house to floods of tears, she was very often counting it.

It can be said, of course, that this is simply a matter of technique; and that the novelist must also develop his. The celebrated American wit, Miss Mae West, once remarked that Shakespeare had his technique, and she had hers. I mention this, however, to illustrate the vast gulf that exists between interpretation and creation, all the more so since on the surface they sometimes appear very much the same. But without the framework that the creative artist provides in his book or his play or his musical score, the interpreter is helpless. The one art is essentially active, the other passive, like criticism.

But it is certainly true that the novelist must acquire technique. I have often likened this to a singing voice. It comes as a gift; but it must be trained, if it is to last and develop. Some people have the idea that writing is the easiest of all trades, and that all you have to do is sit down at a desk and scribble away. It is not quite as easy as that. Most writers are born with a feeling for words, an instinct for them, and this is certainly something that cannot be acquired. But it must be refined by hard practice, and the wearying task of trial and error. With the creative gift there comes nearly always a certain ruthlessness, a determination not to let anything get in the way of finishing anything that you want to do. And you must do it alone; no one can really help you. This often makes writers surly and unsociable; but here again he is not necessarily unique in this. I dislike the idea of the writer being a particular sort of person set apart from everybody else in his everyday life. Other people have to work hard at their various professions, very often alone; but being less vocal than writers and less subject to publicity, no one hears about it.

The point about the writer, however, is that in his writing he must make use of himself and his own experience to a degree that is not always necessary in other trades. In a certain sense, he writes with his blood, and if you're not prepared to do this you'll never be any kind of writer. Any backing away from the consequences of the quest for truth, any compromise, any fear of what may happen to you as a result of what you write, and you will never achieve anything worthwhile. This total commitment is a great deal more important than technique, because naturally if you care sufficiently about what you are doing, you will try to do it well. If a young person came to me and asked: how do I become a writer? I wouldn't tell him – or her – how to introduce characters, or arrange chapters or learn English – a very important requirement nowadays – I would ask him: 'Do you really care what anybody says about you?' The standard answer to this one is of course: 'Oh, no, I don't.' That, however, is something that has to be proven. I would follow it up by asking: 'Do you simply want to get your name in the newspapers, and become famous, or notorious? Because if you do, there are easier ways of doing it than writing.' However, the curious thing about writers who ever achieve anything is that they never ask anybody else how to do it. And that of course is the whole point.

Using himself as he does, being himself his own sole instrument, it is often asked how autobiographical novel-writing is. Obviously some of it is very much so; and this is particularly true of first novels. I must say quite frankly that I distrust them when they're like that. Compton MacKenzie used to say that it's far better for a first novel to be completely unrealistic, even a historical romance, because it shows that the writer has imagination. If you have nothing better to write about than yourself, it's very often an indication of a sterile talent, which quickly burns itself out. I think that equipped as he is to understand, if not necessarily to participate in most human activities, the novelist should direct his talent towards observation. This does not say that he should go about with a notebook, or, God forbid, a tape recorder, making a record of everything that people say and do. This impedes the progress of creation, and is fatal to the narrative, which should flow like a river enclosed by its banks to give it shape.

Yet this is a continuing debate between critics and writers themselves. In his memoirs, François Mauriac writes that all literature oscillates between these confessions of a being turned in upon himself and upon the deep mud in which the person he might have been is diluted, and the so-called classical works, detached from their creator, composed according to an inviolable body of rules, and imitating the great models. To be a writer is not so much to be a creator of characters, or a teller of tales, as to track down an elusive truth through what others have told us about themselves, and to confront it with what we think we know about ourselves.

Here Mauriac points out the subsoil of the creative temperament, out of which come so many blooms, some monstrous, some beautiful, which the novelist cultivates. I myself admire the classical approach in which characters are created through observation and comparison with one's own temperament. Nothing irritates me more than to be asked about such-and-such a character in one of my books: 'Who's that? Is it so-and-so?' Whenever anybody asks me that, I know I'm dealing with a fool; and I do not suffer fools gladly. Most characters in novels that are not strictly autobiographical are composite figures, made up of elements of various people seen through one's own particular vision of life. Was James Joyce Molly Bloom? Was D.H. Lawrence Lady Chatterley? The answer is, of course, no. And yes. There is an androgynous quality in all creative writers, which many people simply do not understand; and I think this is one of the reasons why so many of them are often regarded with extreme disfavour by many. Unless you accept this very simple fact then you might as well give up trying to understand any kind of creative work. Just read it. And if you disapprove, you'll have a very enjoyable time. There is nothing in this life quite as sensual as indignation. No wonder it's so popular.

The novelist, of course, likes his books to be read. He likes to be well reviewed. He likes to think he will be remembered. But ultimately he writes for himself. I've never heard of a writer of any quality catering to a particular section of the public. He develops his own vision of life; his characters are in many ways a personification of this; and if the public don't like it they can lump it. Any kind of compromise with public indignation is fatal to a writer, and particularly to a novelist. If he submits to it, it means that he is twisting his characters to adapt to a climate of opinion that is not his own. The result is false. This works both ways. If a writer sets out deliberately to cater to the prevailing public interest in sex to the exclusion of all else, he is giving a distorted view of life. If, on the other hand, he avoids this very important human impulse, and gives the impression that his characters never indulge in anything more perfidious than three cups of tea when they should only take two, these people are in fact no better than prostitutes since they are exemplifying a totally one-sided view of life, and one that in my view is equally immoral.

I should like to conclude with the hope that the horrible puritanism that has divided races and individuals since the Reformation and the Counter-Reformation is now gradually dying out. I do not subscribe to the view, in spite of the relaxation of the censorship laws in this country, that we are all now marvellously broad-minded and emancipated. A lot of people are now going about clapping one another on the back and exclaiming 'Hurrah, hurrah, aren't we wonderful? I see *Lolita* on sale in Dublin.' This could very easily become the new hypocrisy. Until we look at life as a whole, a one, we are not really broad-minded. Until we accept the fact that our particular culture – if such it can be called – is not the only one, we are not civilized. Until we realize that people are much the same everywhere, black, white, yellow, we are not tolerant. And until we take it as a commonplace that art and artists are part of our daily lives, and not just something filed away in a department labelled 'culture', we are not even educated.

I think that here the novelist can be of practical value in the world. Just as he makes an attempt, in a very corrupt and fumbling sort of way, to create some unity out of his appallingly divided character, so too other people, who are not, fortunately for themselves, gifted in this way, can make some sort of contribution towards bringing a little order into the worldwide mess in which we find ourselves today. And we might begin by asking ourselves: are we any better in our heart of hearts than the most depraved character that any novelist has ever created?

Text of a lecture delivered at St Patrick's College, Maynooth, 9 March 1969 and subsequently published in *The Fountain*

How to Succeed in Literature
Without Really Trying

1. BEER AND BOOM

For the best part of forty years before his death, Sir Max Beer-bohm wrote practically nothing. His last volume *A Variety of Things* dates from 1928, and most of the pieces contained in it were written as far back as the beginning of the century. He remains a shining example of the evils of overproduction and the virtue of economy. With each book he did not publish, he became more celebrated; and when he died in 1956 he had become an institution of the most exquisite and rarified kind, a position he would certainly not have attained if he had produced a quantity of work as stupendous as Trollope's.

E.M. Forster is another name that springs to mind when one considers the problem of how to achieve literary success by doing as little as possible. On the strength of five novels, the last published forty-six years before his death, he contrived to end up as the Grand Old Man of English Letters.

It is surprising that these two authors are not more popular in Ireland, for they represent an attitude of mind that appeals most powerfully to the Irish creative temperament. It has long been established, and accepted without question by the world at large, that we are a nation of poets and dramatists; somewhat less as a nation of novelists. No one, I am sure, would be at all surprised if the government inserted a clause in the Constitution to the effect that for the greater glory of God and the justification of the demo-cratic principle, to which the whole nation is dedicated, every

Irishman has a book in him. But it is a volume of a very particular sort, for are we not also a nation of spiritual dreamers?

Perhaps the reason for the neglect of Beerbohm and Forster among the Irish public, insatiable readers and buyers of books though they are well known to be, is that these two men so nearly approach the ideal so beautifully lodged in our hearts, without actually fulfilling it; and nothing is so irritating as being confronted with someone who seems to share our virtues or vices, as the case may be, without in the last resort practising them. Thus the heavy drinker cannot abide the sight of an alcoholic, nor the celibate the spectacle of a man who avoids women but cultivates a taste for pornography.

For Beerbohm and Forster did at least write something, which is not playing the game if you are a spiritual dreamer. Indeed it smacks of the crude, the material and the vulgar, all of which are anathema to the Irish soul. Why should one do anything when we shall all be dust and ashes in a hundred years' time? Why, especially, should one commit a word to paper when all the world knows that we are, in the words of Bord Fáilte and Oscar Wilde, the greatest talkers since the Greeks?

There are cynics who question this. They come starry-eyed to do the ritual round of our Dublin pubs to listen to the famous wit and wisdom; and depart cockeyed and more than a little liverish. They have no doubt heard of all the books, plays and poems that the habitués, who so gracefully accept their hospitality, describe at enormous length as in the process of composition. Dozens of Dublin characters have over the years achieved a considerable literary reputation by talking of the books they are writing. They dress like poets, they act like poets, and they drink like maniacs. Since the average foreigner, especially the English, associates the literary life with bohemian antics in the fullest Victorian sense, they are suitably impressed, and go away amazed by the wealth of talent that Dublin possesses for a provincial town of its size.

And then they sober up. Yet even the cynics, when they get back home and dose themselves with bicarbonate of soda, very often begin to have second thoughts. London, Birmingham and

Manchester are so dull by comparison. Writers and poets are not much in evidence there; certainly in no such concentrated numbers. The ones who publish, and whose reviews appear in the newspapers, are rarely to be met with. Many live abroad, most stay at home and presumably get on with their writing, for which they get paid. It is really all very prosaic

Nostalgia sets in. After all, these talkers may have something. Certainly they bear all the hallmarks of true poets and literary men in the traditional sense. For one thing, they are so poor; probably starving in a garret. The grace with which they accept round after round of porter is invariably mingled with a certain air of condescension. Is it not well known that persons with the artistic temperament are proud, even arrogant? And is it not proof of a great nobility of soul in these days of fashionable photographers posing as artists, and makers of bookjects passing themselves off, with the aid of the same photographers, as writers, to discover real poets who are too high-minded to prostitute their art by the vulgar act of publishing? Lost in thought, drowning their age-old sorrows in the wine of the country, they are far above the mercenary hackwork of putting their beautiful dreams down on paper. How rich must be their spirits, how admirable their self-control, how spiritual their acceptance of the rat race, and how wholly disinterested their avoidance of it.

By the time our visitor has worked himself into a lather of nostalgia for the good old Dublin days of oral poetry, as he plods his weary way among the go-getters of the welfare state, the hoary myth of Ireland's unpublished genius is more firmly established than ever before; and our poor Englishman wishes he could be one of them himself, with someone like himself buying him drinks, as he unfolds the story of the book *he* would like to write. His cynicism vanishes; his liver is restored; only his envy remains. He may not really believe – not many Englishmen do – but he wants to. And after all, hills are green far away.

As might be expected, the only people who are truly cynical about the unwritten masterpieces of Dublin are the Dubliners themselves. Since they invented the genre, naturally enough they have little faith in it. Those so-called poets in the literary pubs are nothing but a bunch of lousy scroungers, whose principal talent lies in the touch. Besides, every true Dublin man knows in his heart of hearts that he could write a far better book than any of those professional bums, if only he were given the chance. But what can he do, ground into the dust as he is, with the cost of living, the wife's new fur coat and all the kids running amok and quoting passages from Dr Conor Cruise O'Brien straight into his face? His contempt for the famous unpublished is profound. What taxes do *they* pay?

But even such honest citizens have recently been shaken in their scepticism. For many years a famous Dublin character, now deceased, spent a lifetime talking about an enormous book, which he was in the process of writing. Naturally no one believed him. Judge then, of everybody's astonishment when on his death it was discovered that he had in fact left a manuscript two feet high of a huge episodic novel. Discreetly edited and pruned, it was published in London and acclaimed by all the leading English critics as Ireland's answer to *Doctor Zhivago*. It wasn't quite as bad as that; but it did contain passages of great sensitivity and power; and sold like hot cross buns on Good Friday.

After that, no one could be certain of anything. The drunken bore who accosts one in a bar lounge with a story of a great poem or novel he is writing just possibly may produce it in time; and what is worse, do so without dying. There have been several recent examples of this kind of literature. With the result that the myth of singing Dublin and its hordes of embryo bards and storytellers is now stronger than ever. The cynics have been confounded. Money talks; and the Irish *Doctor Zhivago* made lots of it. It should now be possible, on the strength of such a success, to coast along on talk alone in literary circles for at least another ten years. By that time, it may become necessary for another oral genius to die and leave another enormous manuscript, so that the myth may be perpetuated.

But that headstone can be cleared when it is met. In the meantime, it is a mug's game to write at all. For one thing, it makes

one feel quite sordid and ordinary. Anyone, as you will be told in
Ireland, can write a book; and millions have down the centuries –
alas. But it takes a talent of a peculiarly subtle and rarified kind to
achieve a literary reputation without ever putting pen to paper.
Far from being the lazy, dirty, idle occupation that it is generally
supposed to be by all worthy citizens, it is in fact a most delicate
and artful profession, requiring great powers of concentration and
self-restraint. The temptation to write down one's thoughts must
sometimes be almost too much for flesh and blood to bear. But we
have not a monastic tradition for nothing; asceticism is in our
bones. We hold back and the world is the better for it. Decidedly
better. But then, the world does not have to listen, unless it comes
to Dublin; and if it does it has only itself to blame. After all, the
visitor has nothing to lose except his pocketbook: and what is that
when spiritual values are his for the asking?

2. COPYWRITE

Many people have in their possession title deeds to property written out in old-fashioned copperplate handwriting. Hardly anybody reads them except lawyers; and certainly no one considers
them as even remotely connected with literature. They err; for
they are the forerunners of a vastly popular and financially important section of the publishing industry today, as surely as the Hit-
tite hieroglyphics and the Greek alphabet were the precursors of
the modern typewriter.

Little did those humble copying clerks, proud no doubt as
they well might be of their craft, think that with a little more
enterprise they might have ended up as fashionable authors,
hailed by all the right critics and read by all the right people. They
did not copy out the relevant documents with a view to such dizzy
success; but their methods were sound, and are widely used nowadays in literary circles.

More sophisticated in their approach, now that copying clerks
are a dying breed, are those multitudes who spend their working
hours filing cards, often in connection with the interminable government process of tax collecting and collating generally useless

information. Many of those busy citizens do not even know what all these cards contain. Facts, figures, references and cross-references, and more often than not, double-cross data of all kinds, are contained therein. What these filing clerks do not know is that they have at their fingertips a method that could be turned to very useful purpose in the field of literature. They are too modest. Anybody can be a writer today if they know the proper short cuts. It is high time that somebody told them. Why be a filing clerk when you can be the centre of interest at a publisher's cocktail party?

Finally, it is disgraceful how much talent is going to waste in the field of electronics and sound recording. There must be hundreds of such people, pressing buttons, twiddling knobs and transferring tapes in Telefís Éireann alone. Has anybody told them that they too have it in their power to make themselves famous in Madison Avenue and Mayfair? Apparently not. Wage slaves, victims of a system dedicated to keeping the working man in his place; they are masters of a technique by which politicians, pop singers, boxers and self-confessed criminals have achieved acclaim as authors, often with great financial benefit to themselves and others.

It has, of course, to be pointed out that this school is best adapted to the gifts of those who are already well known to the public. It is a sign of the anti-democratic spirit of the age that the most advanced technique of all has hitherto been almost entirely at the disposal of ex-prime ministers, ageing film stars and retired generals; and it is not easy for a sound engineer to rival the incredible antics of such people. But he can try. Life, talking its head off, lies all about him. All he has to do is tape it: go out into the country – if he is a Dublin man this will be the equivalent of a trip to Abyssinia – get people talking about themselves, transfer the results onto a typewriter from the recorder, and he can publish a sociological survey of Ireland, religious, sexual and political, which will be received with great respect by the critics, so accustomed are they to handling bookjects of this kind rolled off the assembly line by professors, statesmen, anthropologists and hundreds of others who, in a crazy world, are solemnly accepted as the ultimate in sanity.

Yet, strange as it may seem, these underprivileged people, the filing clerks and the electricians, never seem to take advantage of the tools of their trade, which have been put to such profitable use by their betters. When these humble people do write books they nearly always do it the hard way – out of their heads and using their own imagination. Some of them even achieve success; but it is a long haul, and the financial results are hardly ever equal to those enjoyed by people who have no literary talents at all, but have access to public or private documents not readily available to the lowly creative artist who has only his own resources to fall back upon. Nor is a genuine writer likely to have already made a name for himself in those extra-literary activities, which may include anything from belly dancing to singing bishops, which nowadays are almost an indispensable condition for success in the publishing world.

No, I fear bookjects – by which I mean articles stuck together from bits and scraps provided by reference books, newspaper files or tape recorders – are largely the domain of the privileged classes. Take the case of Mr Harold Wilson. I understand that he has already received an enormous advance for his memoirs. True, he is married to a bestselling poetess of the daffs and daisies school, and she may provide him with some lyrical inspiration; but in all likelihood it will turn out to be a rehash of speeches, interdepartmental memos, linked together with passages of dictated self-justification: a socialist version of Harold Macmillan's stupefying autobiography. It will be a bestseller, since such projects, like the memoirs of other monumental bores like Churchill and Eisenhower, are really subscription lists, by which a grateful nation repays those political figures who are not actually certified as lunatics while in office. Certainly during their construction one may be sure the files will be flying.

But these are the most obvious examples of non-books, which even the most biased critics have not the gall to classify as 'literature'. Much more insidious are those historical-biographical bookjects, which have flooded the market of recent years. Some are the work of dedicated scholars who have devoted a lifetime to their subjects, much as Housman spent thirty years on his edition of

Manilius. Since obsessive scholarship and grace of style rarely go together, such books are usually worthy but unreadable; and their authors are often modest and unassuming men, even if a little dotty.

All academics are not, however, either modest or unassuming; and they are far from dotty. Collectors of grants from all kinds of tax-free foundations, connoisseurs of the sabbatical year and the seminar cocktail circuit, they fasten upon some writer, of whom the Joyce of *Finnegans Wake* is the prototype, whose work is open to any interpretation one cares to read into it. I have already written of these pests before; and all I will add here is the observation that on the whole they discourage the public from reading those obscurantist writers.

After ploughing one's way through a volume on the significance of Beckett, any reader with sane, healthy instincts would never want to hear the man's name again. In this the commentators perform quite a useful function; except that they often corrupt the natural critical faculties of gullible university students.

But the most pernicious of all the modern book-makers are those amateur historians who cater for a mass market in pseudo-serious style. It is in this particular field that a privileged position really counts. While it is not absolutely necessary to be titled, a handle helps; nor are all members of this new shower society hostesses, but historical biography produced by a lady or sir is an asset, especially if one is photogenic. The public is as impressed by a gentleman who figures constantly in *Vogue* as it would be if a member of the British royal family were suddenly to produce a volume of poetry in the manner of Mary Wilson.

The uses to which these publicity hounds put the methods of the copying and filing clerks are unbelievable. If they belong to an ancient family remotely connected with some of the figures they write about, they are often able to lay their hands on letters and documents, always completely harmless, which lend an air of spurious authenticity to their productions; while for the most part they simply gather a bundle of previous biographies and copy their material unashamedly out of them. This is called research. Since most of the subjects that are now reprocessed in the biographical factories are famous figures in British imperial history, hundreds of books about them, mostly out of print, have already been written. The addition of a few unprinted letters, a chatty style and as much pre-publication logrolling as the funds will allow, are enough to send the snob-critics into a twitter of sado-masochistic rapture.

Since with a few honourable exceptions all of the leading English and American critics are as sterile as dummy eggs, and could not write a page of creative prose if it were to save their lives, this enthusiasm is entirely unconnected with literature. It is a result of the collapse of the British Empire. When an empire crumbles as suddenly and as abjectly as England's has, it generates a tremendous amount of nostalgia, and a certain self-conscious feeling of guilt. The fabricators of bestselling biographies and histories thus have it both ways.

Anything that recalls the great past is welcome, even when it is unsavoury, as witness the recent spate of successful bookjects about England's highly questionable relations with Ireland. The Tories can sigh for the good old gunboat diplomacy; while the socialists can take a legitimate pride in their country's past greatness, now that everyone is supposed to have equal opportunities.

Alas, they haven't. Literature is now big business, and the privileged classes have cleverly adapted themselves to its methods, while the workers who have the tools in their hands are out in the cold with the poets and the creative novelists. It is time they woke up. Copywrite can be had for the asking.

3. USES OF OBSCURITY

Some time ago in these columns I wrote a review of a Beckett book, which caused some raising of eyebrows on the part of those who take their opinions at second-hand. However, it brought forth a letter of approval from a distinguished Irish writer, himself a master of lucid and poetic prose, which drew attention to one sentence in the article. I had written: 'Now, of course, he is world famous, and in dire danger of really becoming the "chic" writer which, in fact, he is.' My correspondent questioned the lucidity of this. 'How can one do that?' he queried, and went on to remark that presumably 'become' here is to be interpreted as 'publicly recognized as'.

In fact, it was sheer sloppy writing on my part; and if I had the opportunity to rephrase the piece I would alter it. But the letter gave me an idea that had never occurred to me before. Perhaps all obscure writing is merely careless writing. It is a thought worth considering: and it ought to give great consolation to all those who want to become famous without really trying. Certainly it was the first time that any sentence of mine was the subject of 'interpretation'; and it is not without significance that it was a bad one.

Do not despair, therefore, if you cannot achieve the lucidity of a Swift, a Berkeley or a Newman. These men have expressed the most difficult and subtle reflections in prose as clear as spring water. But who organizes seminars to study them? No one. Do books pour forth from university presses interpreting the meaning of their various theories? They do not. Are they held up as models for the young and aspiring? On the whole, no. This is very much a do-it-yourself age: so be with it. Everything is on your side. The spirit of the age is chaotic, confused and almost incredibly gullible. It will swallow anything provided it is humourless, pointless, hopeless and capable of as many interpretations as the answers of a politician being fed questions by a tame television interviewer.

Indeed, television is a great help nowadays to the aspiring genius. He can abandon himself to it without any effort at all, acquiring a working knowledge of how to say nothing in the most impressive possible way. All discussions end in smoke; everyone waffles; nothing is ever decided; and all is conducted in an atmosphere of such ritualistic pomp and self-importance that the viewer is left with the impression that he has been assisting at some esoteric rite, the exact meaning of which escapes him, but which is undoubtedly important by reason of the number of people who follow it. It is a triumph of manner over matter. This lesson will not be lost on our eager young man. Passive though his responses may be, he will, subconsciously at any rate, soak up the

very significant fact that whatever you have to say is of no importance whatsoever: it is the manner of saying it that counts.

Forget any grammar you have ever learned. This should not
be difficult if you are a product of the Irish educational system.
Correct sentences will make your meaning clear. This is fatal, and
may expose the banality of your ideas. Wrapped in a cloud of
obscurity your thought may be as obvious as Ella Wheeler
Wilcox; but if it is sufficiently vague you will be given credit for
being in touch with the subconscious, which, as every schoolboy
knows, is just one big mess. In this region anything goes, especially if it is concerned with despair and decay.

If you wish to describe a young man taking a wrong turning
out of a busy street and ending up in front of a cul-de-sac, you will
not state it in such simple terms if you wish to gain a reputation
as a prophet of the times. It is remarkable the amount of symbolic
meaning that can be read into such a momentous adventure if you
allow the zeitgeist to flow through you as you relate it. A short
example may help the blushing to grow eminent with the pale cast
of thought:

> Gibbon was heavy with a load and in dire danger of really
> becoming the sack which, in fact, he is. Off Dame Street, with
> a smell of porter lingering in his ears. Down the Hatch,
> although that was another part of town, a red passage and a
> brown bombshell. This was nowhere and never had been in his
> channel-crossing. It was a heavy cross to bear and his shoulder
> used to be used to it, even when he carried it in another way.
> Not a soul in sound.
>
> Molly Bawn was across the yellow water. Pish-tush. Where
> was he coming after? A blank end. Up the IRA and vote for
> himself. How many Gibbons were there? Neon lights made a
> fiery glow over the top, a cross between and it stank. He would
> never know what lay on the other side. Olé ...

When you have written two hundred pages of this sort of
stuff and waited five years on your civil service salary to have it
published by a private press in Paris, the reviews will prove interesting. Not one critic, unless he happens to be connected with

The Irish Times and writes under the name of Burdenick, will admit that he does not know what the hell it means. They will all treat it respectfully but evasively, for fear they might be missing another Joyce, another Beckett. It is at this point that the author, if he be a canny prophet, will show his true mettle. Under no circumstances whatever will he make the slightest effort to explain what he has written. What are the scholars there for? Sooner or later one of them will take it up, shiver with ecstasy, and apply for a Guggenheim. Happy days are here again: and revelation is at hand. Did Gibbon turn off Dame Street and wander down a side lane and find himself confronted with a blank wall? Gentle reader, he did nothing of the kind. If he did, the groves of academe would be depopulated.

This passage is, in fact, full of symbolism of the most modern and soul-shattering kind, the critic will explain in that private language the secret of which is known only to income tax collectors and academic scholars. Gibbon is Everyman, alone, forsaken and crying out for salvation to the only God he knows who is essentially unknowable, and very possibly dead according to the meaning of the act, which to modern man is intrinsically sexual and scatophagous. He attempts to drown his existential despair in nullifying his reflexes – in plain language, he drinks like a fish.

'Down the Hatch' is clearly a cross reference connoting his search for oblivion with a certain public house in Hatch Street, which his subconscious also mythically connects with his lost love, Molly Bawn. Love, in modern man's psyche, and occasionally also in his civic consciousness, is inextricably bound up – a subtle play of words here – with the organs of excrement.

When he thinks of his Beatrice, fundamental images – a red passage, yellow water and pish-tush – trouble his libido. Here Gibbon is at one with the universal dilemma: mankind is constipated with guilt, and God being dead, no healing purgative can be applied. Gibbon is bursting to unload his guilt, but he is up against a blank wall on which his own name, which is Everyman, is scrawled, and does not know how to do it. Vague images from his lost heritage trouble his mind: the cross and the load are intermingled in his tortured consciousness. 'His shoulder used to be used to it, even when he carried it in another way.' This is a highly significant passage, especially since it is self-evident that in Gibbon's odyssey all passages are passages of the soul through the bowels. In his agony he imagines it is a blank end: but is it, that is to say is it, essentially and existentially?

Here, If the critic is fairly well read, as some of them are, he will bring in a highly sophisticated reference to Wilde. 'We are all in the gutter, but some of us are looking at the stars.' This leads to a scholarly digression on the various philosophical theories tossed off so lightly by the great wit. Masks for Yeats; the sensual soul for Meredith; the theory of repression for Freud; and piles for Gibbon.

But Gibbon does not entirely give up hoping for a sign of deliverance. Loaded as he is with guilt, and trapped in a cul-de-sac – a pun worthy of Joyce – he yet sees the light of salvation glimmering in the symbol of the cross outlined luridly against the neon sky. Does this mean relief is at hand? Is grace imminent? Will the symbolic passage be opened and guilt evacuated?

The answer to this very much depends on the critic's commitment. If he is employed by a university financed by Episcopalian money, or even Catholic money, he will undoubtedly interpret that particular passage as meaning that God is winging His way across the neon-lighted waters of Anna Livia Plurabelle. If he be free to express what he really thinks, he will probably interpret the fiery cross as an illusion born of tribal superstition, and leave Gibbon where he found him, up the wall celebrating the sensual man. What lay on the other side? Olé.

The question, however, remains open, even when it is closed. Dog does not eat dog. The author remains silent; thereby gaining a reputation for inscrutable wisdom. And there is room for another Guggenheim and another scholarly tome. And if the reader imagines that all this is exaggerated, he has not read as many academic theses as I have. But at least I have given a nod to the wise. It is really all very easy. Just scramble it – and shut your mouth.

The Irish Times, 6, 7 & 8 January 1971

Bath Bricks

Not far from where I live in the buffing spa town of Bath, two old ladies reside in separate flats in streets leading off the Circus, that eighteenth-century tribute to the Coliseum; but instead of provision being made for lions and gladiators in the centre, there is a neat round circle of grass, full of dog droppings and five magnificent plane trees. Very English. As are the two old ladies who live nearby. Like so many others, they meet occasionally when out shopping, or just walking, or on their way to their favourite quack. 'Such a caring young man, my dear, and the most wonderful hands.' But these two particular ladies do not speak, although one suspects that they know all about each other. We shall call them Mrs Younghusband and Miss Pettigrew.

They are both about seventy, which is the age the old ladies of Bath have decided upon as a suitable one to live out the declining years of their lives. Too mature to hurry; too early to stiffen in the joints; and the word 'decline' is never used in Bath in any circumstances whatsoever. People do not even 'decline' an invitation; they are 'unfortunately taken up elsewhere'. But we may be sure that when Mrs Younghusband and Miss Pettigrew reach the respectable age of ninety, they will suddenly make the leap over the decades with flying colours, and manifest their triumph over old mortality to all within and nearby their circles.

In this they will have to make a decision that is being forced upon their contemporaries every day of the week. There are now so many nonagenarians in Bath that many of the residents are thinking of making the final revelation only when they become centenarians. In the past few years, telegrams of congratulations have been flying through the air like a swarm of carrier pigeons to Bath from Buckingham Palace.

But this is to digress. The old ladies of Bath nearly all live in flats, and no doubt Mrs Y. and Miss P. occupy space that is very similar in extent; living room is doled out in square inches in this overcrowded city. They would each have a small sitting room, full of family photographs and 'pieces' of furniture from their old homes. It is very OK to have at least one big chest or table or picture that is altogether out of proportion to the tiny room it dominates. 'Our old place was so big you know. We had that in the back drawing room.'

The bedroom will be even smaller; the kitchen minute, and the hallway, cut out from the big landing or entrance hall without, only capable of taking two persons following each other, like the tinkers, in the same direction. For this accommodation, in a good area between the Circus and Lansdown Crescent, or in and about Great Pulteney Street, the ladies will have paid between £16,000 and £18,000 ten or twelve years ago. Today they would have to pay at least twice that.

Mrs Younghusband and Miss Pettigrew are both pear-shaped, which is the most popular shape to develop in Bath; it shows that one has lived well, and it ensures that good clothes bought when they were first approaching plumpness in their fifties, can still be worn, with a little alteration here and a new hem there. They all wear very good shoes and well worn but obviously genuine skin gloves. Some favour cotton gloves in pastel shades for the summer, which can be obtained in one of the two glove shops in Bath: both establishments are well worth a visit, for they exude the very air and appointment of an England that is passing away.

Umbrellas are used when the ladies are nearing the age of revelation, but are only brought out by the swinging seventies on a wet day. To be seen walking with an umbrella before the time of apotheosis is looked upon with extreme disfavour, almost as if one flew the Union Jack for fun out of the window, accompanied by a blast of American jazz from the wireless within. Coventry would follow. 'Quite round the bend, dear. So sad.'

I have been told that Mrs Y. and Miss P. are the widow of an army officer, decorated at Anzio while ordering his men to forward right instead of left; and the daughter of an archdeacon, the granddaughter of a bishop and the niece of a knight respectively. Generally speaking, their two backgrounds are typical of the majority of old ladies who live behind the great Georgian facades of Bath. They are not churchgoers; but then few in this godless city are or ever have been. They believe in the royal family, Lloyds Bank and the necessity of cats, in that order. They both have OAPs, and a little capital sum tied up in Lloyds for the rainy day. Neither eats meat very frequently – 'no longer a health food, I do assure you'. Both buy eggs, vegetables and tea sparingly, rarely sit down in a coffee shop, as their predecessors were wont to do in great numbers – 'too crowded, my dear, all those foreigners', which translated means full of bloody Americans, and far, far too expensive.

The ladies do not take a holiday, which is considered common in the extreme: all those busloads of impossible people rolling off to Greece, Spain (stroked off the map of Europe by the best people) and even India and Hong Kong, where Uncle Arthur used to have his suits made, and Cousin Eric was ADC to the viceroy. No, the ladies go to 'stay with friends', if they have any left, in Hampshire, Shropshire and Norfolk, all very acceptable counties, or they go to a small private hotel in Kent run by the daughter of an old retainer.

They do not read much, and so have little to complain about Bath's public library, which is about half as well stocked as the one in Athlone, and not nearly as well or so efficiently staffed. They go to matinees in the Theatre Royal where by 'standing only', an occupation they are good at, they secure seats at half-price. The only things the ladies spend money on, sometimes recklessly and at the price of many a lost chop or omelette, are flowers, bunches of which in all seasons they may be seen carrying home with a beatific expression on their faces.

While little pots of crocuses, hyacinths and anemones, indeed little pots of every variety of suitable flowers are the most popular, safe and well-bred present one may give to anyone on a *very special* occasion, like a first century, or the diamond jubilee of a wedding, or the birth of a friend's great-great-grandson, or turning up unexpectedly after being presumed dead in Africa – 'We were certain they were eaten alive by the father of that awful man who is president of whatever-they-call-it-now. Such a shock. I bought a pot of polyants.' (Lovely Joycean words that, polyants, pollyaunts; the ladies are not quite sure of the plural of polyanthus, so they have settled on this pleasing diminutive.)

So, all in all, there is a certain sameness about the old ladies of Bath: pear-shaped, piercing of voice, frugal, routine-ridden as all the English are; Tory, cat-lovers and powerful advocates of hats if at all possible. Mrs Younghusband and Miss Pettigrew are exactly like their neighbours in every particular, except one. These two highly respectable women are also witches.

Admittedly, it is not easy to imagine either of them stripped to the buff, surrounded in a slowly moving circle by the members of their covens, equally buffed, and chanting strange old English pagan rites, or what they believe to be such. I have been assured that the atmosphere of these Sabbaths is decorous in the extreme, and that nothing violent or ill-bred, like sexual intercourse while standing up, ever takes place. The whole thing is more in the way of a nature-worshipping club, which also concocts its own herbs, believed to give great potency to those who might feel they are flagging in that respect. And after all, what else does Miss Barbara Cartland do with her sex pills? She is not a witch, so far as I know; but, like her, the covens of Bath are equally dedicated to eternal youth, the worship of fertility gods and goddesses, and the manufacture of love potions, which are about as effective in making people fall in love with suitable partners as the novels of Miss Cartland.

There are, of course, more covens than two in Bath. The West Country as a whole has rather a reputation for magic and mumbo-jumbo and all kinds of witchcraft. Evelyn Waugh, who lived in Gloucester and Somerset, drew attention to it in *Mr Pin-fold*. Indeed it has been said that Waugh was a kind of witch or warlock himself, but I do not believe a word of it.

The witches and warlocks of Bath are a great deal more ordinary than the late Mr Waugh. One day, a friend of mine who knows all about the witches, sat down with me on the bench outside Barclays Bank in Milsom Street, and pointed out some of them to me. First, a fat retired bank manager, appropriately enough; then three ladies out of the same mould as Mrs Younghusband and Miss Pettigrew; a young man who looked like a rugby player and was one, and who joined to be with his girlfriend who, like himself, worked in an insurance company; a retired pub owner from Bristol – the only one of them who looked like he might cast a spell, having one large wall eye and one half-closed, like Mr Leon Brittain.

The others did not manifest themselves that morning, but I gathered that they are all quite ordinary people, from ordinary, everyday professions and trades. It is certainly one way for our two lady witches to meet a painting contractor and a postman with their clothes off. For there is a certain amount of shifting about among the covens; the witches are not ashamed of filching members from one another, and so life becomes a little more exciting for them, and one hopes less routine for the postman. What magic mail, what rare black cats, what shining goats' hooves he must conjure out of his bag on a foggy winter morning, before an appointed door.

There are apparently about twenty covens in Bath, and more, of course, in the outskirts. It has always been so, and no doubt will increase as religion ebbs rapidly from the land, and love-spells and the casting-off of cloth takes over. There are no records of Black Masses in Bath, so far as I can make out, as there are in London, and the witchcraft scene seems to be fairly harmless; a pinching of skin that has grown flaccid, bloodless and bored: a symptom of the times. Not Merrie England at all; just closing time.

All this, however, is the respectable side of Bath. Mrs Younghusband and Miss Pettigrew and their fellow witches are people who might, apart from their daemonic activities, have stepped out of a novel by Miss Barbara Pym. All the old ladies of the town are not by any means respectable; and some of them have never wanted to be.

They are the one-time mistresses of rich businessmen in London and other places where rich businessmen congregate. But London chiefly, because in the old days it was a comfortable train journey from London, but one that necessitated a stay overnight to do business in Bristol. So the mistress, a chorus girl, a secretary, a nightclub hostess, was set up in a dear little flat in one of the discreet streets of Bath; and there, pensioned off, most of them have remained ever since.

They can be seen walking down Milsom Street any morning of the week; always alone, brightly dressed, painted to kill, with hair dyed defiantly red or jet black, and ropes of cultured pearls wound round their carefully preserved necks. 'Some of them tie back the wattles with a clothes peg, did you ever hear that? Well, they do.' No one speaks to them, and they have a professional contempt for one another. The better-off ones take to young men who may be seen escorting them to the theatre, or into one of the better hotel bars.

Bath has always been famous for its gigolos; today they are no less plentiful, and come from all over England, and, of course, also from France, Italy and North Africa to cater for the rich old trouts, with whom they more or less share a profession, in Bath and its flush surroundings. They rarely 'live-in' with the old ladies, although some are passed off as nephews and so on; but most of them stay in a row of high eighteenth-century houses near the centre of the city, and known locally as the Stable Yard. They are always beautifully dressed, these handsome young men, and most of them have girlfriends on the side; although I have been told that the old ladies keep them so rigorously in training that they are mostly too tired to tackle an outside fence.

One small but vivid section of old ladies deserves a mention. These are the 'girls' who attended upon their Mamas until Mama was ninety-five and they in their late sixties or early seventies. Most typically, Mama owned a house in London, which she inherited from her husband; and with inflation it turned out to be worth perhaps £100,000, quite beyond the wildest dreams of the poor, downtrodden daughter, who having come into her long-awaited kingdom, immediately takes off for Bath to hit the high spots.

Most of those unfortunates have never heard of the Stable Yard, and any of them would not know what to do with one of its young men if she found one sent to her for a birthday present. Not many of these ancient 'girls' are remembered on their birthdays, or any other day for that matter. Their lives ended with Mama. Nearly all of them take to drink. I don't know why this should be; but it is a fact well-known in Bath.

There is one of these bereaved daughters who is famous here. Almost any night of the week she and her dog can be seen weaving their way back home from one of the bars downtown. Miss Y-Z helps herself along by clinging to the railings, and often sings to herself; the little poodle, no longer exquisite, but dirty and soiled, staggers along beside her, making a feeble attempt to bark, and burping loudly. Footless. Many people think this sight is great fun; but not me. It is a terrible thing to lead a little dog into drink.

It might be wondered, from all that has been said above, if there are any old men in Bath. Well, there aren't. It is most curious, and there are many theories about it, the commonest being that the old women kill them off in the natural order of marriage. This may well be the case, but one would still expect to see a few newcomers who have not as yet been bumped off; yet one doesn't. I asked one of the old ladies about it, she being a widow of long standing, and she immediately replied: 'Yes, that's quite right. There are no old men in Bath. I expect you mean old majors and generals and admirals and things like that, yes, so do I. Well, all those types settle in Cheltenham, don't ask me why but they do.'

'The races, perhaps?'

'Perhaps,' she said doubtfully.

So all the old jackasses settle in Cheltenham, that is certain, but one would, I imagine, have to go to that sister spa to find out why. In the meantime Bath remains, like Cranford, that well-known Victorian shocker, in possession of the Amazons. 'If a married couple come to settle in the town, somehow the gentleman disappears ...' The author of *Cranford* gives some reasons for this, but they are not convincing. What would the gentlemen do at their evening parties, she asks. I could tell her. They might be found in the back drawing room knocking the punch aft. And as for saying that their absence is due to their business interests in the great neighbouring commercial town of Bristol (in the case of Bath), no one believes that. Some families settle in Bath while the parents are engaged in business elsewhere; but they are not the sort of people who make up the Bath-dweller in the accepted sense.

The old ladies of Bath toil not, neither do they spin. The very word 'business' is hardly in their vocabulary. They often complain of the tradesmen, but this is quite different, and they have plenty to complain about, for Bath is one of the most expensive towns in England. Shopkeepers in Bath do not believe in anything less than 100 per cent profit on anything, and twice that if they can get away with it. The fact is that we are talking of very old ladies and old gentlemen in a very particular sense. In the same sense as the English duchess who examined the crowded dining room of the Ritz Hotel in London intently through her lorgnette, lowered it with a sigh, and remarked to her companion: 'It's all right, there's no one here.'

What she meant, of course, was that there was no one there known to her. And so it is with the old ladies of Bath, witches though some of them may be. They have all retired on private means, and have never engaged in trade. The missing old boys in Cheltenham are in the same case. The French have an even more extreme attitude to this sort of thing; one is either 'born' or one is not. If one is born outside the stud book then one is not really 'born' at all. The English do not bring things as far as this, but, of course, they have evolved the perfect means by which they can identify just exactly where in the caste system anyone was born. All they have to do is listen to one another's accents. It is as simple as that. One of the reasons why they are not entirely at ease with the Irish is that, unless one speaks one of the better-known basic dialects, Kerry, Belfast, Mayo, it is impossible for them to 'place' one. It is the same with Australians and New Zealanders. How much money have they? It is impossible to tell since they all speak the same way. Very tiresome.

For, of course, apart from those who are well 'placed', and so in their own little pigeonhole, whether male or female, for the rest of their lives, there are hordes of men and women in Bath. It is said that an American GI taking a taxi from the station to the upper slopes of Bath, sometime after the last war, was moved to observe: 'Gee, this is the first time I've ever seen a cemetery with traffic lights.'

He would not make the same remark today. Bath is now the second-largest tourist attraction in the UK. For almost ten months of the year it is packed with sightseers of all nations, young, middling and old. They follow a set route, which fortunately does not bring them past where I live. The abbey, the Pump Room, the Roman Baths, Pulteney Bridge, Great Pulteney Street and the Holburn of Menstrie Museum, a whiz round the Grand Parade and on to Queen Square, Gay Street, the Circus, Brock Street and a grand finale at the Royal Crescent. Some also take in the American Museum at Claverton Manor (birthplace of Molly Keane's father, I believe), and now with its smooth and purring curator, a great deal more baronial – in the theatre sense – than ever it was in the days of private ownership. The whole set-up is something that those with an offbeat sense of humour ought to see.

Much has been written about Bath, the most perfectly pre-served eighteenth-century city in the world. The planning was a work of art, simple and varied as genius often is. Square flows into crescent, through a connecting street calculated to rest the eye, and public buildings of chaste and strong proportions fit in admirably with the whole. Nothing offends the eye in Bath in the small area between the abbey and the great crescents. There is a hideous modern hotel on the river, but it is in a part of town that is more medieval than Georgian. One does not have to look at it, and the quarter it looms over, Walcot, is noisy, dirty, idle, promiscuous, occasionally dangerous and always smelly. It is a delightful place, just off the High Street. And one feels that the houses and shops are in proportion to the people and the place. Walcot is like any bohemian quarter anywhere in the world.

But the city itself is largely a fake. A stage setting, a wonderful backdrop, a series of film sequences. Few of those elegant Georgian houses are now used for the purpose for which they were built. Eighteenth-century England was largely a slave state. It is true that labourers were paid some wages, but they had little choice of anything better than long, killing hours of work, and mean food to consume in a hovel or cellar at the end of it. Most of them died young, believing that they were free men. It was one of the great con jobs of history. The houses of Bath were built for a family to live in state, attended by numerous slaves. The society of the eighteenth century was very much an indoor one. The streets were too dirty and dangerous to walk in; and persons of quality were transported from their homes to the Pump Room or the Assembly Room by sedan chair – to have the right 'swing' it had to be carried by 'two bogtrotting Irishmen' – or carriage. All of the houses were designed for ostentatious entertaining, and a style of life totally dependant on a large slave population.

All this is vanished. The splendid fronts of Bath remain. But behind most of them a rabbit warren of small, dark flats lies concealed. Only a few of the great houses are open to the public, and none of them are lived in; the rest are not fit to be seen as eighteenth-century dwellings. The whole of the Bath experience is based on idle, snobbish fancies of the glamour of the past. That particular century was far from 'golden'. People died like flies, while a few architects of genius built a city of breathtaking beauty for ruthless speculators who made a rapid fortune, while thousands of ill-fed workers toiled in the process. And the new rich possessed the city. That's the truth about Bath.

Its climate is peculiar; steamy and hideously hot during the summer: American tourists and others, both fat and thin, frequently collapse and die while staggering up the hills to see yet another landmark. And in the depths of January old people are picked by the dozen from their freezing garrets, stone dead for days.

The dust is awful. Jane Austen, who never really liked Bath, once remarked with relief as she was leaving the place that 'the dust was beyond anything'. It is even worse today. A table left for twelve hours without dusting will acquire a fine coat on which you can write your name. Left a week, the table will simply disappear.

Yet most old people, especially women, seem to thrive in this atmosphere. Think of all those sprightly old girls near their century mark, while marriages of couples in their sixties and seventies are an everyday occurrence. 'We fell in love when we sat on a bench in Victoria Park, spring it was, and all the lovely cherry trees just swept us both off our feet.' The lady who said that was eighty-one, and her newly-wed husband, seventy-nine. There is a flourishing trade in OAP marriages in Bath. The young just dump down in the first room they can find, produce a child, and then if they're in the mood, drift away, while the single parent gets a pension for not marrying, and is found a flat immediately. The young men who drift from girl to girl and pad to pad are doing a real service for their country, and leaving their former bedfellows in style. It is a most interesting development.

Yes, people thrive here in all sorts of ways. Why then, the reader might well ask, do I not join in the general praise for this loveliest of cities? 'If he hates it so much, why does not the bleeding fella get the hell out of it.' Ah yes. But that is another story.

The Irish Times, 18 May 1985

III.

Unpublished Short Fiction

From the early 1960s until a few months before the onset of his final illness in 1987, John Broderick used a 'Waverley Student's Notebook' to record ideas and outlines for novels, plays and stories. The notebook is now in the possession of Athlone Public Library, part of a collection of Broderick's papers and published and unpublished works. The collection includes nine short stories in typescript, some with manuscript corrections. In some cases they are re-workings of the same plot.

Of the stories published here, 'Two Pieces of Sèvres' is one of three versions of its plot, the other two both being entitled 'An Evening in Ravenna'. The legend of 'The Marked Man', which tells that anyone who intervenes to save a drowning man from the sea will eventually be taken by the sea, appears six times in the typescripts. Three appearances are in the form of plays for television, one of which, entitled 'The Man from the Sea', was submitted to RTÉ, and rejected in November 1980.

'The Young Poet' reflects Broderick's veneration of the art and craft of writing. It is a story of art and love betrayed, 'a lark ... set to sing grand opera', and the artist/lover thereby destroyed. The most substantial of the stories in this volume, 'Untitled', is the longest of the typescripts and has particular interest for those who know something of Broderick's life and work. Like Roger Dowling in the story, he was brought up among middle-class merchants in a midland town in Ireland and inherited large interests in a local business. The whole of the third paragraph of the story could have the name of John Broderick credibly substituted for that of Dowling. Broderick himself seems never really to have gone 'in search of freedom' but he certainly had 'the sense of sin'. Dowling's account of his lifetime of deliberate and effortful perversion of good, and the narrator's suspicion that at the end he achieved an even more terrible distortion, reflect the preoccupations of Maurice O'Connell in Broderick's *The Trial of Father Dillingham*, first published in 1974. The story reflects also the writer's knowledge of the novels of François Mauriac, which he greatly admired for their depictions of the demands of religious belief and the constant striving between evil and good. John Broderick understood well the danger for the creative artist of finding the greatest stimulus in sin.

Two Pieces of Sèvres

'Have we far more to go?' asked Bennett, leaning forward and tapping the driver on the shoulder.

'About a mile more, sir. Won't be long now.'

Bennett sat back again with a sigh. The car was really very uncomfortable, with springs that protruded through the worn upholstery like old bones. And it rattled like a cartload of tin cans on the narrow, bumpy road.

'Not many people coming this road these days,' said the hackney driver.

'I'm not surprised,' replied Bennett with a ghost of a smile.

'Haven't been out this way myself for twelve months. Shocking road.'

'It must be pretty tiring on Mrs Morton driving on it,' ventured Bennett.

'She hasn't got a car. Bikes it.'

'It must be ten miles into town!' exclaimed Bennett, appalled. But he made a mental note that she must really be very poor: ten miles of this on a bicycle. And her letter had been urgent. He had learnt to recognize urgency in any disguise. This journey might after all be worth his while. Occasionally one did hit on something good in these old decayed mansions.

'Don't know how they live in the place. All broken down,' said the driver.

'I expect they're used to it. When one has one's family –'

'There's nobody except Mrs Morton and her mother.'

'Yes?' queried Bennett softly.

'And the mother's dying. Stroke she got at Christmas. Pretty tough on Mrs Morton.'

'Very sad.'

'Wonder what she'll do when the old lady dies?' asked the driver, shooting his passenger a sidelong glance.

'It's hard to tell,' replied Bennett smoothly. 'I suppose she'll just go on living.'

'She's had a tough life up to this – Mrs Morton that is. Married some fellow in the British Army, he left her after a couple of years. Then she came back to live with her mother. Father's dead. Mother was a bit of an old tarter. Liked her bottle too. I suppose that's what done her in the end. Gin, I hear. Now, I don't say no to a bottle of stout,' he went on suggestively, 'but I draw the line at gin. Can't take it when you're driving.'

'No, no, indeed.'

'And it's death for the women.'

Bennett agreed.

'Here we are,' announced the driver, turning in at a wide gateway. Bennett supposed that there had once been gates hung on those huge stone pillars: but they were there no longer. The drive was broken and muddy. Then the house came into sight.

'Fine house,' remarked Bennett appraisingly.

'Wait', said the driver, 'until we get nearer.'

The house did not improve on closer acquaintance. Many of the windows were seen to be broken, some of them shuttered, there were blinds on six only; moss clung to the steps almost to the door, rainwater dripped steadily from the hanging eaves, and what had once been a lawn was now a meadow.

'Run-down,' said the driver with finality. 'Run-down.'

'I suppose I'll be about an hour,' said Bennett, climbing carefully out.

Winifred Morton had watched their coming. She was nervous. There was very little now she had left to sell; she hoped they would send a man with at least good manners.

'Heavens,' she murmured to herself as she watched Bennett approach, 'what an old man to send.' Perhaps – but no, he would be all the more difficult. Old men always were. She went to open the door with some misgivings.

'Good afternoon,' she began. 'Won't you come in? Such a wet day. I suppose you're the man from Bennetts.' She took his hat. He kept his coat. The hall did not presage heat in the interior regions.

'Yes,' he replied with a certain degree of satisfaction, 'I am Mr Bennett.'

Mrs Morton did not conceal her surprise. 'I didn't think you would come yourself.'

'I always come myself,' he answered with simple truth.

She led the way into the living room. He followed, blowing his nose, sat down, took out his notebooks, and came straight to the point.

'You said you had some Hepplewhite dining chairs. I think I might be able to place them. How many have you?'

'Seven. They're in the other room.'

'That's a pity. I needed eight. However, we'll see. And the Empire suite, is it in good condition?'

'Well, yes – ' she began slowly.

'I see. Pity you don't have any Louis Quinze. Just now I have several enquiries from America for that. But Empire is slow. I don't think Gray or Stephenson landscapes would interest me, late Victorian you know, quite gone out.'

And so it went on. He inspected the pieces she brought him to see. There was nothing of any value. He knew he had made his journey for nothing. He did not regret it. There was always the chance that there might have been something.

'I think perhaps the Hepplewhite chairs, even though the set is short –' he broke off and looked up at the ceiling. Something was knocking on the floor above, a dull, heavy thud. He looked enquiringly at Mrs Morton.

'It's my mother,' she said. 'She knocks on the floor with her stick when she wants me. I'd better go. Will you excuse me? I'll show you the remainder when I get back.'

She went out. The knocking went on. Then he heard a faint sound, probably the opening of a door, and the knocking ceased.

He looked around the room. Nothing of value at all here. Then on a little side table he saw two blue Sèvres vases, and went over to inspect them, surprised that he had not noticed them before. He had an eye for Sèvres and it was always saleable. But before he took them in his hands he stopped short and peered closely at them. At first he could hardly believe his own eyes. It must be a mistake. But there was no mistake: he would have known them anywhere. Christine. The memory of her came back to him with a vividness he thought he would never experience again. Were they still hers? Had she sold them? Given them? How, how, how? The old man sat down, pale and suddenly cold, holding one of the vases in his hands.

He had given these two vases almost fifty years ago to Christine Gray with whom he had been passionately in love for five years. Almost from the very beginning he had known that she did not love him, hardly cared for him. She had fed him titbits of affection, enough to keep him in perpetual adoration: she was one of those women who could not exist without an army of lovers at arm's length. And he was the least of them.

She had come to visit him once, for a caprice, at his father's shop. The old man had met her at the door bowing, mumbling his time-honoured formulae. Her lover coming from the musty caverns at the back of the shop had been considerably embarrassed; he had on his working clothes and his father did not know who she was. He had disentangled her and led her round, half-vexed, half-joyful at her coming. And pausing before she went, she had admired two Sèvres vases. They were exquisite and had in their journey through life rested, according to Bennett senior, for sixty years on the same table in the Faubourg Saint Germain. The following day, his son wrapped them up and sent them to her. A few months later, her engagement was announced. Bennett, in London, received the news calmly and professed himself cured. The groom, he understood, was a Georgian gentleman in the back plains of County Westmeath. For forty years he pursued freelance art and furniture profitably in the cities of Europe and America, coming back to Dublin during the war. The old Castle society had vanished, nobody had ever heard of Christine Gray, Bennett himself had forgotten. And now, after all these years –

Mrs Morton coming back into the room found the old man sitting still, holding the vase in his hand.

'I'm sorry for keeping you,' she said.

'I hope your mother is more comfortable now,' he replied, rising and setting the vase down on the table again.

'Oh, she's quite all right. She calls sometimes for no reason at all. I see you've been looking at the Sèvres vases.'

'Yes. They're very interesting.'

'They belong to my mother. She is very much attached to them.'

'I suppose so,' he heard himself saying. So Christine was the old woman upstairs, thumping on the floor with a stick, waiting for death. He wondered vaguely how she looked now. But he pursued his business with that part of his mind that was anchored firmly in the present.

'As I was saying, the chairs are the only things I am really interested in, and their being incomplete is a drawback. Also they're not in very good condition.'

'They could be restored easily enough,' Mrs Morton began wearily.

'I do not deal in restorations,' said Bennett mildly. 'I will give you twenty pounds for them.'

'Twenty pounds!' Mrs Morton paled.

'It is really more than they are worth.'

Suddenly the knocking began again. The hollow sound vibrated through the still room. Bennett looked up at the ceiling, and asked Mrs Morton if she wanted to go to her mother again. The knocking unnerved him. But Mrs Morton did not want to go. She sat down and, holding her head in her hands, was quietly crying. The knocking went on.

'Don't you want to go to her?' enquired Bennett again.

'No, no, no.' Mrs Morton struggled hard to regain control of herself, wiped her eyes and stood up. 'She calls me for no reason fifty times a day. She was all right five minutes ago. Let her knock,' she burst out with sudden ferocity. 'I'm sorry. I had been expecting

so much from your visit. Twenty pounds is so little. I've been
through such a lot. My mother's so ill, and now it doesn't seem as
if she can last much longer, and there's nothing – ' she broke off.

Nothing to bury her with, thought Bennett. Well, at least he
could do Christine that last service. He turned and went to the
table on which the vases reposed.

'Do you think your mother would part with these?' he asked,
pointing to them.

'I don't suppose she'd mind if she got a good price for them.
What would you give for them?'

'They're very attractive. I think I could dispose of them. I
will give you two hundred pounds for them,' he said quietly.

'Two hundred pounds,' she repeated in a dazed voice.

'I am of course taking a risk,' he went on, reeling off the
shopworn phrases without thinking. All he wanted was to get this
embarrassing business over and done with. The knocking which
had ceased for a few seconds began again, louder and more insistent. 'Are you sure you don't want to go to your mother?' he asked.

'I'll go later. She'll be alright. Do you think the vases valuable?'

'They may be. Will you take that for them?'

'Yes,' she said eagerly. 'Yes, I will.'

'I'll take them with me now.'

She hunted about in a press in the corner of the room looking for wrapping paper, while he sat down to write out his cheque.
The first time he had ever lost money knowingly in his life. He
signed his name, surprised to find his hand quite steady. The
knocking was now continuous; the old woman was determined
not to be left alone. I am too old, thought Bennett, too old to
savour this situation.

Mrs Morton had unearthed some paper. The vases were
wrapped up, the cheque exchanged. They moved out to the hall,
out of sound of the knocking. Bennett bade goodbye, arranged for
the chairs to be collected, put on his hat and walked to his car. His
chief emotion was the desire to get away as quickly as possible.

Mrs Morton closed the door quickly and ran upstairs. When
she got to her mother's room, the old lady had ceased knocking and

was lying back exhausted on her pillows. Her face was ashen grey and her mouth was twitching slightly. She spoke with difficulty.

'Why didn't you come? I wanted you.'

'I couldn't get away. I was finishing up with the dealer. What is it you want?'

'A drink. I'm thirsty. I forgot to ask.'

'Mother,' exclaimed Mrs Morton, holding up her cheque, 'he gave me two hundred pounds for the two Sèvres vases. Isn't it wonderful?'

'What did you ask for them?' asked the old woman.

Her daughter poured out a drink of water and handed it to her.

'I didn't ask him for anything. He offered me that for them. I was amazed. Who'd ever think they were worth that?'

'You should have asked for two hundred and fifty. If he gave you that you may be sure they're worth twice.'

'How was I to know they were valuable? You never said they were. I thought you got them for a present.'

The old woman struggled into a sitting position. She was pale with anger.

'You're a fool. You should have asked more. They belonged to your father's first wife. He gave them to me after she died. Some man gave them to her. Some rich man who wanted to marry her. These vases may be worth a fortune. And you gave them away.'

'How was I to know?' wailed Mrs Morton wretchedly. 'You never told me anything about them. I didn't know they were valuable. Why didn't you tell me?'

'They must be priceless. That dealer saw it and tricked you. Oh, you fool!' and the old woman began to blubber with impotent rage.

'Nothing I ever do is right, nothing, nothing ever.'

Mrs Morton walked over to the window with trembling lips and looked out at the grey landscape and the slowly-falling curtain of rain.

The Marked Man

The storm was over. Two women came down to the beach from one of the three cabins that huddled together in the shelter of a little hill about a hundred yards from the sea. They made their way along the shore, their heavy boots crunching into the damp shingle, their bright red petticoats showing as they bent down picking up bits and lengths of sticks thrown in by the sea.

They worked silently like this for a while, until their aprons were filled with faggots. Then Mary Cullen, who had led the way, straightened herself up. Her daughter Nora went on gathering until she too was finished. She looked out at the sea.

'The Lord save us, 'twas a terrible night,' she said. 'It has the sea beat.'

'The sea is never beat, Nora,' said the old woman. 'The sea is only resting and waiting.'

'God help all seafaring men that were sailing the sea in the teeth of the great storm.'

'God help all them that's waiting for their men to come home after the great storm.'

'God help them, surely. There's many a man floating today on the cold water, and many a man clinging to an old oar, or a bit of stray stick maybe, out under the lonely sky.'

'Four days and four nights I waited for your father to come out of the teeth of the storm, and when they brought him in and laid him on the table, I was glad that the waiting was over. My pity is for them that wait.'

'The sea is a terrible cruel thing, surely,' said Nora.

'Whist, girl!' said Mary sternly. 'Don't be complaining of the sea. The sea is greater than you and me. Sometimes when I wake in the lonesome dark I do be thinking of them that'll never come back, and then I hear the thundering of the waves and they beating up against the black rocks, and I do be comforted, listening to the great roar of the sea.'

'Thank God that Stephen Óg was under his own roof last night, and not out on the water battling against the black night!'

'Thank God, Nora, that your own brother, Sean, wasn't away from his own roof in the storm!'

Nora crossed herself and murmured thanks. But she was thinking of Stephen Óg, with his strong white body, and his red, curling hair, and her lips tightened, and she crushed the bundle of faggots against her breast, thinking of the infant that would lie there when she and Stephen Óg were married.

The two women stood looking out over the green-grey sea, thinking their separate thoughts. The waves broke at their feet, and slipped back, pursued by their own damp shadows on the shingle.

Further down the shore, the big breakers curled lazily round the rocky base of Cuileen Head, and further out, almost where the grey wing of the sky dipped over the horizon, a small black object bobbed up and down like a floating bird.

Nora squinted her eyes and leaned forward.

'What is it?' asked Mary.

'Look!' said Nora, pointing with her finger. 'Out there.'

The old woman searched the wide expanse of water for a few moments before she, too, saw it.

'Can you make out what it is?' she asked her daughter.

'It looks like a great seabird.'

'It looks like some sort of a vessel.'

'I'm thinking that it's some strange object brought in from the sea.'

'It's no creature of the sea. It's a queer thing entirely.'

'It is surely,' said Nora, staring harder than ever.

Suddenly they heard a shout further along the shore, and

turning round, they saw a figure clambering over the rocks at the base of the head, and waving at them.

'It's Stephen Óg!' exclaimed Nora. 'What can be up with him?'

The young man got clear of the rocks, and began to run along the beach towards the two women.

'What is it, Stephen Óg?' asked Nora, going forward to meet him.

'I was up on the head and I saw the thing out on the sea. Did ye see it?'

'We did,' answered Nora, 'but we couldn't make out what it was.'

'It's an aeroplane, and there's a man on it,' panted Stephen Óg, his eyes bright with excitement. 'Ye can't see it rightly from here, but up on the head I could see it, and the man sitting on top of it, and he waving.'

'I'm going up to the head to see it,' exclaimed Nora, dropping her apron of sticks. 'Will you show me, Stephen Óg?'

'I'll go up after ye,' said Mary. 'I want to tell Sean and the rest.'

When she went up to the head shortly afterwards the whole village went with her, her son Sean, the mother of Stephen Óg and his sister Bride, and old Mag Moran who had lost four sons to the sea, and who lived alone in the third cabin of Cuileen.

They all lined out along the edge of the head that jutted into the sea, huge and flat-faced like a whale. The spray from the slowly-breaking waves splattered on the rocks beneath them like sudden gusts of rain. The seabirds flew up screaming from their nests in the cliff. The green-grey sea stretched out below, vast and silent.

And in the middle distance the aeroplane, one wing dipping into the water like a tired bird, the other slanting upwards, floated on the calm waters.

'Look, look!' shouted Stephen Óg, 'You'll see a man as plain as daylight on the aeroplane. Look!'

'Haven't you the fine sight,' said Nora, laying her hand on his arm, and leaning forward. 'I can hardly see him.'

Then they all saw him.

'He's standing up,' said Bride.

'No, he's not,' said Stephen Óg, 'he's kneeling up.'

'That's right,' agreed Nora, 'he's kneeling up.'

'That aeroplane is sinking,' said Sean. 'I don't think it'll float much longer. The man is waving to us.'

'The Lord save us!' exclaimed Bride. 'What's going to happen to him at all?'

'We'll have to row out and take him off,' said Sean. He turned back from the cliff and made as if to go. But his mother broke away from the little group, and grasped him by the arm. Her fingers dug into the sleeve of his coat.

'No son of mine will take a stranger from the sea,' she said in a strong, high voice. 'The sea looks after its own.'

'The man is drowning,' said Sean, going pale before his mother's burst of fury.

'The sea looks after its own,' repeated Mary. 'That man belongs to the sea, and no son of mine is going to take him from it.'

'I can't let him drown, mother.'

'What power have you to go against the sea? The sea is greater than you and me. The sea gives and the sea takes. Night and day the sea is watching and waiting, looking after its own, and seeking for its own. Are you mad to reach out and take what belongs to the sea?'

'It's sinking, mother. I'm thinking of the cold waters and they sucking him down.'

'If you interfere with what belongs to the sea, the sea will get its revenge.'

'Let me go, mother.'

'No. Isn't it bad enough to be waiting for you to come home into the cold night without knowing that you're a man marked for it by the sea?'

'Listen to your mother, Sean,' said the mother of Stephen Óg. 'Don't be tempting the sea.'

'The young men is all for defying the sea,' put in old Mag in her deep, quivering voice. 'But it's the women that have to wait. Four sons I lost to the sea: Michael, and Thomas, and Brian, and Eamon, that was my firstborn, drowned in the green depths of the sea. Don't be for tempting the sea, Sean. The sea looks after its own, I know.' And she relapsed into incoherent mumbling.

'Your father challenged the sea,' broke in Mary again, lowering her voice to a husky whisper. 'That's why I'm afraid for you. It was on the islands when I was a girl. He rescued a stranger from the sea, and I laughed at them when they told me that the sea would have its revenge. I laughed because I was young, and because your father was the finest man that ever was seen on the islands, and he an inland man. Tall and straight and strong, like an oar held up in the sun. I laughed, but that was before I got the wisdom of the sea. Four nights I waited for them to bring him back to me and the cold moonlight dripping from his face.'

'Don't go, Sean,' breathed Nora.

'Don't go,' pleaded Bride. 'Sean, Sean, listen to us.'

'Is it what ye want me to stand here and watch a man drowning in the clutches of the sea? Is that what ye want?' Sean tore his arm away from his mother's grip and stood back. He faced them, his face as white as the wings of the seabirds that flashed overhead.

'He's a stranger that the sea has marked, and you're my son,' answered Mary.

'Are you coming, Stephen Óg, or are you afraid too?' asked Sean, turning to where Stephen Óg was standing with Nora by his side.

Stephen Óg took a step forward, but suddenly Nora threw herself on his breast, and wrapped her arms around his neck, sobbing wildly, 'Stay, stay for God's sake stay, leave the sea to its own. Let him go if he wants; stay you.'

'Stephen Óg, listen to Nora,' said his mother.

'Four sons, and two of them never got in the sea,' moaned old Mag.

'Listen to your own,' pleaded Bride softly. 'Leave the stranger to the sea.'

Sean hesitated and looked at her with trembling lips.

'Leave the stranger to the sea. Don't mark yourself in this place,' repeated Bride in a low thrilling voice.

'Listen to Bride, Sean,' said Mary.

Sean hesitated for a moment longer, looking Bride full in the face. Then he tore his eyes away and began to run down the slope.

Nora screamed as Stephen Óg made a movement to follow him, and tightened her arms around him. 'Heart of my bosom, don't leave. Stay and don't tempt the sea. Think of the watching and waiting in the cold night.'

Bride sank down to the ground and began to sob. Mary crossed her arms on her breast and began to sway to and fro moaning softly to herself. Old Mag began mumbling the names of her four sons over and over again like a litany.

On the grey waters the aeroplane still floated, but one wing was already submerged, and the other was slowly tipping up into the air.

Sean clambered madly down the rocks. For a short while those on the head could not see him. Only the waves beating on the cliff broke the silence. Then suddenly they saw his long black curragh nosing out into the sea, out and out with long steady oar. The distance between the two black objects on the great silent mirror of sea grew less and less. The watchers on the head followed the race with cold eyes. They watched the two blobs become one, and separate, and then as the distance between them grew again, Mary broke the silence.

'I must go back,' she said, 'and get a bed ready for the stranger that Sean will be bringing home from the sea.'

They followed her down the black rocks, and when they came onto the shingle, Sean was already pulling up his curragh. Stephen Óg helped him lift the stranger out, and carry him into Mary's house. They put him to bed in Sean's bed, and the women put his clothes to dry at the fire. There was a great bustle about the house. Everybody crowded about the bed to look at the stranger.

Suddenly Sean stood up and went to the door.

'I think I'll go down and pull the boat up rightly out of the water for fear there be another storm in the night,' he said.

A silence fell on the house. They watched him go out the door. Their eyes were still and anxious and strangely resigned. They listened to his footsteps on the stone path outside, dying away into the dull, insistent murmur of the sea. Now and forever more he was a marked man.

The Young Poet

Cassandra, standing behind the morning-room window, watched him come up the drive. Several times during the past two days she had regretted asking him to come, but now, seeing him again, she knew she was glad. He carried his cap in his hands, nervously, Cassandra supposed, and the sun shining pitilessly on his bare head made him appear like a young actor coming onto the stage for the first time. Indeed, he was like a young actor Cassandra had seen last year when she and her father had gone to London for the Queen's golden jubilee, the same black curling hair, the Grecian forehead and nose, the full curving mouth, the large flashing eyes. It was hard to imagine that Willie Maxwell was a peasant, and had never been out of Mayo in his life.

Mary Curley, Cassandra's maid, came into the room. She, too, had seen the young man's approach.

'I see one of Jimmy Maxwell's sons coming up the front avenue. What business has he?' she demanded. Mary was displeased at the idea of one of her own class using the front avenue, when she and her relations had to use the back one.

'I asked him,' answered her mistress with a slight smile. She was well aware that this unexpected reply would throw Mary into a flutter of curiosity.

'You asked him! What for!'

'Two days ago I stumbled over him lying in a ditch reading a volume of poetry – Keats to be exact. He was the first person I'd met in Clera since I came back from school who read Keats. I was intrigued. Then he told me that he had only got the lend of it from the schoolmistress at Inchbeg, and that he had to return it that evening. He seemed quite upset. So I told him to come along and browse in the library if he wanted to. So here he is.'

'You're being taken advantage of, Miss,' declared Mary firmly.

'I don't think so,' laughed Cassandra. 'I needn't have asked him if I didn't like.'

'No matter. And besides what will your father say to the likes of him using the library?'

'You know perfectly well that my father never uses the library. I don't suppose he's been in it half a dozen times in his life. Neither have I for that matter.'

The doorbell rang. Mary made no move to open it – (the nerve of him using the front door) – so Cassandra went and opened it herself.

'Good morning,' she said, smiling.

'Good morning,' he answered, blushing and twisting his cap violently in his hands. 'I – I don't know whether I should have come.'

'I was expecting you. Won't you come in?'

She led the way across the huge tiled hall, and threw open the door of the library.

'Oh!' exclaimed Willie on the threshold, 'I never saw so many books in my life!'

'Yes,' said Cassandra, pleased at his wonder, 'it was got together by my grandfather, who was a great book-man. He used to sleep here, when he grew old. It hasn't been used much since.'

'I often heard tell of it,' said Willie, coming into the great dim room as if it were a church, 'but I didn't think it was so big.'

'It seems a pity to have all these books going to waste, I'm sure there's a volume of Keats somewhere.' Cassandra went down along the dusty rows. 'Come along,' she called back to Willie, 'and help me to find it.'

When at last they found it, and she gave it to him, they were both as delighted as two children successful in a treasure hunt. Willie was confused and happy, and could hardly find words to express himself. His gratitude was touching. Cassandra found the role of patroness very pleasant.

After that she gave him a great many books. Sometimes he came to the castle for them, and sometimes Cassandra brought them to him in the ruins of an old cabin in the bog where they had agreed to meet. Cassandra began to look forward to these meetings. She was an only child living with her father in a huge house, and cut off from her nearest neighbours by several miles of wild countryside. Her father was old and infirm and interested mainly in his ailments. Willie Maxwell was a welcome diversion. He had a sense of fun; was a wonderful mimic, and the fact that she could play the benefactress, and treat him in a high-handed manner which she would not have dared to use towards one of her own class, flattered the autocratic streak in her. She began to have a proprietary interest in him.

'What do you want to do with yourself?' she asked him one day, after he had brought her back a copy of *The Duchess of Malfi*.

'I don't know,' he replied, stopping and frowning.

'But you must have some ambition,' she insisted. 'Don't you want to make something of yourself?'

'I'd like to be able to write,' he said at last.

'Then why don't you?'

'I have tried, but I'm not satisfied. Not when I read what other men have written, lines like "cover her face: mine eyes dazzle: she died young".' He repeated this softly to himself several times until Cassandra began to be annoyed. She was never very pleased when he went into trances over something he had read in musty old books that she lent him. She liked him to talk about herself.

'That doesn't seem very wonderful to me,' she replied crossly 'I'm sure I could do just as good myself.'

One morning about a week after this meeting, Cassandra found an envelope addressed to her pushed in under the front door. She opened it and took out a single sheet of paper. It was a poem of fourteen lines. She read it through. Then she took it to her room and read it through again. It had been written by Willie Maxwell, and a little tremor shook through her as she read it. It was an appeal as exquisite and ardent as any that had been made by another lover-poet to another Cassandra three hundred years

before. Today it is in every anthology. But the young girl who read
it for the first time that morning did not know that she was holding a great love poem in her hands. She only knew that Willie
Maxwell loved her. In this way Cassandra Barlow, daughter of the
Big House, took a peasant lover.

It had been an enchanted summer. As they stood in their
trysting place watching the October sun go down, Cassandra and
Willie felt as if they were looking at the death of a friend. A little
chill shivered across the darkening bog. Willie kissed her gently.

'There will be other summers,' he whispered.

'But first of all there will be a long winter,' said Cassandra,
who never lost her strong sense of reality.

'There's something I want to tell you,' she went on. 'You remember I sent that poem called "Glenowel" to *Brockett's Magazine?*'

'Yes, I remember. You sent it first and then told me.' He said
this in a pained voice. They had quarrelled over it.

'Well, this morning I got a letter from the editor enclosing a
cheque for two guineas, and asking for more poems like it. He said
he would pay more for longer poems, narrative poems; yes, that's
what he said he wanted, narrative poems. This is the letter.'

'I don't want to write narrative poems.' He took her hands. 'I
only want to write about you.'

She allowed him to kiss her and stroked his black curls ten-
derly. But a few moments later she returned to her point.

'You're a very foolish boy, Willie. If you want to write poetry
you must write something really worthwhile like *Don Juan*, or – '
she cast about for something else really worthwhile – 'or *The Rape
of the Lock*, or something about Helen of Troy. Yes, why don't you
write about Helen of Troy, or Dido, or Cleopatra, or somebody
like that: write a good long poem with plenty of action. You know,
you might become famous.'

'I don't want to become famous. I only want to stay as I am.'
Willie looked at her pleadingly.

But Cassandra swept on, devoured by her ambition for him.

'Yes, you might become famous, and make money, and write
books. Wouldn't you like that?'

'I don't know,' said Willie, weakening.

'You must write an epic. That's it, an epic.'

In this way Willie Maxwell began to write epics about Helen of Troy, and Dido, and Cleopatra, and succeeded in producing some of the most remarkable literary curiosities of his time, weighty narrative poems on classical themes written by an uneducated Irish boy who had a pure lyrical genius. The lark was set to sing grand opera.

'Anybody can write about birds and trees and mountains,' declared Cassandra. 'You must aim at the heights.'

'I like writing about the little things,' replied Willie, who was unhappy about the whole business. 'I find it easier. I don't want to write long poems.'

'Because you find it hard. I'm afraid you're lazy. You will never achieve anything unless you work and work. You must keep at it.'

And Willie went wearily to work on his latest epic. And the Victorian public found it very much to its taste. Willie had become already wildly famous. Requests from editors arrived with gratifying frequency. He began to make a little money. Even the short lyrics which Cassandra allowed him to turn out as a sideline never went long without a publisher. Cassandra had a great contempt for these short pieces, and some of them Willie had to compose in secret. Today it is these tender little verses, together with the five sonnets he wrote to his mistress, that keep his name alive.

Cassandra basked in all this glory. She dealt with Willie's correspondence, and saw that he got full market value for his wares. The literary men who began to visit Willie found that first of all it was necessary for them to pay a visit to Miss Barlow, and compliment her on the insight which led her to the discovery of such a genius in such an unusual place. And indeed all of them were agreed that she managed her protégé very well, and that without her his poetry might never have become known to the world.

But she was not satisfied yet. She had a methodical mind, and it offended her sense of proportion that Willie had never completed the cycle of six sonnets. When she had accepted the first one he had promised to write five more and dedicate them to her.

'It seems a pity', she said, 'that you haven't finished the sonnets. Quite a lot of people have remarked on it. Then you could print the six complete when they bring out your book.'

'I thought you didn't approve of such little things like sonnets,' said Willie with a touch of bitterness in his voice.

'Now Willie, don't be difficult. You know perfectly well what I mean. If you are going to publish these sonnets you must complete the set, particularly as you actually say in the first one that there are going to be six. You know that line about a bouquet of six coloured roses.'

'I wasn't thinking about getting them published when I wrote them.'

'Perhaps you weren't,' said Cassandra patiently, 'but if every author took that line, nothing would ever be done.'

'I don't know whether I'll be able to write it now.' Willie looked at her searchingly, and then glanced quickly away.

'Nonsense, of course you'll be able to write it. If you can write fifty pages about Helen of Troy, you ought to be able to write a little thing of fourteen lines – ' she broke off. 'What are you looking at me like that for?' she asked sharply.

'I ought never to have listened to you in the first place. You know nothing about poetry. And you know nothing about love. If you did you wouldn't say a thing like that!' He was pale with rage. Cassandra's lips tightened, and her eyes flashed. She stood up from the settee on which she had been sitting. Her voice was biting.

'There was a time when you thought I knew a great deal about poetry. But, of course, that was the time when you where finding your feet. You were glad of an audience of one. In those days I was useful, as well as being a very adequate lending library. Your other remark was truer. I don't know anything about love. If I did I wouldn't have permitted myself to take lessons from you.'

For a few moments they faced each other, their lips trembling. Then Willie turned, and rushed blindly from the room.

Three days later Cassandra came in from a walk to find Willie's brother, Pat, waiting for her in the hall. He was excited and trembling.

'What is it?' she asked quickly.

'It's Willie,' he stammered. 'He's gone.'

'Gone! Where?'

'He didn't sleep in the house last night, and this morning we found he had brought all his clothes in the little tin box my father got in America. I thought, maybe, he came here –'

'Why would he come here?' broke in Cassandra sharply.

'Well, I thought maybe – did he say anything to you, Miss, about going away?'

'No, he didn't,' said Cassandra, leaving him abruptly.

His family never heard from him again. He disappeared completely from the face of the earth. There was a mild sensation. When Willie's book came out in the spring, with a puzzled preface by a famous novelist, it had a brisk sale.

Cassandra kept her silence. She did not reply to the tempting offer of an American magazine to write an article on the lost poet.

A year afterwards, her father died. She refused several earnest and attractive offers of marriage and drifted into early middle age, a cold, self-possessed spinster. She rarely left her western castle, and as day followed day in the ordered round of her existence, time passed smoothly by.

She rarely thought of Willie Maxwell now. It all seemed so long ago, an escapade of her youth, that she found it hard to believe it had ever taken place. But the poetry was there, and occasionally on winter nights she read it over again. She still preferred the epics, and remained puzzled when the critics disregarded them and praised the shorter poems. Recently, a young man in some American university had actually written an article about the missing sonnet, and had even provided one himself as he thought Maxwell might have done it. She thought this vulgar. But there was a great deal of vulgarity nowadays, and there was nothing anybody could do about it.

Cassandra became a very old lady. She was still straight and active, but her eyes were deeply sunken, and her once charming face was a network of wrinkles. She had lost all her teeth, and she looked like a placid and retired old witch.

One day she was walking in the garden when she was interrupted by Mary Curley, who had remained with her all these years. Mary had been troubled by rheumatism for some years, and Cassandra had not seen her walk so fast for a very long time. There was evidently something the matter.

'What is it?' asked Cassandra.

'The butter, Miss – '

'Well, what about the butter?' It was Cassandra's thrifty habit to bury a firkin of butter in the bog to preserve it for the winter months when milk was scarce.

'When Tom was digging to put down the firkin he came on ... Oh, Miss it was awful!' and Mary broke off and covered her face with her hands. '

'What in the name of goodness has happened!' exclaimed Cassandra. 'One would think you had seen a ghost. What is the matter?'

'Well, his spade hit against something,' went on Mary, swallowing hard. 'It was a corpse, and you know, Miss, a corpse in a bog never rots.'

'Yes, go on.'

'Tom says it must have got drowned in the bog-hole, and got covered – '

'I will go down and see,' said Cassandra calmly.

'Oh, no, Miss, you mustn't,' burst out Mary.

'What do you think I am?' asked her mistress. 'Go and get me my shawl.'

It was not very far from the house under an old rotting oak tree. Tom, the gardener, was standing over the spot. When Cassandra came near he uncovered the face of the corpse. It was the face of a young man of twenty-five, with black curling hair, a Grecian forehead and nose, and full curving lips. The old woman looked at him. A chill ran through her and she clutched her shawl. Her shrivelled face was almost as clay-like as his.

'We don't know who it is, Miss,' said Tom.

'The Lord save us,' whispered Mary.

'It might have lain here for a hundred years,' went on Tom.

'I found a little box not far from here, but the water that had got into it rotted whatever was in it.'

'What's that?' asked Cassandra, tearing her eyes away and looking at Tom. He saw that she was weeping. He repeated what he had said.

'He kept his promise,' whispered Cassandra. 'He was coming to deliver it before he went away.'

'What's that, Miss?' asked Tom. But Cassandra did not reply and continued to stare at the corpse. Suddenly she spoke.

'All these years, not a hundred yards from the house, while I grew old, and he ... '

'Did you know him, Miss?' asked Tom.

'Yes,' answered Cassandra. 'I knew him long ago.'

'The Lord have mercy on his soul,' whispered Mary. Then she touched her mistress on the arm, frightened at the expression on her face. 'I think we ought to be going in,' she said. Cassandra allowed herself to be led away. But when she had gone a few yards she turned.

'Cover his face,' she said. 'I knew him when I was a girl; he died young.'

Untitled

In the beginning was *The Word*. I don't suppose many people
remember *The Word* now. It was a monthly literary magazine put
out by some enthusiastic young students of Trinity College,
Dublin, before the war. As is the way with university students,
they had neither money nor business ability, and it is surprising
that *The Word* existed for as long as it did. It survived for nine
months. The first number dealt almost entirely with the work of
James Joyce and Roger Dowling, two authors whose books were
banned in the country of their birth. I was asked to write about
Dowling since I was the only one who had read everything he had
written. I had been able to do this because my parents had spent
their holidays in France every year, and I was able to buy his novels there, and bring them back to Ireland innocently mingled with
the works of Charles Dickens, which I had brought out specially
for that purpose. I have the article by me now.

It is, of course, immensely enthusiastic. It is also very long. I
was at that time a callow and over-clever youth with little or no
experience of the world. Many of the conclusions I drew would
embarrass me now if I heard them expressed by somebody else. I
would think them cheap and pretentious. But it must be, in view
of what happened later, that I hit accidentally upon some points
which had up to then escaped the notice of the critics who had
occupied themselves with the same subject. Instinct is a dangerous thing, and no author of experience would think of relying on
it completely; but it sometimes flashes to the heart of the matter
with a sure directness that escapes the mature and complex mind.

Dowling had published seven novels and two volumes of short stories, all obviously inspired by the life of the richer middle-class merchants in the large midland town in Ireland where he was born. He had been an only child, his mother died at his birth, and he had been brought up by his spinster aunt. His father died when he was sixteen and left him his large interest in the local woollen mills, shares which he was still in possession of at the time of his death. He had been educated privately, and the few people who knew him remember him as a young man who seemed to them to be quite ordinary in every way. At twenty-five he left Ireland and never returned.

He was the first Irish author to tap a hitherto neglected mine of material. Irish life up to this time had been treated as if it consisted of a passionately poetic peasantry, and a romantically rakish Anglo-Irish gentry. The solid, Jansenistic, purse-proud, insular, ruthless, hypocritical, conservative junta which has emerged as the ruling class since the Rebellion, had remained unchronicled for the simple reason that it had not produced a renegade of genius from within its own ranks. Roger Dowling was the first child* among them to take notes. He wrote about them with a clinical detachment, a profound acquaintance with their household gods, which could only have been done by a man who was one of themselves. He never made use of profanity as Joyce did; he was never angry; there were no scenes in his books which could be called obscene. He simply reached out and with a sure, steady knife ripped down the curtains from those ugly, prosperous houses he knew so well. And the occupants did not like what they saw of themselves. The tawdry motives of life, stripped of the comfortable trappings of convention, are never very pleasant company for those who will not admit that they possess them. The skilfully constructed stories of lust, avarice and hypocrisy which Dowling wove out of his family background were unforgivable because they calmly assumed that the Irish middle classes possessed exactly the

---

* This is a rare misquotation by Broderick: the Robert Burns line is 'A chiel among you taking notes.' A 'chiel' or 'child' in Burns's vernacular means 'a young man'.

same kind of vices and virtues as their counterparts in any other country: and the one thing which no man brought up in this sort of atmosphere will admit is that he is like the rest of men. Passion is all very well in France: our breasts are calm.

This, then, was the subject matter which I dealt with in my article; this, together with the few remarks which impressed Dowling and caused him to write to me.

I received his letter six months after the publication of the article. I had just finished college, and was looking forward to a holiday in Italy which I had long promised myself when I should have graduated. I was about to set out when I got his letter. I still have it, and I may as well give it in full. It is quite short.

> *Villa Mannheim,*
> *Place Autry,*
> *Avenue de la Californie,*
> *Cannes, A.M.*
> *France.*

Dear Sir,

> *I read your article about my work while in a dentist's waiting room in Nice. I learned afterwards that the dentist has a nephew in Trinity.*
>
> *I was flattered at some of the things you had to say about me and very much interested in some others. I think you have come nearer to what I have tried to do than any other critic I have read. If you are ever in this part of the world I should be very glad to see you if you care to come and have lunch with an old man.*

This letter made me the happiest of men. I was tremendously flattered and excited. I showed it to all my friends and boasted of it at great length. And as is the way with young men, who set out on a journey not so much to see a particular country as to find adventure, I immediately cancelled my arrangements to go to Italy, and resolved to spend my time in Cannes instead. Could anything be more exciting than getting to know a great man, who was also one's personal idol? I began to dream of the enthusiastic praise which he would give to the manuscripts I would humbly submit to him; a letter to his publishers would follow, recommending the work of this brilliant unknown: and I was on the road to fame! Youth is essentially selfish, and I was really interested in Dowling in relation to myself, and to the impression I was convinced I would make on him.

The Place Autry was a small impasse. Three houses opened on to it. The Villa Mannheim was the centre one. It was a typical, yellow-stucco Riviera villa, with a red roof and green shutters, iron balconies on the upstairs windows, a flight of steps to the front door flanked on either side by a cypress hedge. It was quiet and nondescript. I walked up and down outside several times to calm myself before venturing to ring the doorbell.

It was answered by an elderly Frenchwoman in a white housecoat. She was pleasant and friendly. She showed me into a small room off the hall and told me to wait. The room had a highly polished floor, a few skin rugs, a round mahogany table and some prints on the walls. A French window opened on to a terrace overlooking the garden. It was faintly like a convent parlour. I was nervous as one always is when kept waiting, and I remember I kept moving one of the rugs around with the tip of my shoe. Then the door opened and Roger Dowling was in the room.

For those who are interested in what he looked like I suppose I may as well try to describe him. He was not by any means good-looking; if anything, some people might think him distinctly ugly. He was small and flabby, with a dark, coarse skin, and a funny round blob of a nose. But you forgot this when you looked into his eyes and listened to his voice. He had not lost his Irish accent, which was warm, flexible and expressive. But it was his eyes which were his most striking feature. They were very dark, wide-set, frank and compelling. His smile too was very charming and lit up his somewhat plain, heavy face. From the very first I felt completely at home with him. He possessed the gift of putting one immediately at one's ease, a gift which may be commonplace and, like charm, entirely superficial, but it is always welcome to a stranger. He took my arm, and led me out on to the terrace.

'So you are the young man who discovered what I was thinking,' he said.

'It was very nice of you to ask me to come,' I replied.

'To tell you the truth I did not expect to see you so soon,' he said with a smile. 'Dublin is a long way from Cannes. But my invitation was perfectly sincere for all that. You know you are the first critic I have ever invited to my house, and you will also probably be the last. I suppose you can stay for lunch?'

I replied that I could indeed.

'Well, then,' he said indicating a chair, 'sit down and I'll get you some drinks and tell Marie there will be another for lunch. It will surprise her, I think.'

From my chair on the terrace I had a splendid view of both the Golfe Juan and the Golfe de Napoule, with the jagged peaks of the Esterels in the distance, and nearer, the jumbled red roofs and the white walls of Cannes. It was a perfect summer day, and it made one feel at peace with oneself and with the world just to sit there idly in the sun. Dowling came back with a tray of drinks and some cigarettes.

'I expect you smoke?' he asked.

'And you?' I replied, politely proffering my own packet.

'Oh, me, I never smoke. But help yourself. Marie will have lunch quite soon. In the meantime we can talk.'

It would be tiresome to go into the details of how we got to know each other better. We got along very well, and whatever is the source of those natural springs of friendship, we both of us felt, I the young enthusiast, he the old wanderer, that we had tapped them in each other. I don't know if it was then, that first morning, that he decided to tell me the things he did afterwards, or whether he had a vague idea of using me from the time he had read my article.

That is something he never told me, and I don't think it matters very much in the long run. What is important is that this man who had stepped aside from the world had made up his mind to publish certain things about himself and had chosen this oblique method of the second person to do so. What exactly was his reason for doing this must ultimately remain a mystery. I cannot tell; I can merely conjecture, and that is what I shall try to do when I have told this story.

After the first visit, I came the next day, and the next, and in a little while became a constant caller. But it was not until ten days after I had first met him that he brought up the subject of my article again. I remember we were sitting on the terrace in the afternoon over our coffee. Suddenly Dowling leaned forward, tapped me on the knee and spoke.

'Why did you say that I never went back to the town I was born in because I was afraid? Why did you say that the people in my novels love and hate each other without ever reaching out and touching each other? Why did you say that they are all, those creatures of mine, filled with a sense of the insufficiency of passion almost before they come to love? Why did you say that none of them have the capacity for pleasure, that they use it as a knife to wound themselves?'

'I too was born in a town like that,' I somewhat pompously replied.

'You could not know these things,' he went on. 'You might sense them. It is strange that nobody has ever hit on those points before when dealing with my books. I have had a good deal of praise and a good deal of blame, but I have a feeling, I suppose every author has it, that I have not been altogether understood. And yet you could not understand these things, you are too young.'

'We can often understand things without experiencing them. I cannot say how I came to these conclusions, except that they, those characters of yours, appeared to me like that.'

'You do not sympathize with those people?'

'Yes, yes, of course I do,' I said earnestly.

'It is just that you have never experienced those emotions yourself? Of course you have not, they are not the emotions of a young man.'

'That is true. But perhaps I recognized an affinity. I know

these people seemed to me to express things which I have felt, but have never formulated.'

'That may be the answer. You may, too, have just hit on it. I know that in some ways my novels are not balanced in the same sense that I attribute certain emotions, certain discoveries of self to my characters, which they could hardly be so consciously aware of, and which I myself only came to grips with after long years of pilgrimage. But that is something you have to accept, it is one of the conventions of the form I have chosen in which to express myself. These good people back home would not express all these things in so many words, would hardly in fact feel them, but what I want to insist is this: that the seeds of all these things which you have sensed are there, in those people, in the society they live in, in the breeding that has gone into them.'

'I agree. I do not quite know the particular "things" you are speaking of, but I understand you.'

'They are the seeds of decay that are embedded in every bourgeois society, the insect heap on the other side of the solid rock of convention, the hypocrisy that is inevitable, and the mental reactions that go with it. I have all these characteristics myself, the conscious and the subconscious; but I have used them differently, and have come to this along a different road.'

'Yes?'

'Listen. I have written seven books, all of them based on the types of people I was born and brought up among. They are the people I know and have never written of any other. In a sense I was writing about myself. Let me tell you something of the journey I took. It was, in a way, a terrifying journey, because although the road was strange I had only the same light to guide me as the one I would have had if I had stayed at home, settled down, reared a family and never read a book in my life.'

'Then you were afraid to go back?' I exclaimed, not without a feeling of triumph.

'Yes. I had got too far away, and in another sense had never got away at all. To go back would have been a fiasco. I realized that, and I accepted it when I went away. But I did not think I would come up against the precise difficulties that I did. They were unexpected. I went in search of freedom. I was young and I felt that if I stayed any longer at home I would choke, become complacent like all the rest of them. I wanted to throw off the shackles of the middle-class morality into which I was born. I was determined to see and taste life. That is a fairly common reaction among young men. They feel they are chained and they want to burst out. I suppose you feel that way yourself?'

'Yes,' I admitted. 'But I don't know if I have the courage to do anything about it.'

He looked at me and smiled. 'Ah, it needs courage, and even more – ruthlessness. You are a wise young man.'

'Oh, I think I'm pretty average.'

'Perhaps you are,' he replied frankly. 'But somehow I think I was much more naive at your age. The young men of my generation were, or so it seems to me now. I'm fifty-eight,' he said suddenly.

'A child as authors go,' I replied.

'I wish that were true. But I have nothing more to say now.'

'Nonsense.'

'That's why I am glad you have come here. I should like to tell you something of my life, and when I am gone you can contradict all those people who have their own theories about me.'

'A manifesto?' I smiled.

'If you like.'

'Well, you can talk away to me.'

'More than that I want somebody to talk for me. I have got too far away from men and affairs. I have no desire to go back.'

'That's a strange thing to say.'

'From your point of view, yes. From mine, no. It would be impossible.'

'That I can't understand,' I protested.

'How could you? We have got ahead of our story. I gave up my religion as soon as I left home. Of course I had ceased to believe long before that, but to please my aunt, who was very pious, I went through all the motions of it. I fooled her completely, or at least I think I did. I came to Paris to be a citizen of the world. I wanted to be absolutely free of my past. I wanted to find love.'

'Did you find it?'

'That question reveals the hopeless inadequacy of words. There is never enough of them to express our meaning when we want to get below the surface of things. Love, love, love, yes, I found lots of it. I also found I couldn't accept it.'

'Why?'

'Many people have a foolish idea that to commit sin is the easiest thing in the world. They spend their lives dreaming of all the wonderful things they would do if they could only shake off the chains of convention. They do not know themselves. It is not easy.'

'I'm afraid I'm not so sure about that,' I laughed.

'A man brought up in the rigid doctrine of Irish Catholicism, with its strong Jansenistic streak, can never sin happily. The very use of the word "sin" in any context tells its own story. To commit even the most heinous sin and remain conscious of it is a submission to God as definite as confession. That's why the old pagan ideal is so attractive to so many people today. It was free from the sense of sin.'

'I see,' I replied primly. 'And yet many people are brought up nowadays to disbelieve in the sense of sin, and they don't seem to be any happier.'

'That is because they substitute happiness for God, without knowing anything at all of the nature of it. It's the old story of the inadequacy of words. It means one thing to one person and something else to another. The word "freedom" is today used in so many different ways that it has ceased to mean anything at all. For me at one time it meant dissipation.' He darted a piercing glance of his brilliant dark eyes at me. I felt as though an arrow had pinned me to my chair. 'Have you ever been to a brothel?' he asked.

I blushed, hated myself for doing so and became confused. 'I, well, I, you know - '

'I can see that you have not.'

I confessed rather miserably that indeed I had not.

'I shall not easily forget the first time I went to one. I had

looked forward to it for months. It was to be my first great gesture against the old life. I did not realize then that this desire was
really more important to me than the desire for pleasure which I
had indulged in imagination for weeks. When I got to the door of
the house I felt a sudden panic, and wanted to call back the cab,
but I laughed at my childish fears and marched in, utterly at odds
with myself. I seemed to be moving in a dream, in which I had a
frantic desire to wake up, but could not. I was cold and clammy
with sweat, and all desire for pleasure had long left me. I wanted
to get away as quickly as I could from this strange place and those
grinning, painted faces. I chose the first girl who came. I cannot
even remember what she looked like except that she was friendly
and gentle. But afterwards I was at once sick, and desperately
angry. I knew I had made a fool of myself and that they were
amused at me. They called a cab and sent me home to my hotel. I
did not stir out for two days. This was sin! This was the pleasure
for which I had waited so long!

'Then it seemed to me that all this was so new to me it was
only to be expected that I should be awkward at the beginning. I
decided that I was over-fastidious, silly, childish. I laughed at
myself. So I forced myself to go again and again, always to different houses, and then as I grew more adept I sometimes went back
to the same ones. I thought perhaps that familiarity would help me
to overcome the loathing which, on every occasion, and no matter
in what company, I felt. I made friends among these people. Many
of them were simple and kindly. I learned much about the mechan-
ics of pleasure, an art like any other. I grew worldly-wise, and
achieved a certain aplomb. But I never enjoyed myself. There was
no time even in my most abandoned moments that I could not
have wished myself elsewhere. I hated myself for being so prudish.

'I whipped myself into going back again and again. I pursued
pleasure with a grim determination. But I never learned to like it.
I could never lose myself; I was forever acting a part: I was constantly deluding myself. It was always necessary for me to do this.
But I resolved to break away from my background, and I perse-
vered in this terrible noviciate with the same singleness of pur-

pose as if I were studying for the priesthood. It was the hardest thing I have ever done in my life. I would dress myself for the evening's dissipation with the same deliberate act of will as an old clown who makes up for his part with a cancer in his stomach. At one time I thought that I was going against my natural inclinations, that I was in fact homosexual: but this sordid device so horrified me that I thought I would go mad. I rushed back to a woman for whom I felt some affection and lived with her for some months.

'But gradually a change had been coming over me. I began slowly to realize that, try as I might, this life would always remain torture for me. I began instead to seek out my old haunts for a reason quite different. I knew now that for me what is called pleasure would always be pain, and I began to revel in the torment which nightly I inflicted upon myself. I also began to regard that demi-monde of the spirit in which I lived in quite another light. It was now a penance, a pilgrimage, a denial of the self. I was like a pious Catholic rising early in the winter frosts for six o'clock Mass and Communion, fasting on Fridays and Wednesdays, making all the steady round of prayers for the several seasons like the good women at home: like my aunt who finished the Thirty Days' Prayer to begin it again, and always said the fifteen decades of the rosary and the Stations of the Cross every evening before the church closed. I expect all this seems very strange to you?'

'Yes,' I replied. 'It is very strange. But I think I understand. What happened? How long did you remain living this kind of life?'

'For years,' he said. 'I deliberately set out to dissipate myself, and I found in the end that I was applying the same standards to this way of life as to the kind of life I would lead if I had stayed at home and denied all my appetites. The more I struggled to be free, the more I hated the deadly heritage which had made me like this. But that does not say that I didn't change. You do not lead that kind of existence without being affected. I changed very much. There was no going back for me. That is the terrible thing about life: that we must keep going on and changing, and that there is, in fact, no returning to the point we started from. If we return physically as some have done, we find that all is changed within us, the old answers no longer satisfy, the old faces irritate, restlessness pursues us. Take what you want of life, says the old Spanish proverb; take it, and pay for it. We always pay. We discover that it is necessary to push on into the inexorable jungle that is ourselves, and we are forced to go on hacking our way blindly, knife in hand.

'I tried to find a new set of values, and when at last I did find them I discovered that I was only able to grasp them with a mind that was set rigidly to a different rhythm. If I went back, I should go back terribly changed. The mind plays us strange tricks, and is not mocked. I believe that James Joyce laughed when it was reported to him that Maritain had said that the structure of his mind was Catholic. Joyce did not believe the structure of the mind could be anything. Perhaps he, a virtuoso of words, boggled at the use of the word "structure"; it may be that he could not see the meaning for the construction.

'Because Maritain was right. That is something the Jesuits have understood profoundly for centuries before Freud. If Joyce thought he had beaten the Jesuits at Clongowes he was very much mistaken. I was never a Jesuit pupil: I had to reach all these conclusions myself, which is I suppose a sort of bitter consolation. I was set by blood and upbringing in a certain way, and I chose another course. I have kept that course and I do not intend to change it. But I am like a man walking in the same direction as everybody else – whose insides have been twisted round. But I shall go on. I am no longer equipped for the old world. If we are to break it down it needs somebody to make this blind path. If I went back again it would be as a kind of twice-removed experiment. It would in a sense be a perversion as deliberate as anything that had gone before.'

'That I confess I do not altogether understand,' I said. 'Surely it is more simple than that. Tell me, did you ever fall in love?'

He laughed. 'I was coming to that. Yes, I did. It was inevitable, or so it seems to me now. Don't you think so?'

'I think it was a good thing. Any love is better than no love.'

'That is true in a sense. But I think we can only love or hate ourselves. I may have been unfortunate in the people I have loved. None of them loved me, and the few persons who did fall in love with me left me unmoved. When I was twenty-nine I fell in love with a married woman ten years older than myself. I thought I had found some peace at last, and for a time I did indeed experience more pleasure than I have ever experienced since. Rochefoucauld tells us that we are made happier by the passion that we experience than by that which we inspire; and that is very true. This woman did not love me and eventually left me. I felt drained of emotion.

'I attempted to form the same sort of liaison with other women, and with some of them I did in a sense fall in love, or what passes for love in the general term. Each time I hated myself a little more for prostrating myself before a creature I knew to be utterly worthless. I have often observed that men who tend to be intellectuals always fall in love with those who are exactly the opposite. I began to suspect this human passion which condemned me to drag myself along at the heels of some creature, charming perhaps and full of vitality, whose only link with me was a body I found I wanted less and less. I began to feel that awful sense of loneliness which inevitably comes to every man who is not content with the daily bread of humanity.

'I may have been unlucky. I am prepared to believe that human love shared on the same level must be at the summit of those experiences that stand outside the mystical. And yet I am not sure even of that. I think it is only possible for those who are unaware of anything better. At any rate I found myself thrown more and more on myself. I had to make myself self-sufficient. I began to read and eventually to write.'

'You did not leave Ireland to become a writer?' I asked.

'A young man with means who sets out to travel has always the ambition to be a writer. It is a good excuse. Few of them realize it. I started writing because otherwise I think I should have gone mad. I could no longer pretend that the society in which I moved even vaguely interested me. At the parties which I now sometimes went to, I more often than not found myself sitting alone in a corner, watching the others with a kind of grim amusement. They seemed to me to be creatures naked in a glass case; I could turn a bright lamp on them, I could examine every part of their bodies; but I could not reach out and touch them. More and more I lived with the figments of my imagination. I went back in my mind to those people I was born among. They came to life, and then I began to write about them.'

'Did you cut yourself off from your friends? I mean did you in a sense become a recluse?'

'Yes, I became a hermit, as every man must sooner or later who wants to come to grips with himself.'

'But why did you withdraw in the physical sense too? Or did you? Surely you must have kept some friends that you visit and that sort of thing?'

'I have lived here quite alone for twenty years,' he answered quite simply.

I was appalled. 'But, good heavens, that's not possible!' I exclaimed. 'You must have had somebody to talk to.'

'I have Marie. I know a few people in Paris to whom I write. Some of them are girls I used to know in the houses long ago. They are old women now and are glad of a helping hand now and then. I talk to the children in the road here. I feel nearer to children nowadays. I know the grocer and the baker and the barber: it is enough.'

'But surely a man like you would want intellectual conversation.'

'That above all I have especially avoided,' he laughed. 'It is nearly always a set of opposite platforms, and the loudest voice wins. I have my books.'

'Yes, but that kind of life must produce eventually a distorted outlook on life, especially for a novelist. You have to live among your material.'

'Perhaps', he said with a funny little grimace, 'you are confusing journalism with creative writing. I have lived among my material. I think I know a good deal about it.'

'That is true,' I admitted. 'I suppose it's just the thought of anybody being so much alone horrifies me. There is so much to be had from life and the world around us.'

'These are the sentiments of a young man. I had them myself once. They are generous.'

'Will you admit that you are disillusioned?' I demanded.

'No. I do not hate the world. It is a very pleasant place, if you are clever enough to make the most of it. I merely thought it was a great waste of time mingling with people, and reaching out to them, and knowing that I could never reach as far as I wanted to. I am no more alone here than I was in a crowded drawing room in Paris.'

'I do not think I want to understand that,' I said.

'You are too young. One day you will,' he answered.

'Do you expect to live like this for the rest of your days?'

'I do not expect to be any more alone, or any less so. But there is one more experiment that I want to make before I die.'

'Experiment?' I asked.

'Experiment,' he answered. 'It will be the full turn of the wheel.'

That night when I was leaving him, I was going back to Ireland the next day, I asked him quite suddenly, 'Why don't you go back to the Church?'

He looked at me for a long moment, and then spoke. 'That is too easy,' he said.

I never saw him again. The war intervened. I was busy at my job. I did not write to him nor he to me. Then two years ago he died. I found myself thinking more and more about him. What was that final experiment he had meant to make? Could anybody tell me about it?

I doubted it; but that summer I went to Cannes for my holidays. There was a faint chance that if I could find Marie she might be able to tell me something of this strange man.

Marie was not easy to discover, and my time was almost up when I traced her to a small restaurant in the old port at Nice which she kept with her sister. She recognized me the moment I came in. She fussed about me a great deal and introduced me to her sister. I came straight to the point.

'I came to talk to you about Mr Dowling,' I said.

'Mais oui, of course, Monsieur,' she replied. 'He was very fond of you. He often spoke of the Irish gentleman.'

'Did he?'

'He said that you were very intelligent. I think it was a good thing when you came.'

'Why?' I asked eagerly.

'Monsieur, he always led such a quiet life, reading and walking, and writing. I always said he did too much reading and writing.'

'But he was a writer, Marie. He wrote many famous books.'

'Was he?' she replied indifferently. 'He never told me.'

'How long were you with him?'

'Twenty years,' she answered. 'I thought, perhaps, he was writing his journal.'

'In a way I suppose he was,' I answered. How easy it is to disappear! 'Did he see nobody at all?' I went on.

'There were never any visitors until you left. Then our life changed. It was much more agreeable. Though of course there was more cooking to be done. But I never minded that.'

'What do you mean?' I asked curious now and uneasy.

'Monsieur went out much more in the world after you left. I was very glad. There were always people in the house.'

'What sort of people, were they writers and people of that sort?'

'Oh, no, Monsieur,' said Marie a little shocked. 'Nothing like that. They were people of the neighbourhood, the most respectable.'

'Respectable?'

'Oui, Monsieur, that is so, the very nicest, and every Wednesday they played bridge.'

'Bridge!'

'But, yes, Monsieur, it was very jolly and comfortable.'

'Tell me,' I asked, 'did Monsieur le Curé come too?'

'Yes, of course, Monsieur le Curé came to bridge every

Wednesday too. Monsieur was very pious after you left. It was a miracle. It was very good that you came. Monsieur le Curé was very agreeable.'

'Was Monsieur le Curé with him when he died?' I asked.

'I do not know,' answered Marie. 'Monsieur went to the hospital. I was not there when he died.'

A frightful suspicion began to dawn in my mind. 'Marie,' I urged, 'Did he leave any message for me? Did he leave any letters or journals?'

'Mais non, everything was burned.'

I groaned aloud.

'Is Monsieur ill?' asked Marie anxiously.

I cannot remember how I managed to get rid of her. I wanted to get away as quickly as possible. Experiment, experiment, the word went whirling round in my mind. I felt cold and ill. I could formulate no coherent thoughts. If what I suspected was true, it was the most monstrous thing that man can conceive.

It is only now almost two years after that I can set down in some sort of order the terrible suspicions that have tortured me since. If Roger Dowling had gone back to something of that kind of life which he set himself deliberately to break with, if he pursued it as an experiment, I do not care to think of the process of perverted puritanism which led him to do this. The awful thing is that it would be a perfectly logical extension of what had gone before. He was a man who had turned away from the background and the God of his youth; but he could not escape the dreadful sense of the repression of the self, the all-pervading consciousness of sin, which is so prominent a feature of that faith and of the people who practise it.

In a sense he had never escaped at all. Deep in his vitals was always the desire to curb, restrain, conceal his true feelings; and of this he was always aware. If he did not know himself so well, he would have been a happier man. He was a living example of what may happen to a man who has in him the seeds of a saint, and who deliberately turns his back on God. For him, pleasure, above all the pleasure of the flesh, was never tolerable unless he could connect it with the sense of suffering.

This is the way in which his ingrown spirit of Jansenism took its revenge. He was unable to sin happily, and determined to break from the chains that bound his youth, he pursued his fearful course until at last the very loathing which this course inspired in him became the only consolation and justification for it. He was like a holy hermit who as an additional penance forces himself to sleep with the most depraved of creatures. The hermit would never have done it because he would have been upheld by the interior light which is above all the sane and healthy. Dowling's standards were neither sane nor healthy. They were sincere, very courageous, and in a nature like his, given the course he had mapped out for himself, inevitable. Few people have gone so far on a self-appointed path.

He reacted to love in the same way. He found, as all men of sensibility find out sooner or later, that passion is not enough, that it is a monster in the breast that feeds on its own flesh. He fell in love with people with whom he had little or nothing in common; coarse, insensitive and vulgar. He saw he was making a fool of himself. And he also began to discover that kernel in himself which it is impossible to share with another. Some people call it the soul; I do not know what Dowling called it. At any rate he was aware of it, and as with every other discovery of his life, he was unable to treat it with moderation. If he was alone, then he would be absolutely alone, physically as well as spiritually. He withdrew and gave himself up to himself. And the greatest and most besetting sin of his life, one I think which he was unaware of, intellectual pride, would not allow him to go back.

All of this is reasonable enough. It is merely a summary of what he himself told me. What I have to say next is based on my own conjecture, and can only be regarded as such. I hope it is wrong, I have very little to go on. He made quite sure that he would elude the world in death as he had in life. I think I am justified in saying that Roger Dowling hated the society which gave him birth. He hated it with the baffled rage of those who know that they will never escape absolutely from the object of their hatred. This became more and more clearly defined in him as he grew older. He was a man of almost superhuman strength of character, and he never quailed under the strain of the awful pilgrimage which he had set himself, the pilgrimage to freedom from his inherited beliefs. He was self-sufficient of everything – except his ancestry.

And if he would not be rid of that then he would take the most terrible revenge on it that a baptized Catholic could take. He would bring back his new faith of no faith and cast it in the face of the old. I do not know what other that the experiment he spoke of can have been; the change in his way of life in his last years was not accidental. He would turn the wheel full circle, and take up that solid Catholic life he had left so long ago. But how different this new dispensation would be. He would take up those old threads as being completely changed, sceptical and sophisticated.

Herein was hypocrisy come to its awful logical conclusion. Nothing could have been more hateful to this man of immense erudition, and boundless imagination, than the tea-drinking, bridge-playing, church-going conventions of his childhood. In complete revolt he had associated his personal solution with a complete absence of them. Why then should he deliberately live that life again except to take his mocking revenge, and to make his last irrevocable gesture? Why the respectable neighbours? Why the bridge parties? Why was the Curé a constant visitor? So that he could play the horrible comedy to the bitter end. Did he quite consciously choose damnation, or did he, and that would be infinitely worse, carry it about in his breast and refuse to believe in it? We shall never know. That last act is outside our province, certainly outside mine.

I did not go to see Monsieur le Curé. Could he have told me anything? He could have told me that Dowling had received his Maker on his deathbed. Could I, suspecting what I suspect, take any comfort in that? I was afraid to ask the Curé, afraid that Dowling had carried his hate and his iron resolve to the very brink, and accepted his Maker in the last most dreadful deceit of all, the final diabolical gesture. I think he was capable of planning it. I only hope that some weakness came to his aid before it was too late, and that in those last moments when eternity loomed before him, some simple ancestral instinct, which he had fought so bitterly, rose irresistibly in his proud heart and forced him to cry out for forgiveness. Perhaps he realized that this hatred, this straining of bonds was a more complete acceptance of Him and His word than the passive indifference of a conventional existence. The last moments of Roger Dowling are outside mortal province.

That is all I can write or tell. It may be that I am completely wrong. It may be that long before he died he came back to the old way, that the 'experiment' doubled back on him as so much else did in his life. It may be that God became a bridge player – and won.

The story of my friend will trouble me until I die, but these reflections which I have written down will ease my mind at any rate of some of that burden. It is incomplete, and if I were asked if it was a story, or a tract, or an extract from a diary I would hardly know what to reply. In a sense it is a love story in which love and hate are inextricably woven, in which the pursuer is both pursuing and pursued; the action of which is no less tense because it is unseen. This is a theory which some people will be out of sympathy with. But it is true.